# #YESTOLIFE

## What Would EL Do?

**Dr. EL March**

# About the Author

My name is EL. My name is by choice and not by birth, as is the path of spirituality I follow. I was born in Tehran, Iran into a mixed religion and diverse family where my mother was the driver and my father took the back seat – and thank God for that. Most of my life I can say that I have been in hiding. My mother pretty much was the protector of the children and the family secrets. From outside and to others, our family looked normal. Internally, there was so much that we never spoke of to anyone, and there was no transparency.

We rarely accepted guests or even went to a family get togethers because of the way our life was arranged. My circle of trusted people was limited to my mom, and my eldest brother. Everything was private and hush-hush. My growing years were especially kept in secret. Without going too much into the details of the story and turning this into an autobiography, truly, not even today as I write this, many of my friends, family and relatives know me and my past.

Maybe one day I will be bold enough to put the whole story into writing. I spent most of my days in an ashram and was home schooled. In that I had the advantage of choosing the topics that most applied to my field of studies and what would be relevant in living my life. In today's schooling I see that kids are forced to take topics they hate and this makes school the place they loathe and they cannot wait to get out of it or they play sick not to attend it. For me it was otherwise. I looked eagerly forward to it. The kids today do not like school because of all we teach them that may or may not play any role in their real life. By real life I mean not the physical life, but the actual spiritual life that needs to take precedence.

They learn everything that they will never use, except for some. They learn about the differences of race and religion, which they are better off not knowing. The learning is not directed at what the interest and passion is, hence the school system fails. The school does not teach them how to deal with their emotions and how to learn from everything and how the issues are resolved or the art of communication and being a human. I on the other hand had the subject of "Sense of Assistance" as a greater part of my curriculum than the other children because in the world of humanity, that would be what would determine how I lived.

I did not need to learn history in a great detail but only the stories that I could learn from and apply to the future. I did not need to recite all the kings or presidents names from the past. I was fully engrossed in learning about human physiology and psychology, observation of nature, weight lifting using brain muscle, sense of service and acceptance, and emotional quotient.

In this manner I managed to finish 24 years of schooling in 12 under the direct supervision of this old man I refer to as my master today for the lack of a better expression. My actual school days were only a handful. It was not until only a few years back, after years of living in North America that I even dared to use the title of Dr. That title was supposed to be hidden until such date as needed; and I am not even sure if was needed to be revealed at all.

For years I have worked in the IT industry and when any of my colleagues would hear the title, they would say: "You are a doctor? What are you doing here?"

I remember a couple of years ago, a childhood neighbour of mine found me on the internet and got in touch with me and was asking all sorts of curious questions as she did not know anything about me and she was surprised.

But what remains a question and it has at all time in my mind is: Why do you want to know who I am before you read? Every book and article we read, we tend to try and find out about the credentials of the person behind it. Well, I am trying to change that in this book by saying, all anyone needs to know about me, is that, just like you, I am another face of God. Just like you, I have a belief and a personality of my own. Just like you, I live and breathe.

Who I am today is not who I was yesterday or who I will be tomorrow. None of the things you are looking for in my past or present define me and certainly none of them can define what I do or do not know, if I am wise or just a fool, or if the message I am trying to relay is good or bad. We have never questioned our spiritual leaders in their credentials, why start now?

I am me. I am not my past; I am not my credentials; I am not my lifestyle; I am not what I own or how much I have in the bank. I am me. I am the "me" in MEssenger. My ego separating me from the rest, has made me into someone who wants to see all prosper, however they define prosperity. I do not have a major in English language, so you will see grammatical errors and run-on sentences and improper punctuations. I am the one who decided, my book has to be my words. The way I speak and feel and write, not some made-up version. My writing did not go to a makeup artist or a plastic surgeon to look good and be appealing. My writing is my feelings and my belief. My writing reflects my desire to spread the message of joy, happiness and prosperity.

All I say, has been said many times. But the objective is trying to relay the message from a different perspective. Perspective matters. There is only one holy book, but many ministers and variety of translations and views. The view that captures your heart and resonates is the one you adopt. In this book I have tried to offer my own view and description. If I can touch one person's life and bring joy to it, I have accomplished my mission.

I hope you enjoy this book and get out of it, what you wish. It is nothing but my beliefs and understanding of life. It is from the experience of others that we learn and decide whether a road is to be taken. When the newscaster lets you know that a bridge is broken and few cars have fallen off; this is a deciding factor for you not to go that route so that you will not fall. My writing is nothing but a newscast. Just as any newscast can be simply a different perception of the incident; so is this. You can step to the site of the incident carefully and examine to see if you wish to continue or take the suggestion of avoiding the bridge. You must do so with this as well.

Read my experience, explanations and suggestions. Carefully examine it. Now decide whether it will benefit you or not.

You see, our perception is our mental vision. Our perceptions rule our lives. We get into fights and arguments sometimes even if we are actually agreeing with something and someone simply because of a misperception. In other words you cannot see the backyard looking through the window that is looking at front yard. You cannot do macro photography with a regular lens and expect a sharp beautiful result. Your action shots will be blurry on a regular shutter speed. You get the point.

Seeing that perception and communication are the two most important aspects of our daily lives, I intend to focus around these two topics throughout this book. The process of perception allows us to experience this life as an individual. Think about everything that you perceive every day. You see things you know, you touch things, smell the aromas, and hear the sounds and all of these help you create your bag of experience. So perception includes our five senses as well as our cognitive process. Perception plays the role of a sensor. It not only creates your experience but also it governs your reactions to all actions and experiences. Your fight or flight responses depend on it; and for that reason, how you react in situations, how stressed or relaxed you feel and ultimately your physical health depends on this.

One last word: The material discussed in this book is solely dependent on my perception and life experience and is not intended to replace the advice of your healthcare provider. The reader is responsible in choosing to take or not to take the suggestions offered or implied.

# Introduction

Over the period of past few months, I have been rethinking my life and my mission. Even though I have been true to my mission all my life, I felt there is more to be done. This of course brought me to think about where I am and what the best plan of action is.

Out of these thoughts and contemplations was the birth of EL-SOS services. My intention by creating this organization is to help those in need of mental, spiritual, relationship, family or business help.

I have spent the past 35+ years of my life around creating business processes and helping companies along with their day to day issues. I also alongside this, have helped people with their various personal matters. I have always seen both of these works as one. In the business world my dealings have been with incidents, problems, change, configuration, release, service level management and process development.

The way I see it, the personal side has been the same. I have dealt with people facing emotional and spiritual "incidents" and "problems"; I have helped them "change" their views and lifestyles, I have "reconfigured" some of their thoughts /emotions /diets /perspectives and I have shown when would be a good time to "release" all troubles and reminded and helped them hone their social agreements and revisited their old beliefs and updated them and at times written material for them to keep as guides.

This has been by wearing two different hats but very similar end results and work efforts.

I have spent a lot of time writing books and articles on various topics and now the last thought that has come to me is to write a guide book specifically for those who are thinking about changing their perception in life and better communicate with the world around them.

What better subtitle can I pick for this book than "What Would EL Do?" What I reflect here is out of my very own experience and studies in life and what "I" would do in such situations. I strongly advise the reader to take all that I have discussed with a grain of salt. Not every method is for everyone.

I will be starting by what I feel to be a strong factor in why we feel the way we do and why do we do the things we do and just let it all flow. So don't be disturbed at times if the flow takes you where you are not ready, and just try to relax and read. At times you may even feel angry for what I would be saying. Its' OK. Let it out. Let it flow. All I would like to do, is to introduce the concept and an idea. The rest is up to you. You can agree or disagree. You can use or toss the idea. The "ask" is for you to "think". That's all.

I am also making this book different in the way it is setup. You are all probably used to seeing a preface, an introduction, then the list of chapters, perhaps an index and some footnotes. Well I have news for you. Most of that will be missing here. It is a free flow book, so get ready.

# First things first…

I always like to first examine the core beliefs about life, existence, and who you think or perceive you are? Where do you come from? Do you ever have any control over anything in your life? Do you believe in fate? What part does tradition play in your life? How influenced are you by the society? Who is most influential in your life? What did they teach you? Have you questioned your religion? What part religion plays in your life? Are you afraid of thinking? Are you a victim? What occupies your thinking most of your day? What is see no evil, hear no evil to you? Are you seeing all positives, all negatives or half and half? How do you see yourself in the future? Are you fearful and anxious? When you talk to your friends, what are the topics (Troubles in life? Joys in life? Sympathizing/empathizing? Memories?)

For us to delve into all these questions and go through them one by one, there is one major thing that needs to be addressed first. That is: looking into the detail and seeing the big picture. This is basically what everyone is calling understanding microcosm to realize the macrocosm. Same thing said a bit fancier.

Where does this detail start? Where do we find this detail that everyone raves about? Simple! Within you and your surroundings. You don't need to go far. I will start you off with some of the main info and the rest you can dig out if you are curious. Hang on to your seats, here we go…….

It starts with your body and how it is put together and your physical being. I know this might sound boring to some but I promise it will be well worth it at the end. Just hang in there with me. I promise I will be writing this in the simplest terms, so much so to offend your intelligence…LOL

Everything we need to know is based on the understanding that the smallest piece of the Universe is called an atom. Atoms are like dense marbles and their character is determined by the character of the items that the atoms contain. So in this, at all times we are dealing with physical parts and pieces that you can take apart which are the atoms.

The reason an Atom was called an atom to begin with, was because this word has a Greek root, meaning: Undividable. The assumption of course was the atom is the smallest particle in the Universe and you cannot divide it any smaller than that. Back in 1895, the first awareness came out that maybe the atom is not the smallest thing. Maybe there are other things inside the atom. So we started to look at things like the nucleus and the electrons. At this point this changed a lot of theories in physics because before this, physics thought the atom was undividable.

Then the scientists found out that there are really no physical electrons inside of an atom. That was our "perception", because we wanted to look at this in a material way. When the physicists started looking at this closer, they noticed that electrons are really like energy waves. Like ripples on a pond and that the nucleus wasn't physical either. The atoms are filled with whirlpools of energy like microscopic tornados collectively swirling around each other.

So what this means, is that there is really no structure to an atom. An atom is just a whirlpool of energy.

So now wait a second, if atoms make molecules and atoms are made of energy, what are molecules made of? Next question is: if molecules assemble a cell and cells assemble the whole body, what is our body made of? Result of these questions: <u>EVERYTHING</u> in the Universe is made out of energy.

So if now you say, hold on a minute, this wall is hard, and if I hit it I break my arm. It is hard, I feel it, it has to be material. I will give you an example: when you look at a tornado from a distance what do you see? You see a cloud of swirling dust that is coming towards you. If you are travelling in the direction of this tornado and it hits you, you blow into pieces. It literally hits you harder than a brick wall, that you considered material. It is exactly like hitting something visibly solid.

Now I want you to imagine that same tornado, without any dust particles in it. It is clear and it is coming towards you. You don't really see it because it is clean, but when it does hit you, it is still going to feel like a brick wall and it will definitely feel solid guaranteed, but there is nothing solid about it.

So the forces of the whirlpools of energy within the construction of a wall, are so strong that you cannot put your hand through the wall, because all the atoms that make it, are little tornados which have force fields. Everything in the Universe is made out of energy even though to our perception, it is concrete like☺☺☺

At this point I am going to add a bit more of a twist into this: energy interacts with energy even though they appear to be separate from each other.

Explanation: Let's say you take a rock and drop it into a pond. You will of course see the ripples of waves. This is energy moving through the water and not water moving itself. To understand this, if when you drop the stone in the water, you have a cork floating on top of the water, you would see as the ripples hit the cork, it would move up and down but remain in the same place. If this was water moving, the cork would move with it.

So now, what would happen if two energy waves hit each other? For this experiment, take two rocks that are the same size and weight and drop them in the water at exactly the same time. When the rocks hit the water, the ripples from the rocks will start joining each other. When these two waves come together, the result is a wave that has added up the power of the two waves. This is called "constructive interference".

In our second experiment, take the same two stones and drop them into the water, but not at the same time. Drop one and then the next. What you will see happen is a different kind of joining, where the height of one ripple hits the lowest point of the other ripple, in that case they nullify each other. This is called "destructive interference".

So now going back to atoms, every atom is radiating energy because it is spinning like a tornado. Waves are broadcasted from each atom just like the ripples of the wave on water all the time. Here is a scientific fact: every atom and molecule, gives off light and absorbs light. Meaning the vibration of atoms are in the range of light.

What does this mean to us? It means that every atom in your body is generating light right now. And the character of a single molecule in your body, is the pattern that the atoms make. And now these molecules add up to be cells, so the shape and health of a cell is dependent on what it contains and how constructively the molecules are interfering with each other. And your body is made of cells and its health is dependent on how your cells interact with each other.

So at any given moment, the energy you radiate, shows how healthy you are and how constructively your cells are interacting with each other. You are a generator of waves, but in the meantime you are a recipient of waves as well. So why is this relevant? Well I said that there is constructive interference and destructive interference. You may be more familiar with the terms "good vibes" and "bad vibes"☺☺☺

When you come into contact with someone who gives off energy that is like yours, and vibrates to the same frequency, you feel good because of the constructive interference and you both feel powerful after you have separated and gone away. Someone with destructive interference can drain you completely when you have left them. We literally soak up the energy around us.
Human is the only creature that depends on language to communicate. All other creatures read the vibration. We are also able to read vibrations, but because we have become too accustomed to "physical" reality we have forgotten how to do so. We have also been programmed not to pay attention to our feelings and listen to people. But by denying our feelings we have really forgotten the use of one of the most important tools we had been originally offered.

Why is this important? It is important because at all times you will know if you are somewhere with constructive interference, which is going to support you, or you are being subjected to so called "bad vibes" that will throw you off course in all matters of life; health and otherwise.

Science and physics have given the doctors all kind of facilities, like CAT scans, MRIs, Mammogram, thermography and Radiation Therapy. So what is a mammogram? It is not a photograph, it is an energy profile. So the character of the energy they are reading is the character of the material you are studying. So when you are looking at a CAT scan or a mammogram and you see these different colours which tell you about the different frequencies, and you say, "Oh, there is cancer". Are you physically seeing the cancer? No. You are only seeing the vibrational energy of a cancer cell.

Wherever we are, we are being influenced by energy fields. We are a part of the entire field of Universe. As Albert Einstein said, "The field is the sole governing agency of the particle." Now remember that our thoughts, words, emotions are all part of this field; which will play a major role in the nature of the particles that Einstein is referring to.

When you meditate, you give off energy. Here is an interesting research: you are all familiar with Electro Encephala Graph (EEG) where they attach wires to someone's head to read their brain activity. There is another way of reading these activities which is called Magneto Encephala Graph (MEG). The difference is that this reads a magnetic field instead of electric field of the brain. In EEG they needed to have contact with skin to read the electric currents of the brain but in this it is understood that the brain also has a magnetic field which can be measured from a distance. In this the probe that is reading the brain activity is not even touching the body.

So the significance of this is that your thoughts are not really contained in your head. Another thing they have found out, is that if you take a magnetic field and direct it back into the head, you can influence brain activity. They can actually scramble the target's thoughts. This of course takes us back to Einstein's words, "The field is the sole governing agency of particle", bringing us into understanding that our thoughts can give <u>form</u> to particles.

# Who do you think you are?

I would like to go back to the set of questions I asked to begin with, and the first one I want to dig into: Who do you think you are? Are you this solid moving, breathing thing that goes to work in the morning to make ends meet?  When you are asked who are you, do you answer, I am a mother of two, or I am a doctor, or I am Nancy or anything else to identify yourself?  Do you really know yourself?  Do you really understand what it means to be a whirling tornado of energy in motion? You are made of some 50 trillion cells which means you have 50 trillion tornados happening inside you.  This is an incredible field of strong energy you are carrying around.  Do you ever get a chance to recognize that? Do you ever get a chance to think about that? Do you realize the beauty of this energy and strength? Do you give yourself enough credit for it?

So tell me now, seeing that you are this solid field of energy in motion, what and who can stand in your way? Does any tornado ever worry about anything in its way? Does any tornado play a victim? I just want you to think about these questions.

The next question I want you to think about is: where do you come from? Before your parents decided to create this ball of twirling energy, where were you? The science has clearly defined energy as: "Energy can be transformed into another sort of energy. But it cannot be created AND it cannot be destroyed. Energy has always existed in one form or another."  What? Say that again? "Energy has always existed in one form or another."  So does this mean that we always existed? And "Energy can be transformed into another sort of energy." So does this mean I can be something else next or I was something else before? "It cannot be created AND it cannot be destroyed", wow, so I am ongoing?

Isn't that the exact same thing the religions describe God as? Which brings us to the next topic of "what part does religion and tradition play in your life?" Do you consider yourself part of a well-known religion, or a complete atheist, or none of the above? Here is the funny part: no matter what you relate to, even if it is just a big bang theory, you cannot escape the topic of energy. Anything solid around you has a rate of frequency within which they vibrate. The experimental botany talks about and researches the natural frequencies of trees and how to measure them. (Journal of Experimental Botany, Vol. 48, No. 310, pp. 1125-1132, May 1997). The plants, wildlife, stones, and anything you see and many you cannot possibly see – due to the range of vision - have their own energy and special frequency. Your own body is comprised of different energies. One frequency creates the liver cell and another the muscle cell and another the kidneys and so on. Look back at the talk we had earlier about CAT Scans or MRIs.

So now, if our so called physical world is all about energy, and what we call Universe is also that, as well as the God of your certain religion, where do you end and God begins? Where do you end and the Universe begins? Energy as we know it, does not have a clear cut line or a border around it. It is due to this, that we can hear each other in a distance. If there was void between us, we would never hear each other or any other noise for that matter.

If you are an atheist, you have it easy. Why? Because you have not been fed a whole bunch of non-truth about a creator. You see what is around you, you deduct from what you see and if you read enough material in your lifetime about energy and quantum mechanics and quantum physics, you would clearly understand that the God everyone is striving to please is only a part of the energy you call "you". It cannot be outside of you, beside you, above you or interfering in any way in your life. It is pure and simple. The simplest form of energy I like to always refer to because it is so familiar to us, is electricity. Electricity, does not reward or punish you. If you place your wet finger in a socket and a jolt throws you a few feet away, it was not punishing you, but that is what electricity does. If you get to light up your house, or make a toast, it is not rewarding you, but you have learned how to use this energy to your advantage. If we fly a plane against gravity, the gravity is not rewarding you, but you have learned how to manipulate this energy. If your few thousand pound ship does not sink in the sea, it is because you have learned the laws of buoyancy.

For the more religious crowd, God has always been portrayed as one that can reward and punish. Can also sometimes be kind enough that at times of need will/may lend you a hand. He is quite judgmental and can make or break you for what you do, or who you are. The fear of God is so deeply engrained in so many individuals that it actually interferes with their daily lives.

I would like everyone to TRULY examine their belief system and the reasons of why they perform certain rituals, or are allowed to do some things and not another. One important factor that I would like you to keep in mind for any of the holy books is that, they have been mostly written at a different time in history, and a different continent of planet where the language and the narratives mean completely a different thing. Some expressions translated to any other language, often takes a completely new meaning.

I follow the non-denominational religion, where there is no division and we are all one, based on the earlier explanation of the "energy". I have interest in all religions and findings and am completely flexible to change my views at a drop of a hat, if what is being said makes sense.

Looking into the major and minor religions they have much in common. Well first of all there is a God existing in all of them. The omnipotent (all powerful), omniscient (knows everything), omnipresent (in all places at the same time), and omnibenevolent (only does things that are good for all). I agree with all of them because from the stand point of a "Source Energy", of course it would be all powerful as it is the one that everything is made of and hence has the control over the frequency of the vibration to change from one creation to the next. Of course it is all-knowing. Wouldn't you know it all if you were a part of EVERYTHING there is, which also speaks to being present everywhere. And of course it does things that are all good, as an energy would never hurt itself so to speak.

Good and bad is only a separation in "our" minds. There is no real meaning to "good" or "bad", only choices.

As I mentioned in the case of electricity, you will not be seeing an electrical jolt, sitting, moping and feeling guilty because it has zapped you. It has done, what is needed to be done. That's it. It is not good, it is not bad, it just is. You will not see one cat or dog or any other wildlife passing by another one of their species and boasting about how good they have it, and how pitiful the other one is. Because these are only human differentiations and it comes from the choice. We have the "choice" to choose, as we are a different frequency of this ever-lasting energy.

Now back to the holy books and the questions we might want to think about. The very first topic is of course, is the matter of God being loving and punishing you for your deeds at the same time. I guess as a human, we have no other way of looking at things but in a form of parenting. He is the father, and hence for the sake of tough love, he will punish me to keep me on the straight and narrow. Does this ring a bell?

If yes, I would like you for one minute to think about this: what is outside of this energy that we call God?

As a human, when we want to build something, we reach inside first, think about what we want to make, then reach out of ourselves and get the material for it, and make it. We also at this point, write a manual on how this item can be used and what will make it last longer or break. A user's guide so to speak. Now what happens if you are the "source" of all things? You think about it, and then you reach within you to create it. If you compare the "Source" to us, then you would feel that he is reaching out to create something, then the subject of "parent" and "child" becomes valid. But if you look at God from the "Source" perspective, where he (and I am using "he" for the lack of better term. Energy is not gender specific) does not reach out of himself and all is self-contained; so will be the rules and regulations. The creation happens and the options and conditions of

17

how this creation will be living is provided, just like a built-in users' manual.

So if I simplify our creation; let's say you make a pen. The user's manual will specify how to hold the pen for the best ink flow. What temperatures are best suited so that it would not leak. What is the maximum flexibility of the item before it breaks, etc. Now, someone buys this pen and if this person takes this pen and dunks it into hot water – where it was not recommended – what happens? The pen of course at this point is done for. It will not work. Would it be a fair statement to say, "The creator of the pen is punishing the user?" Because this is exactly what we do, on the subject of God. Say for example, we abuse our body, and when it stops functioning, and we have health issues, we ask God to lend us a hand to rejuvenate the body. Does this make sense? And if he does not, is he punishing us? We manage to mess up our relationships and then when we are feeling lonely or in trouble the first things that pops up in our head is, "Why has God forsaken me?" Does that make sense?

On the other hand when we made the pen, we warned the user that certain things will render the pen useless. So now here comes the "choice". I have, as the user, the option of using something properly, or improperly. But that is my choice. You have created this pen and left it for whomever wants to pick and use it; and provided all the possible options. If a user decides to break the pen, seeing that you had made that option available, you would have nothing to say to that. That is what the user decided to try and they did. It was not good. It was not bad. It was "just" a choice.

The flip side of this is that if we look at parenting and compare our God to a parent, then we have a different story happening. So we give birth to a new generation. Then we feed them, shelter them, clothe them, raise them, and educate them. We "expect" them to behave a certain way, and to pick a certain trait, and manage their lives the way "we" imagined them to. If they deviate from our expectations, then there is hell to pay. At times we might even be ever so offended, to disown them. If your perspective of God is as a parent, I can see how you would mistake the functions.

Yet another view of the parenting would be, the open-minded parenting. We have given birth and done all that needs to be done to provide for the new generation with support they need. We also have offered choice to the fledglings to go ahead and choose whatever they want, and no matter what, they have the support and love they are seeking to continue making choices for themselves. Do you feel any fear of punishment in a relationship like this? Is it scary? Now look around you in nature. Which one of the above methods, do you see most happening in nature? The scary one where you are punished, or the supportive one where you can choose? When you look at this small, yet various instances and pictures the nature has provided you with, which one would you say is likely for the Source to support?

Yet another twist to this story, is that if the "Source" does not reach out of itself to create anything, what is it we are made of other than what is existing within the Source? And if the "Source" has created this frequency version of itself, what is this lower frequency, seemingly solid body, is capable of doing? What can a piece of apple do that the whole apple can't? The only thing has to be, that a piece of apple is not the whole of the apple, but has exact properties of the whole.
So if you are the piece of the whole "Source" what is it you cannot do? Seeing that you are made of energy based on what we talked earlier on the subject of atoms and molecules and cells, what within you, can you not fix if it goes wrong? Every ailment we suffer then becomes "In-curable" or curable from within.

Now I want you to think about God punishing or rewarding one more time. What does that even mean? The "Source" of this energy that comprises all within and around us, has provided the choices and the avenues and the so-called menu to pick from. A restaurant owner offering you a menu can never punish or reward you, for choosing

19

any meal out of the menu. Every choice, is just that, a choice. Everything goes and everything is accepted.

What we have agreed on, as a society to live and work in peace, and the laws we have created, to create our harmony, only applies the period of time we are here as the physical being. The laws of energy are different. They are those of acceptance. There is no good; there is no bad; only variations of frequencies that will bring about various results. Cause and effect. The boomerang effect. The Law of Attraction. Or whatever else you like to call it. Simple, yet certainly powerful. So behaving in a low frequency manner, will result in low frequency happenings – this is what we consider bad things. And behaving in high frequency manner, will result in high frequency happenings – this is what we call happy and good things.

This of course also covers the topic of, do you have control over what happens in your life. The answer is: it depends on how you behave. So maybe I have to expand on the word behave, to say that it includes: words, actions, emotions, feelings and thoughts. All of which are considered energies and energy altering and so altering the state of your living as well as health and prosperity in general.

After the paragraph above, what does it mean to be a victim? The only thing you can become a victim of, would be your very own actions, words, emotions, thoughts and feelings. This of course puts "you" in the driver's seat and in charge. This is a huge undertaking and responsibility. You no longer can blame "anyone" for "anything". Wow! So now what? What occupies your thoughts most of the day? What do you talk about? Remember that your thoughts and talks, also rule your feelings and emotions.

When you talk about cutting and squeezing a lemon on ice and adding sugar and water, your body shows a reaction by producing saliva and you can almost taste it. The same goes for any other words you utter, or whatever you think about. You may not see a definite sign, like the saliva production, but it definitely produces something, a reaction to the thought and words.

A quick explanation of what a hormone is: we have something called an Endocrine system which contains endocrine glands and they make chemicals called hormones and pass them right into the bloodstream. You can think of them as chemical messages.

The hormones then, from the blood stream, communicate with the different parts of body by heading towards their target cells, to bring about a particular change or effect to that cell. The hormone can create changes in the cells and the adjacent tissues. The endocrine system works with the nervous system and the immune system to help the body handle different events and stresses.

Now that we have the very basics of what a hormone does, let me get into this a bit more. Emotions are called "energy in motion". This is your internal GPS. Your thoughts and emotions affect every hormone and cell in your body. So your thoughts create emotions, which produce hormones accordingly, which affects your body and brain, which produces feelings, and which in turn will decide on our actions. Your thoughts are super powerful.

Perception →Thoughts → Emotions → Hormones → Feelings → Words/Actions

The effect of vitamins, herbs, healthy eating, acupuncture, exercise and all other good things, can be undermined with the thoughts you might be having. Thoughts have a profound effect on your health, physically, emotionally, spiritually and mentally.

We can start our very own healing process by showing compassion to ourselves and loving ourselves. The best road to healing, is through high frequency thoughts, and getting rid of low frequencies like: shame, anger, anxiety, worry, and blame, just to name a few. Having said that, perception is at the root of all the feelings I just mentioned.

Please understand that no emotion is considered "good" or "bad". The goodness or badness of something, depends on what it makes "you" feel like. If you feel uplifted and happy, you will take positive steps towards bettering your life. If you feel distressed and unhappy, it will take you in the direction of desperate actions.

# A bit more about Emotions

Oriental medicine, associates the emotions with the Yin organs. Each organ is connected with a particular emotion. For example: fear relates to the kidney, anger to the liver, sadness to the lungs, joy to the heart, and anxiety to the spleen.

Two organs bear the impact of all emotional difficulties – the Heart and the Liver. The Heart is associated with love, warmth, and the formation of relationships. It houses the Mind, or Spirit, which governs general stability. Emotional stress and shock can lead to mental disturbance, anxiety, and unstable behaviour.

The Liver governs the free flow of Qi. Emotional stress and general frustrations restrain the liver and block Qi. This can cause pain, stuffiness, or obstruction anywhere in the body, as well as depression or forceful explosions of feeling.

Although people consider emotions as being only psychologically based, scientific discoveries have shown that emotions are physiologically based. According to the Longman Dictionary of Psychology and Psychiatry, an emotion is "a complex reaction pattern of changes in nervous, visceral, and skeletal muscle tissues in response to a stimulus. As a byproduct of feeling, an emotion is usually related to a specific person or event and involves widespread physiological changes, such as increased heart rate."

The physiology of emotions can be affected by structural factors. A muscle contracting, when and how you want it, is normal physiology. When a muscle is in a state of constant contraction (or spasm) at an inappropriate time, this is abnormal physiology. Similarly, when an emotional response is happening at an inappropriate time, it is also abnormal physiology. We feel different emotions in different parts of our body, and in different ways.

Although the primary locations for the physiology of emotions are in the brain, spine, and autonomic nervous system, emotions affect any and all parts of the body in a physiological way.

Normally, a person who has a stressful life event experiences the emotion and stores the event as a memory. When the emotional response is expressed, the biochemicals flow freely and all systems continue to work together.

At times however, after an event, we don't just return to our "normal" state of being. Our bodies hold on to the response and "lock it" in our nervous system, as a conditioned reflex to stimuli, associated with the event. When emotions are repressed or denied, the network of pathways gets blocked, stopping the flow of vital feel-good chemicals.

This can cause weakened conditions that may manifest either in a specific dysfunction or a general influence on body function. It may promote, worsen, or even cause recurrences of illness, behaviours, and imbalances. The end result is often ill health.

# A Non-Denominational View to God…

To me, God translates to: pure energy that is ever present. This energy is our essence and what we are made of. We have been told for many thousands of years through all religions that we are made in the image of God, yet never properly contemplated what that means. Now with the advancement of the science and Quantum Physics, it is proven that nothing exists in a solid form and it is all energy that vibrates to different frequencies and even the empty space between two, is made of energy, hence being able to hear or see something. The rate of vibration decides how solid or liquid or visible something is.

## Is it possible to get close to God?

It is impossible for us not to be close to God. We are a piece of the same energy. This is why, God always loves you and protects you, as you would any part of you. This is why you can never be alone.

## Does God really care about you?

God cannot, not care about you. Asking a question like this is like asking: would the ocean care for the drop of water in it. You are a part of the whole. The whole cannot separate from you.

## What is God like?

Beyond what we can imagine. As physical beings, we are not wired to fathom the vastness and the operation of this tremendous energy. The energy that I would like to refer to as "The Source" or "The ALL"; is all there is, and in its essence it is "Just".

## Is God uncaring and heartless?

Energy is about justice and not about emotion and drama. If you stick your finger into a light socket and you are zapped, can you in any sane way declare the electricity or the socket uncaring and heartless? It makes no sense. The energy will do what energy is required to do. None of the emotional drama that we attribute to it, will play a role.

# How does God feel about the injustices we face?

It does not! There are no injustices in the world of cause and effect. What goes around comes around. You receive what you send out, or some equivalent frequency of it. What we face, is simply the mass frequencies we have sent out, over the period of time that is haunting us now. We have the need to dramatize and make it someone else's fault, hence we complain of injustice. In the "Source" created environment, everything is just, because the energy from which it is created, is just. Calling anything an injustice, is pure blasphemy and violation of the rules!

# Does God want you to know who he is?

This was a question asked in a book I recently read….LOL Why would the Source would want the truth hidden from you, when so many prophets have come to tell us about our powers? The more you know yourself, the better this energy source can experience through you. It is a natural understanding then that it would definitely want you to grasp who you are and your relationship to it.

# What is God's purpose for mankind or the Earth?

If the car you design can tell you what your purpose of its creation was, so can we. This is an age old question without any answers but only speculations. All we can do is speculate. For me this is how this unfolds:

When the Source was just the Source, there was nothing more than that. The creation allows for experience. Since the creation is of the same nature as the creator – the energy – the experience is even more so meaningful. Every single bit of existence is completely and fully experienced. When the infinite number of all experiences are exhausted, that is when the whole environment is wrapped up a new creation starts over again.

# What will life on Earth be like in the future?

This was another question in that same book that I read. My thought on this: the life on Earth in the future will be exactly the way it needs to be. I know this sounds a bit sarcastic and facetious, but how can you answer it other than that? The life on Earth will be exactly as we make it. Where are our vibrations heading? Are they going towards peace, joy and prosperity? If yes, then the Earth in the future will be a peaceful, joyful and prosperous place to live on. If our energy is directed towards, separatism, hatred, revenge, anger, control and me-ism, then I will leave it to you to guess what kind of Earth we would have, and what kind of life we would lead.

## Will I get what I want if I pray to God?

You can pray all you want to the electrical socket about sparing you, and the minute you stick your finger in it, you are toast. Prayer only works when you take responsibility for your actions, words, feelings and emotions. When you understand that you are the creator of your reality, your words, feelings, emotions and actions are your prayers and they will take you exactly to where you wish to go. So pray right, and if you feel your prayers are not answered, re-examine yourself.

## Can God punish us or be angry at us?

Let me give you another example: you have created a buffet for a party that is about to arrive. Will you punish or be angry at some of them because they choose one item in the buffet over the other? How can God get angry and or punish you if all you are able to do, is choose from the menu that was originally provided by it? In the infinite number of choices that we have in life, one thing we do not have access to, is the menu that is above and beyond what is provided. If you had that option, then anger and punishment would be an option for the Source. God is not some cantankerous old man, sitting there with a whip, waiting for you to take a wrong step. God is the source of your creation. It is within you and all you have is this energy, no matter what shape it takes. This image of God was created for us for the purpose of control. Fearful people are so much easier controlled than the ones who understand themselves and their relation to God and their true given powers.
We have been told that we get punished for our "sins". What are sins? A sin is when we make a mistake or take the so-called wrong path; or miss a mark. If you know something is going to have ill effects in your life and you do it anyhow, you have committed a "sin". You don't need the church or the mosque or synagogue to tell you that you will have undesirable results. When you understand what the potential of electricity is, and understand the consequences of

playing with it, and you still play with it and it zaps you, you have been in essence punished for not using your knowledge. Unless of course your desire was to be crippled or dead, in which case you have taken the proper action and it will no longer be a sin....LOL So you see, it is not God punishing you for your sins, it is the nature of the energy at work.

## Why Does God allow suffering?

This again was another question I read. Is it really God "allowing" suffering? Again, I encourage you to take a look at nature of things. The nature of an energy signal is to land on whatever allows that same frequency as a receiver. If someone or a nation have low frequency, they are the best landing fixture for the low energy happening. Asking the Source to reach out and interrupt the nature of energy, is only a human understanding in asking for favouritism. This would be equal to saying that if John and Terry are jumping off the CN tower today, one will be floating before hitting the pavement and the other will go into pieces because God did not think Terry should really suffer. The nature of energy does not allow for that kind of distinguishing facts. That is only the human part of us speaking. To the Source, all that is happening is just so, there is no distinguishing factor of "suffering".

# Your Life is Waiting….

Life is constant.  You do not get up one morning to find Lake Ontario in another province or the tree in your backyard does not disappear overnight to your neighbour's yard, and the desk you are working on does not flicker in and out of existence due to Quantum physics' observer theory.   This is showing us that even though everything is made of energy and the solid material is just a perception, there are still some unchanging principles that have made this possible.

For those who look for evidence in holy books, if these unchanging principles and laws did not exist, you would not see such references as: "believe and all things are possible" instead we would have something like, "As long as it is Saturday, the Saturn is rising."  If we make our reality, we are not doing it part time. Your life is a blank canvas waiting for your creativity and expression.

We all have different paintings.  The only reason that some matters seem the same in most paintings, is because we accept and adhere to someone else's beliefs, and generate our thoughts, perceptions and emotions according to that; and in that, we share the same object in our painting.  If you do not want the same, then change your thoughts.

Your life is waiting for you to live it the way that you want to. Your words are a form of action, which would also lead you to, where you want to go.  Your words are your thoughts, "crystallized". Your words often reflect the thoughts that you most intensely believe in. For example if you find yourself saying, "The job market is bad and the good-paying jobs are hard to find", this will definitely manifest in the life you lead at one time or another depending on the intensity of thoughts and emotions.

We normally speak two different kinds of words: the spontaneous words in conversation which identify our beliefs and the intentional words such as mantras and affirmations.

If you really want to get to know someone, listen to them carefully and diligently while they offer spontaneous words, and you will begin to learn their most intimate beliefs.
You are not here to merely make "ends meet" and survive.  Take full advantage of this adventure that is all paid for.  Don't try to pay for a

trip that is already paid in full. We are not here to break even, we are here to be happy and enjoy and have fun and build the sand castles and thrive and grow.

You having everything you want, is only self-centred if, you believe in scarcity. Come, get on with it, your life is really waiting. We are living in a magical Universe. Your own body alone has somewhere around 50 trillion cells that operate day in and day out without fail. This is only one person, what about all the other people, living beings from insects and birds to larger mammals and then there is vegetation and the inanimate things around; all of which are made from the same material we are, and they are also operating day in and day out without fail. Can you even grasp the vastness of this project???

Had it not been for some very basic laws that are consistent, nothing would be operating at a reliable and steady rate. It is quite overwhelming to think of all the invisible, unknown things that support us and make our life even possible. The irony lies in the fact that we must trust these invisible forces to do their part, and we tend to trust them only to a degree that we have to. Whether we admit it or not, the truth of the matter is, that we do trust them and the question remains: how many of your life's manifestations are you willing to leave to the unknown???

The key is to trust it 100% and you will see that your life becomes effortless. I guess this kind of trust, we call faith. Faith that the sun will rise tomorrow, the earth will continue spinning, the stars will still shine, and the oceans will still be there, and your hearts and lungs and kidneys and all 50 trillion cells of your body will operate flawlessly through the night, even though you have no awareness of them. Now fit into this line of faith, that you are always provided for and protected and abundant and you got yourself an awesome life.

Incessantly remember that the "greater you" always extends beyond your physical body, and you are alive in the Universe, and the Universe is alive in you. In this sense it will always plan on your behalf because it is the bigger you. The Universe longs to see you smile and be joyful and hear your laughter bring vibration to every atom comprising it. It roots for you, cheers for you, and loves you every step of the way.

The Universe yearns to see you happy and fulfilled and the only law that it will prevent it from reaching into your deck of cards and rearranging it to see you that way this very second; is the law of attraction. It is a set rule that whatever "you" focus on will be done. Hence, the variety in experiences. The consistency and integrity of the ruling laws must be observed otherwise as we discussed earlier all will fall apart.

So now, all that is required from you is faith. If you take a look at nature you will see the enormous beauty of it. Why is it placed there, if it is not for you to enjoy? Can you fathom for one second to put aside all the old teachings that you have received from multiple sources telling you that, "you are here to learn lessons and you will be punished for what you have not done right?"

Turn within. Listen to your heart. Reason with all the evidence nature has provided you with. Liberate from falsehood and find your power and peace. The game of life is rigged in your favour. We are here to thrive not survive.


Anytime that you pray for something and it comes true, take a look at your level of belief in the fact that it is possible for it to come true and you will see that "you" are responsible in making it manifest. You are powerful. Interfering in your business of co-creating would be against all laws.

I once heard or read an analogy, which I reiterate here as it makes such wonderful sense to me. If you imagine yourself being a pilot; you really did not invent aviation or the flying process. You did not even help build or test the plane and you did not orchestrate the formation of the airline company, hiring the attendants, the ticket agencies, the run way, the control tower, etc. all you do is show up a few hours prior to the flight for departure procedures, hop into the cockpit, power up the engines, aim and fly. During the flight you would be the one turning the yoke, or the rudder and flicking some switches.
That is all you have to do in starting to live now. You have shown up, you are being taught the life procedures, now, aim and live and delegate the rest of the stuff to the Universe as you did with the flight.

Let me ask you a question, if you could have ANYTHING in your life, anything at all what would that be? – Except for a specific person. Now whatever you dreamed of, do you have ANY doubt in the magic of the Universe to deliver it to you? Do you think that maybe and just maybe not even God can provide that? The funny part is that most of us innately know that if it were up to God to give us things, he would, because he is kind, giving and loving. To Him all is possible. The only doubt you might have is in "your" capabilities. (Please Note: God, or Source Energy, or The All, does not have a gender. The use of "he" is specifically due to need for some sort of reference.)

Well in a way you are right. You as the physical you, cannot manifest a darn thing. Unless of course you have the hand of Universe at work. So put your mind at ease in thinking that it is actually you doing anything. If you really understand what I am saying you will get the point I am trying to make. We create nothing at the physical level, we create everything in energy level. But most of us are level confused.

We always think thought that we must carry the weight of the world. But it is time for us to reverse the effects of this brainwashing.

Here is a thought that you might find worthy: dwell in spirit. Instead of trying to take care of everything physically, turn it over to the Universe. Let it resolve it for you. The real work that needs to be done on any matter is far beyond physical reach.

The next time you do any visualization, include the Universe in there as your ally. If thoughts of unworthiness ever creep up on you, please do understand that, "that which is not worthy, is not here". If you are still around, you must be still worthy. You are divine, the Universe is loving and all your thoughts become things.

Faith means you believe. You believe that you are not alone and the infinite wisdom and incalculable powers of the Universe are yours to work with to any degree that you allow yourself to. Whether you ask for a little or a lot, you receive.

# Faith

How do you define faith? I have heard many say, "faith is believing in the unseen", or "when you are blindly going without knowing but trusting that God will take you through it." To me, faith is not actually believing in the unseen or blindly following anything. Faith ONLY can happen if you actually know what you are following and the "seen" or "unseen" part of it, does not really only translate to your physical eyesight, even though there is plenty of physical evidence.

Faith, can only be through knowledge. So, for the religious crowd, in any of the holy books you will see the phrases about "choice" and "dominion", being often repeated. What does that actually mean? Have you ever really stopped to think, what kind of power this provides you with? To have choice? And then being said that you have dominion over Earth and animals? How many of us practice the choice? Do you get to choose your life? When was the last time you made a choice? If your life is ruled by parents, friends, society, media or anything else that seems to rule our lives these days, then you have not really made choices. You have just followed the norm and what is expected. And if you follow the norm, your next reaction can only be of victimhood, and not taking responsibility. Faith can only be true when you take an absolute responsibility of your life and make choices.

For us to take responsibility, the core understanding of what we truly are, and the comprehension of the environment around us and learning from anything and all, is a necessity. It is only when you understand how you fit into the whole thing, and you realize your role and position, that you gain great respect and understanding towards all; hence have dominion and make choices. This is when faith comes to be. Faith comes from your understanding, and not from your will. Faith comes from "getting to know". In this faith can never be blind.

Having said all this, even the non-religious crowd, should get the picture that in order for you, to know that it is all about choices, and things do not happen in some random manner, they need to dig into the specifics of energy and the operations of it. When you see and understand how energy operates, you gain faith in how things will be played out. Faith is not only for religious. Faith is the matter of understanding how things work and what outcomes you can be expecting.

Look around you, learn about any and everything around you. See how the small learnings translate to you understanding the big picture. This will bring about a deep sense of faith, that no one can rob you off of. You will then get the sense of what and who you are and nothing can ever play a role in creating anxiety, depression, shame, sorrow, envy or anger. Knowing translates to peace and loving. Knowing is rewarding. Remember Faith as we talk about different subjects in the upcoming pages and chapters.

# Acceptance

I cannot emphasize enough the value of understanding and learning about your environment. Once again, it is only then, that you start the process of true acceptance. We, as human beings, have been taught from early ages to carry a big chip on our shoulders called supremacy. We are told we are the highest in the food chain for the fact that we speak, we have a certain mental capacity, we decide, we choose, we can define what is good or bad. We are the ultimate of beings.

Let's look at all this for a second. We speak, yes, but so do everything else. Even trees and plants communicate. We have mental capacities, but so do, cats, dogs, horses, pigs and monkeys. We decide, really? If I am following the fashion, and what is acceptable and not acceptable in the eyes of others, and what I am expected to do – marry at a certain age, the marriage must be between a man and a woman, have a white picket fence house and 2.5 kids and a dog, have a certain kind of title and make a certain amount of money – did I really decide anything? Or followed to the next topic, did I really choose anything?

If during my growing years, I have been told what is good or bad, and what is acceptable and not acceptable, isn't that how we train our dogs as well? So what exactly makes us supreme? If we can look around us without a judgment in what we do or do not approve of, and learn from it, now that's different. Learning without judgment comes from understanding what we discussed before and the fact that there is no definite line in where you end and something else begins. When everything becomes so intermingled with your very own existence and not separate from you, this makes passing a judgment on anything, judging yourself. It sort of reminds us of what we used to say as kids, "I am rubber, you are glue, what you say bounces off me and sticks to you."

So understanding yourself and your surrounding is what keeps you away from judgment and brings about acceptance and with it peace.

# Patience and Tolerance

Patience is referred to as a virtue. I of course would like to introduce a different view of it. After all, it is all about perspective right? So, are you ever, tolerant or patient towards something you love and adore? We always tolerate and are patient about the things we are resistant to. We are not patient about good stuff. We are always tolerating "bad" behaviour, or show patience about something that otherwise we would punch the daylight out of. Being patient is nothing but making a judgment, in other word, not "accepting", and hence resisting what is in front of you and causing what you resist to persist. If you are being patient and or tolerating something, try the previous part of this book on "acceptance". Acceptance contains unconditional love within it.

# Communication

There is a lot to be said when it comes to the art of communication and verbal jousting. Having a background in training and psychotherapy has made the importance of this subject quite clear. Concise communication is not just putting your point across, but also the art of listening. This is our tool and gateway to many things, from business to healthy and happy relationships.

Proper communication makes arguments and "broken phone" conversations a thing of the past. The one who uses this tool effectively knows how to use logic and reasoning to calm situations, without having to blame anyone. Just look around you. How many of us today are into the blame game to clear our own name, and blame it on someone else? What causes this, is the lack of knowledge in how to properly communicate without accusing.

Even though one of the most popular and talked-about subjects, few of us know how to really communicate. I have seen people who are unable to speak, but they are wonderful communicators.

Amongst all curriculum at school, and understanding that communication is of utmost importance and vital to our future lives, the topic is not properly discussed or taught during the school years.

Communication involves a transmitter – this is the person sending the message; and a receiver – this is the person receiving the message. There is of course the "message" element – this is information of some form; and noise, which is anything that interferes with the information being transmitted to the mind of the receiver.

Other components include: feedback, which happens consistently in a verbal and non-verbal fashion during a conversation; replication – duplication of the same image in the receiver's mind - which is hoped for but perhaps is more of ideal than achievement; and last but not least, understanding – a guesstimate of what the message means.

Excellent communication is the ability of the sender to replicate the message in the receiver's mind without clouding the matter with irrelevant chatter. Also it is the responsibility of the receiver to clarify any communication that in his/her mind is not properly communicated. The transmitter, however, accepts the responsibility for the end results of the communication. This means the transmitter needs to make sure to speak in terms that the receiver comprehends.

I am certainly simplifying this beyond belief for the mere fact that the perceptions of both the transmitter and the receiver matter. Everything that is transmitted first must go through the perception sieve before the receiver can make sense of it. The other side of this complicated subject is our language of need. Not only the transmitter must communicate in a certain physical language that is comprehendible by the receiver, but also the transmitter must be aware of the "need" language of the receiver.

We communicate through our needs and emotions more than we do through words, and physical movements. It is a must for us to understand the receiver's needs and frequency prior to transmitting a message for clear landing.

All of this is of course of no significance if a person is uncomfortable in the communication process to begin with. This can happen at times of low self-confidence or in occasions where the transmitter is trying to put the blame on someone for misunderstanding, or they might have a stage fright of whom they are transmitting the message to and their perception of the power or hierarchy.

So to summarize the whole thing, the most effective communicators:

- Bond and relate – meaning they do not just relay the message they came to relay or prove; they are dynamic and know what this particular audience is looking for and when they will be losing them intellectually and emotionally. They make you feel like you are the only person in the world.
- Involve – not only they initiate the conversation, but they drive it, give it direction, and encourage others to take part.
- Neutralize – they are able to lower the defenses of the receiver. This does not make them manipulative, but genuine, self-confident, humble and authentic.
- Focus – they organize their communication; carefully structure the stories to be delivered to hold the receiver's interest and drive their point home.

- Clarify – they simplify complex subjects without being patronizing.
- Emphasize – they understand the span of attention and they artfully reinforce the key points at certain intervals. This needs to happen without coming off as redundant.

Learn to communicate effectively.  Your life depends on it

# Addiction

When the topic of addiction comes up, we naturally and immediately think drugs and alcohol. Here are few more addictive material I would like to throw in the bunch:

Anger, anxiety, worry, depression, resentment, jealousy, fear, people, things, pleasure, sex, shame, judgement, blame, regret and all other high or low level frequency feelings and emotions.

When we take drugs or alcohol, we are introducing a chemical compound to the body to get a certain feeling that ignites an emotion to produce a high. This "high" feeling is what takes us away from what is happening in our life currently and numbs us, to what goes on around, hence we become addicted to it. In a case like this the chemical is man-made. Even if one is addicted to pain medication, you know by now that the more of the medication you take, the more resistant you become, and the dosage will need to increase. We somehow become numb or resistant to these chemicals due to the flexibility of this beautiful body of ours.

Our bodies are a huge laboratory, which creates hundreds of chemicals on an ongoing and daily basis, depending on how we feel. For us to experience happiness, the body creates and releases to the bloodstream, chemicals such as: dopamine, serotonin, endorphin and oxytocin. When we face fear, our body produces epinephrine or adrenalin to cause increase in heart rate, muscle strength and blood pressure and metabolism balance. Our body creates melatonin at times of wanting to rest. Thyroxin for growth. Gastrin for digestion. And many, many more.

The way our body deals with our thoughts is to generate a chemical reaction, that will end up creating a feeling, which will lead to an emotion. So for us to experience a certain emotion, a range of chemicals are produced. As we get dependent on that emotion, the body becomes resistant to the chemical, wanting more and more of it. This brings about addiction, to a variety of emotions, from anger to resentment and all the above-mentioned.

When someone is addicted to anger, eventually everything will bring that feeling about. This is how, the person is getting the natural "high". When people meditate, they also get a natural high. So it all depends on what frequency you want to be hooked to, and tune into.

Emotions with higher frequency tend to be closer to the speed of light, hence bringing more health to the system. Lower frequency emotions, bring about dimness in the cells causing disease. I have also discussed this here under "mind powers". The purpose of this section was to bring awareness to the addictive emotions and their side effects.

In the world of today, we have all become adrenaline and cortisol junkies. We have made everything into something serious. From all creations around us, we are the only ones with deadlines. Under a normal circumstance, back when our forefathers were cavemen; their most dominant stress was to run away from animals that would eat them. So, every once in a while, when threatened, adrenalin was produced, and they ran for their life. Today, even if we do not have the stress of work, daily jobs, kids, mortgage, bills, etc. we go to an amusement park and grab a ride on the rollercoaster.

This leaves our body in a state of constant fight or flight; the adrenal glands exhausted, and us feeling tired and unmotivated. We have become so much so addicted to adrenalin and cortisol, a few people in the circle of my associates whom I know for fact, would NEVER be able to just rest and do nothing. Resting and meditation is completely out of their range of frequency. Add to this our eating habits and you have yourself a ticking time-bomb.

We see more and more ladies trying to conceive and not being able to. They go through injections and stress to have a baby; yet not for one moment they consider taking a closer look at the reason behind it. One major factor behind female sterility, is the hardening of the uterus lining. Stress and over production of estrogen plays a major role in this. Relaxation has helped many to be able to reproduce. A study by Dr. Herbert Benson's team found that a program for infertile women based on the relaxation response, led to "decreases in anxiety, depression, and fatigue as well as increases in vigor." Along with those benefits, the same study found that 34% of participants became pregnant within 6 months of completing the program.

So, examine your thoughts, feelings and emotions to pinpoint any addictions you are experiencing; or the ailments you might be suffering from.

# Range of Emotions

## Anger –

The feeling of Anger is similar to depression and it only worsens any situation for you. This emotion is quite destructive and definitely needs to be addressed and not suppressed. When you suppress anger, the next time it appears much denser than the first. Try to understand your anger. Understand that "you" are the source of it and not someone else. You may feel someone else caused it, but it really is your "perception" of an action or word someone presented to you that has caused the anger. Your perception can be at fault at all times. Things are not always as they seem. Even if you feel justified with this feeling, how much good is it doing you anyways?

Instead of asking you why you were angry, I am now going to go right to the core of it and ask: who were you angry at? Were you angry because someone said something bad to you, or did you wrong? Were you angry because someone did not follow your direction?

If you feel, someone said or did you wrong, you are feeling victimized. We talked a bit about this in previous pages, but let's look into it a bit more now.

Our perception of what is right and wrong comes from years of information gathering. From the moment we are born, our parents, family members, all media, school, friends, and associates let us know, if they "think" we have done something wrong. Especially in the earlier stages of our lives, we are quite susceptible to all these suggestions and we keep a real good database of these in alphabetical order in the back of our head.

From this point onwards, when someone else says or does something that does not fit within our list, we call it "wrong". When the deed fits within the list, we call it "right". The list we have is only congruent in some areas with others and it is all dependent on your upbringing, and environment. We call these our "values" and "morals".

From there onwards, we carry a measuring stick around. Every single thing that comes our way, MUST go through the process of measurement and declared either "right", "wrong", or "neutral", in cases where we have no reference or when we don't know how to pigeon-hole it.

So basically you are saying what "I" cannot measure, or what does not follow my "beliefs", is "wrong". With that same token, and the example of the restaurant I gave earlier on, if someone orders chicken instead of Shrimp, you would be highly offended. Your feeling of being offended soon translates to anger and onwards.

Anger is about - yet once again – not understanding, and not accepting. I get it; we all get angry at one point or other. The main thing is, how long do we stay in these feelings? Soon after anger hits you, take a look and see what is the core of the matter that is making you feel this way? The centre of your anger may have nothing to do with the topic. Once you understand what you are really angry at, it becomes easy to resolve it.

Always keep in mind, that other people being different, in ANY manner whatsoever, does not justify anger.

## Anxiety -

You are going to hear the words "Faith" and "Acceptance" to nauseam. LOL. Simply because anxiety and faith do not occupy the same space at the same time. You are either understanding Faith, or anxious. Panic attacks caused by anxiety, are quickly remediated by Faith. I encourage you to read the section on Faith, enough number of times to soak it in and completely absorb it. This is fundamental to your success and quality of life; meanwhile it has no bearing on whether or not you are religious. I wish I could create a different word than "Faith" to use in my writings. This word currently is associated with religion and unfortunately overused. Faith is combination of trust, assurance, confidence, reliance and belief wrapped in one. Even though they "can" be religion related, they are not.

Let me give you an example of a different word: diet. The minute we hear this word, we think about weight loss. Diet simply means what "you" as an individual, fit within your way and habit of feeding yourself. A "diet" can be quite fattening. So misinterpretation of the common words can be deterring factors.

# Blame -

The only way we can release ourselves of this act, is when we actually take responsibility for our lives and our deeds. It seems easier to blame something, someone, for what is happening around us. However, in the long run, there is a huge toll to pay.

The blame game, will only render you as a victim. A victim is always considered someone who is harmed, injured, hurt, by an action outside of themselves. They feel alone and attacked. They need to compete to win. It is dog eat dog world. They will be on the fence and defending themselves on the slightest of the matters. Everything is an accusation. Everyone is out there to get them. They are constantly in attack mode with an invisible sword in their hand. No trust, no confidence and all fear.

Just reading about it makes me anxious….LOL  The question is: do you really want to lead a life like that?  The trouble is that English dictionary only identifies the words "criminal" and "culprit" as antonyms to the word "victim". Hence leading people to believe that they are either the criminal or the victim. I would like to add another antonym to the word victim and that is: Accountable.

If you look at the synonyms of the word "accountable", you will come across: blameable and liable. I would like to be liable and blameable for my own actions, hence taking credit and responsibility in how my life turns out.

Here is the deal: you can live like a victim or an accountable person and they would both be completely OK. It is definitely a matter of choice. As an example I had a gentleman in one of my courses who was 5' tall and when I talked about the fact that we are not victims, he said, "of course I am a victim. I am 5' tall and want to be a basketball player. Can I?" Well, to his surprise the week after I showed him a video of a girl without legs hence only probably 3' tall that was quite successful in the field. Was he a victim? Not at all. But he "chose" to blame his height in not pursuing what he wanted.

The bottom line is, you live, whether you are a victim or a victor. Which one do you "choose"?

## Depression -

This is an interesting topic. This is the emotion that is telling you that you have no control over your life and you are trapped. The unfortunate part of this feeling is that the "depressed" will continuously think the depressing thoughts and hence feel more depressed. And the situation gets only worse, due to the emotions that are projected. This is the time to break the vicious cycle and realize your power and stick to the feeling of power until the situation is resolved. It's like riding a bike, if you need to keep your balance you need to keep moving.

Some people face depression once in a while and some are considered chronically depressed. Looking at this topic medically, there are many causes for this issue ranging from abuse and conflict to major events, genetics, illnesses and or side effect of certain medications. As for the genetics, I am not on board with this, but then I have talked about it in another book in length. If you are interested in the topic, please read: Divine Love the Final Landing! Or research epigenetic findings. Some research has showed that people with this disorder have a higher level of stress hormone – cortisol – than others.

An abundance of hormones such as cortisol or adrenaline, can interrupt the function of other hormones like serotonin, melatonin, estrogen, progesterone, testosterone, etc. hence causing the entire body to be out of balance. To counteract the effects of cortisol and adrenaline, production of DHEA, GABA and endorphin is suggested that happens during meditation and relaxation.

When we relax, our body releases chemicals and brain signals that make our muscles and organs slow down and increase the blood flow to the brain. Relaxation is not about being a couch potato, sleeping or just being lazy. This is more of a mentally active process that leaves the body relaxed.

The most common and non-invasive procedures are: meditation, muscle relaxation (tense and relax), visual imagery, deep breathing, and yoga. Use of aroma therapy as well, has been quite successful in the treatment. If your depression is due to anxiety, then please re-read the anxiety section. Always keep in mind that you cannot undo yesterday and live tomorrow today.

Seeing that this is a larger topic to cover, let's also consider the following when it comes to curing depression through spirituality:

Stats show that over 70 million people are suffering from effects of depression, in sharing feelings of: resentment, uselessness, lack of energy, inability to sleep, and a poor attitude toward life in general, amongst other symptoms. Depression causes a pessimistic view of things. The glass is half empty. It also discourages enthusiasm and stifles one's initiative. It may also produce despair and bring about sickness in the mind and body. It can make one choose rash and thoughtless actions that a person may later regret, and would not have done otherwise. Much of the time such thoughts are completely unnecessary. Hence, it is vital that we help cure depression so that people can live with more happiness, ingenuity, energy, and are therefore able to reach a higher potential in life.

Depression has many different causes for each individual, so it must be analyzed and understood. What can we do to help cure such an attitude?

Spiritually, there are many ways to help take care of this condition. So let us take a deeper look at this. What are the general causes of depression? Well here is a quick list:

## Physical, Biological or Medical Factors

1. Physical factors like digestive problems, diabetes, anemia, or other diseases which cause discomfort. Parasites are another biological factor that will deplete a person of their energy and well-being.

2. Sometimes the diet is the cause and culprit. There may be a lack of vitamins and proper nutrition. Or there may be too much of something, like sugar, which can also cause highs and lows in blood sugar levels, which will certainly create changing mood shifts.

3. There is also the depression that new mothers may feel, right after giving birth to a child. The hormones are often quite imbalanced at that time and a new mother may feel a multitude of changing feelings about things.

4. A weak nervous system, or overwork and tension are also some of the causes that can alter one's outlook on life.

## External Factors

1. In this category, something as simple as the weather or a cloudy day can cause melancholy and depression. These are individuals suffering from SAD (Seasonal Affective Disorder).

2. Some are very much affected by their unsatisfactory social status causing them to feel miserable.

3. Seeking approval from family, friends, and others in general can cause major depressive thoughts.

4. Being controlled or being threatened.

5. Hanging out in the circle of negative people or listening to music with dark lyrics or messages, or listening to the ever-depressive daily news will also cause a person to have the most negative outlook.
6. Feeling of being a victim to any situation.


## Psychological or Emotional Factors

1. Constant thoughts on one's bad habits or mistakes that they wish they could have corrected, or had never done, which still haunts their memory with guilt. Or feeling of guilt in general.

2. Emotions that come up, such as anger, revenge, jealousy, and envy.

3. The inability to face or deal with difficulties or worries about the future. Current regular exposure of population to regular fear and anxiety will also cause despair.


## Metaphysical Factors

1. Other unknown causes like believing in curses that have been cast can affect one negatively.

2. I have often dealt with depressive people who feel they are being influenced by other subtle influences, like ghostly beings, that may affect them in the wrong way.

3. Feeling disappointed in a role model or spiritual master or religious organization that someone may belong to, if things do not go well, can also cause deep scars and depression that can affect a person for years.

4. Misunderstanding of what God is and how it interacts in our lives has been a major cause of depression. Feeling abandoned by God.

These are only few of the causes that I can think of that may bring about a feeling of depression or misery in a person. And what is worse, if the depression is not remedied, then it can become chronic and escalate to feelings of suicide. When someone in despair feels that all of their basic defenses are broken and there is no one to turn to, nor can they find a comforting voice to console or support them, then they may conclude that there is no way out but through death. If their cry for help, is not heard or seems to be ignored, or if they do not know where to find help, then they may consider suicide as a way out.

Almost everyone goes through depression at some point in life. Some are not able to overcome this and so they look for medical and psychiatric treatment. Unfortunately most often they only end up with a bunch of harmful pills to take for the rest of their lives, with more than few side-effects.

Often times, we neglect to realize that the nature's law of cause and effect operates with relentless precision. Many of the difficulties that we encounter in life, are nothing but what is governed by this law.
In spite of what a person who is suffering from depression may think, it is actually very easy to overcome depression from a spiritual point of view. It is not at all as difficult as we imagine. And this is a major issue, since it is all a matter of perception, or point of view, which is based on the mental temperament. Our minds have the mysterious power of magnifying a problem and making it appear frightening and bigger than life. Do not listen to the warnings of your mind. Reject them ruthlessly and throw them out.

Often, developing our level of spiritually can lay the foundation so that if we are depressed, we may change our perception which may allow us to rise above a depressed state of mind.

At the height of spiritual realization you will understand that all there is in the end, is love. Universe manifests based on compassion, which is to help and support you, only if you are open to it. Only if you are willing to perceive it, like the sun shining on everyone, unless they hide from it. But it is up to you to learn how to adjust your vision. There is an old Buddhist saying that if you have a problem and cannot solve it, then why worry about it? And if you have a problem that can be resolved, then why worry about it?

As we have heard before every problem is only a temporary illusion. They may have a cause and a beginning, but they also have an end. They are all temporary and it is not to our advantage to get so wrapped up in the illusion that we forget the real life.

Perhaps at this point it is a good idea for me to clarify the meaning of "Spirituality". Spirituality and religion do not necessarily go hand in hand. I know many religious individuals that are far from spiritual and vice versa. Our ability to create satisfactory meaning out of the events in our lives has been well-established as a factor in mental health. Spirituality is often defined in terms of meaning and purpose in life, illness, death and other existential concerns. When defined in this way, spirituality has been shown to be strongly protective against depression.

People receiving treatment for depression often rate their spirituality as one of the most important parts of their recovery.

The reason for this is that God in religion is often portrayed as an "angry and vengeful" external being that is waiting for you to do something wrong and he pulls the whip out. Also I have heard in many occasions that people are taught that they are sinful. They were born in sin, they live in sin and they die in sin and unless they do something really drastic they will rot in hell. Is that really something that oozes joy? Depression under such learning is almost inevitable.

We have all felt gloom sometime in our lives. We may occasionally become depressed about our job, marriage, love life, family, finances, world events, etc. But typically this feeling dissipates in time, and life goes on. At least till the next crisis. When the feelings continue lingering this causes it to deepen, and become chronic, diminish the quality of life, impair functioning, and keep us from moving toward with our goals, dreams and desires.

As I once read somewhere in an article, despair follows a formula: D=S-M: in other words, Despair equals Suffering minus Meaning. This implies that despair can be treated by helping the patient, attribute to, or discover, some meaning in his or her personal suffering, misery and symptoms.

So basically when a psychiatrist diagnoses the patient's despair as a result of his or her clinical depression or bipolar disorder, he or she has provided some meaning to their suffering, and also some hope for chemical salvation.


# Envy -

Envy is the culprit and reason behind another feeling we call jealousy. Even though not all jealousy is envy based. Envy is when you want, what someone else has. Jealousy usually is when you are worried that someone will take away what you have. In envy, usually there are two people involved. Let's say you and your neighbour. In jealousy usually there are three people involved, you, your husband and the neighbour.

You can feel envy about something you do not have, but jealousy usually is about something you already have. Envy of course can bring about a sleuth of effects like: distress, discontent, bitterness, resentment, and depression just to name a few.

For the religious crowd, you have seen the following references within Bible or any other holy book you follow:
"Thou shall not covet thy neighbour's house. Thou shall not covet thy neighbour's wife; nor his man servant; nor his maid servant; nor his ox; nor his ass; nor anything that is thy neighbour's." exodus -20:17 KJV

This saying has been around for centuries and repeatedly recited in the Ten Commandments. I am certainly hoping that, if you are religious, you have actually given this some thought as opposed to just narrating and memorizing it. Keep in mind that the abovementioned feeling is not only a religious statement, but something to follow for everyone. This is a normal human option.

Now for the rest of us, and the religious, here are few helpful suggestions in getting rid of envy:

> _You can have it too_ – reviewing what we have talked about regarding energy, nothing really is out of your reach. The only difference between you and the person who has what you want, is resonance. They are closer to the frequency of what you want to have. So when you are envious, you are really shooting yourself in the foot. Envy has a low frequency rate. Meaning it will take you further from what you want. However, understanding that everything is available to everyone, and shifting your energy will bring what you want, closer to you.

> _Shift your view and perception to what is good in your life_ – as the old saying goes, we can see the glass half empty of half full. You can concentrate on what you _don't_ have, to what you _do_ have. It is an absolute choice. However concentrating on what you don't have causes depression and resent. Where being thankful for what you have brings more things to be thankful for. Adopt an attitude of gratitude. Some people will be happy for the fact that they _have_ a glass; regardless of it being full or empty.

Look around you and learn from your pets. You can buy a few hundred dollar cat condo, and the moment you open up a package you have received, they abandon the condo and enjoy the box. They seem to be happier in choosing the basics, and not being worried about the neighbour's cat having a bigger, better, fancier condo.

_Don't compare your life_ – one big issue we face now-a-days is the issue of comparison. What we have vs what they have. The house, the car, the job, the career, the wife, the husband, the baby, the bank account and the list goes on. How stressful is that? No matter what we have, we are always one step behind many others.

To conquer envy and all its side effects, we must abandon the idea of competition and comparison. In an energy world, where everything is available to everyone, competition is like a broken pencil - pointless. Comparison is to say, "I need to be or have what they have." So let me examine this. Would you like to have "EVERYTHING" the other person has? Including any ailments? Including the things they have hidden in their closet, possibly? Sometimes the grass on the other side is only painted. It could also be artificial turf. LOL 99% of the time, we only envy "some" of the things the neighbour has and we want the rest of our own stuff. In this, you have to recognize that you are an individual, different than all the rest and your ego can attest to that. You are only one of the spices in the kitchen of life. You cannot be salt and pepper at the same time. That defeats the purpose. You cannot be a Labrador retriever and a Chihuahua at the same time. The differences are the spice of life. We complete each other. We make the world flavourful. We are all needed, just the way we are. Be yourself! You are you!

*Get rid of those who compare you to others* – throughout your life, you probably had to face the fact of dealing with parents or caretakers, who constantly compared you to Jim and Jane. If you came home with a B+ you were asked and told to do better. Neighbour's son came home with an A++ what are you doing with a B+ making your mother ashamed?

This mentality engrained in us in childhood, carries all the way to grave. We are always competing and comparing because we need to prove ourselves to those around us.

*Understand that advertisers like to fan the flame* – We have made envy the base of our lives, advertisements and sales.

Envy plays a big role in the financial dollars we pull in at the end of the company's fiscal year. Buy this, to look like her; buy this, to be acceptable; use this, to live like this and absurdly enough, buy or do this, to be "happy".

As consumers, we fall for this trick over and over again. The number of diet pills and the exercise machines we buy and leave are quite high. We see what the person in the commercial looks like, we envy the figure, looks, level of happiness; and then immediately pull the credit card out. We buy clothing that we see on a figure like mannequin and fail to look like that, we become depressed about our own look, and the cycle of dissatisfaction continues. Please understand the value of envy in sales but not in your personal lives.

*Be happy for other's success* – Even if you have a tough time doing this at the beginning, fake it, till you make it. Being happy for someone else's achievements and success, takes your energy to a higher frequency in realization of your unity with the entire mankind. In this, you bring about your own success.

# Fear-

This is one of the feelings that creeps up on us when we are faced with situations and events through some adventures. At times when you feel fearful of something; don't just feel it, but use it. Every unpleasant feeling that you experience is screaming that there is a belief or false understanding underneath, which needs to be addressed. This is the best time for you to find out what causes that fear and get rid of it.

Not all fears are that obvious though. For example, fear of failure, disappointment and being hurt are there, but they do not show you themselves in the same fashion as, the fear you feel when a lion is chasing you. These are virtually invisible fears. To clear these fears, you need the "blender method". You are your own best friend. Be honest with yourself and find out what these deep beliefs are and if they are not working for you, blend and solidify a new one.

# Grief –

This feeling comes about when we think that we have "lost" something. That something can be an individual who was important in our life, a pet, and belonging of many types.
This emotion takes your will to live away from you. Time usually is the best remedy for it. It is advised of course that you do not re-live the thoughts of loss continuously, and in this, you will be able to come out of it quicker.

One false belief that amplifies grief is that the loss that has happened is permanent. No loss ever is. Remember that we are all going to leave this physical reality and become one with those who already left. On the other hand, understanding the option of choice that we are given, makes the reasoning behind what we perceive as loss, easier. Everyone has equal opportunity to make a choice. For example, people die at variety of ages; someone dies when they are 140 and the other at the age 25 or younger. Both of these characters in life, have made choices leading them down that path and if you respect that individual, you respect their choice, and in that, you require not to grieve.

When you really and deeply look into the subject of grief, we are really not grieving for the "gone" but the fact of, how am "I" supposed to live without it. Where do "I" stand now? Loss in any form creates a void. We as human beings are not equipped to deal with void. We quickly want the space filled. During the time of this transition, we grieve.

Look around and see those who have lost a life partner to death or divorce. The very first feeling that arises out of this is dealing with the "lost" routine. I used to make breakfast. We used to travel. We used to catch a certain show on TV or radio, etc. Doing any of the abovementioned functions without the participation of the other individual, somehow at this point feels pointless and even painful.

As an example of what happened to me, I can address transitioning of my mother. For the past 30+ years, on a regular basis, she called me every Saturday to talk for an hour and our communications always ended in laughter and "I love you". When she passed away in 2013, even though not expected, I knew that she was ready for it. She wanted to go. But knowing that was not making it any easier on me. I realized that it was not so much that she was gone, as it was, I want my routine back. I want this loving voice at the end of the line to tell me she loves me, she prays for me and all is going to be OK. I want to hear her laughter. I want, I want, I want.

It is what "I want" and the change of pattern and routine that is making me feel the way I do. In any perceivable loss, first and foremost we think about the things that we no longer will be doing. I also know people who mourn the loss of their job and some even retirement.

Sometimes during grief we feel disappointed that something miraculously did not save us or the loved one from this happening; or we may condition ourselves to talk about all the negative points of the person/pet/things while they were in our lives, to make us feel better, that they are not around anymore.

As harsh as this may sound, everything is about change. Without change we will not survive a minute. Changes in our body and cells, changes in trees, season, air and the environment in general. Change has been, is, and will be around us ALL the time. It is our level of adaptability to change that defines how quickly we can move on. To lessen the duration of grief, understanding change and flexibility becomes mandatory.

## Guilt -

The feeling of guilt is only useful if you have learned something from it. This feeling is not for punishment reasons. Remember that no wrongdoings will ever take away from your divinity. No matter what you have done, divine love is always with you; as you have done nothing outside of the choices and experiences that the ALL has presented you with. You might have upset the social laws and agreements; but you have not achieved anything outside the box of choices.

At this point I will normally hear someone say, "EL, are you saying that the person who has committed, theft, rape of murder is still divine and good?" I would say, "Committing theft, rape and murder breaks the social laws and agreements we have to live together in a peaceful environment; but, it is all part of what we "can" choose to experience and do. This is why understanding yourself and your relation to the Source is so very important. If you study and understand the laws of energy and the cause and effect, you would never make those choices purely because of the outcome that will await you. Simply put, you do not board a plane if you know ahead of time it is going to crash, unless if you are a suicide bomber that is going to make it crash."

Saying that everyone, regardless of their choice is divine, does not propose that I am approving of the choices that are being made; it just means I am accepting of the choices they are making and the results they will bring about. This is why also assumptions become unnecessary. We see someone who is ill and weak and immediately our heart goes out to them without respecting the choices they have made in life to come to the point they are. This is why also sympathy is not required but compassion is.

No matter what emotions you are going through, they are amazing tools provided for you to gauge your alignment with joy. Feel the feelings you have and do not put them on hold and use them as a guide in where you are. Your purpose in this physical reality is joy. How near or far are you?

Try to not allow your emotions define you. If you just went through a breakup with someone you loved, if you start defining yourself as not worthy of love and unworthy of a good relationship, you are allowing your emotion to define you and you will start believing it, and cause further heartbreaks in the future. Events are only one moment of your life, they are not your entire life.

Whenever you want something in your life, the truth is that you are looking for that thing, because, you choose to allow that thing to make you feel a certain way. We are quite inspired by the way we want to feel. Emotions are the reward of any time and space journey and they add depth and meaning to each event and experience.

Embrace and get to know your emotions and appreciate them in understanding how far you are, from where you need to be. Also remember that at the time the deed was done, you were not who you are NOW. We constantly change. The "you", from two minutes ago would not know what you will know two minutes from now.

## Hate –

This term is widely overused. We use "hate" for anything we dislike. First we need to understand the difference between dislike and hate. Dislike is a feeling where hate is an emotion.

Dislike is something we are entitled to, hate however needs a bit of clarification. I can dislike a person, or a thing. Meaning I do not want this person or thing within the circle of my current physical experience. Hating something means you do not love that person or thing at all and do not want them to exist.

So seeing that from what we discussed earlier, and the topic of energy and the fact that there is no dividing line where you end, and something else begins, hate really becomes not available. Let me give you an example.

A woman looks into the mirror and says, "I hate my nose". Really? Do you hate your nose, or do you dislike the shape of it? If you really hated your nose, losing your nose would be alright. Yes? Is it? So in general, you love all the differing frequencies in your body, that generate various organs, but you might have objection to how they have turned out. In other words, you love your body and the energy that creates it, but you don't like the way a certain part looks.

The same can be said about EVERYTHING around you. The energy of anything, considered alive or otherwise, is not separate from the energy that creates you, as you. You cannot really "Hate" anything because you would be cutting your nose off in spite your face. The only available option is: love. However the matter of choice, gives you the possibility of "disliking" something.

The more you recite the word "hate" to yourself, the more disconnected you will feel; which in turn brings about a lot of emotions that may not work for you in manifestation of your dreams and desires or physical health.

At this point you might say, "I hate my wart." Seeing that you want it actually gone. Here is the news: hating anything, fighting against anything, will ONLY give it strength. You see this in the world of politics as well as health, peace, etc. The one that people usually "hate", is the one that most of the time wins the campaign. The disease that we "fight" against, have only become stronger. The peace that we ironically "fight" for, has turned into wars of many kinds. Once again looking into the field of energy, the two similar energies have gotten together to become constructive. Even though we think about destruction.

# Hope -

This is another overused term. We hope for things to go right. We hope for things to happen. How does the word "hope" resonate with you? Let's go with the religious crowd first. As per the holy books, "In the beginning God created the heaven and the earth". Would you be able to say or change this to: "In the beginning God hoped to create the heaven and the earth?" Does it sound solid to you or create a sense of confidence? It pretty much leaves 50% to failure. So every time we are "hoping" for something, we are actually expecting a 50-50 result. It can go either way.

Once again let's examine the field of energy. There is no room for hope in there. It is solid action. And if we are a part of this field of energy, where does hope really stand?

# Jealousy -

We touched on this topic a bit earlier. This is when you have something, and you feel someone may take it away. The only way out of jealousy is trust. To give you an example, often people are jealous of their partners. In this, if another male or female slightly interacts with their spouse's, the jealousy takes hold, and they are raged, and even though it may not immediately happen, an upcoming fight is inevitable.

In this situation, the person does not trust the partner. You might say, and I have heard, "That is not true, I trust my partner, I don't trust the other person." I say, "Poppycock". In this equation, there is only you and your partner the third party is innocent. If you "trust" that your partner, will not break the vows of fidelity, there is nothing and no one that is going to change his/her mind. Hence jealousy becomes unnecessary.

In the case of items that belong to you, once again is about "trusting" the other party. If you do not trust someone, you may feel they might steal from you. The bottom line is, to abolish jealousy, either learn to trust, or let go of what you are jealous of, for the sake of your and their well-being.

# Joy -

Funny I should bring this up, in the range of all the low-frequency emotions you might say. Joy is a high frequency emotion. The one that will align you for success. One thing that I need to discuss, is when people are actually afraid to be joyful. Yes you heard it right. They are "Afraid".

I remember growing up, probably around the age of 7 or 8, I was partaking in a game and having a lot of fun. A lot of laughter and enjoyment. After about 5 minutes of fun, my friend's mother walked in and claimed, "Stop laughing so much.  Much laughter will bring many tears of sorrow."  OK then.  There is a wet blanket if I ever saw one.  BUT for my friend that became a belief and a fact.  She quoted that many times in the years to come.  To a degree that it became a self-fulfilling prophecy.  With any joy in her life, a sorrow followed.

Since then I have come across many who feel, joy is fleeting and a sign of disaster.  These people believe in this theory so much so, that they actually filter out the times that they have been joyful without any mishaps.  People who are considered perfectionist for example, try to stay away from joyful activities.

There is nothing that will be more uplifting than experiencing pure joy.  In the state of enjoyment, there are no pits to fall into, and all complications fade into thin air.

## Judgement –

We have touched upon this topic as well, but due to its importance let's take another look.  We learn from very early stages of life what is acceptable and what is not.  Way before we start walking, our first reaction revolves around, turning, and checking the parent/caregivers' reaction around what we do.  If they smile and they are happy, we have done well.  If they frown, uh oh!!!

From there onwards, we carry a backpack full of "OK" and "uh oh".  As we grow older this bag is heavier and heavier and more topics are added to it; most of which we have never stopped to re-examine.  This information has been gathered through various encounters: parents/caregivers, schooling, religion or lack thereof, friends, social media, and media (TV, radio, newspapers, magazines, internet…..).

Through our judgement, we decide what we do, or don't want to participate in.  This is perfect.  This makes an individual who he/she is. Our judgements in participation makes us unique.  The trouble starts when we feel that everyone else also MUST follow what we have in our backpack; and when we start using our very own measuring stick in forcing what "others" should or should not do.

Granted that we have a set of measures that we have agreed upon as a society, which we need to stick to, for the sole purpose of keeping the peace. The societal backpack should not be mixed with our personal. Even if we thought, that we know, every feeling, every emotion and every happening in someone's life – which would be a complete bogus claim – we still cannot measure their actions based on our belief system.

Once again this of course calls for the review of the section on "acceptance".


# Regret -


Regret is a form of self-blame for outcomes that have been less than desirable. In a case like this, the less chance someone has of redoing the action, the longer the emotion will linger. This emotion used as a learning tool, can prove to be quite beneficial. The trouble begins, when we hang on to the emotion and forget the learning and continue to cry over it.

Just recently I read a writing that went something like this: when I say a joke the first time, it is funny and you laugh hard. When I repeat the joke, you laugh still, but not as hard. As I keep repeating the joke, you no longer laugh. So why do you keep crying over the same thing over and over again?

I thought that is the best way, to describe regret. We cannot undo what has been done no matter how hard we try. Advertisers harness the power of regret, in people and in product sales. Remember the depressing ads for insurance companies? They focus in what happens before and after funeral and how not buying policies have left their family in despair? Or even simpler the V8 © commercial on saying, "I could have had a V8" to motivate the user not to regret it later?

Follow this rule of thumb: If there is nothing you can do to change a situation, let it go. And if something can be done, do it now. People in death bed, give you the best stories on what they regret not doing or what they should have or could have done. Late Dr. Wayne Dyer recited a very meaningful phrase to say, "Don't die with your music in you." As Bronnie Ware mentions in her book – The top five regrets of the dying: a life transformed by the dearly departing – there are five main regret factors:

1.  Wishing to have the courage to live a life true to themselves, not the life expected by others of them;
2.  Wishing they had not have worked so hard;
3.  Wishing to have had the courage to express their thoughts;
4.  Wishing to have stayed in touch with their friends;
5.  Wishing they had let themselves be happy.

## Resentment -

In resentment we continuously replay a feeling in our head, and the result becomes an intense and consistent anger. In this we tend to relive and re- experience every moment emotionally. We feel someone did something to us that was unnecessarily mean, hurtful and thoughtless. Sometimes even what people did not do for us; or have not done enough for us.

This feeling can even be towards someone that at one time you were really close to. Here is one thing I want you to keep in mind: the moment you start resenting anything and or anyone, you immediately become a slave. This thing or person occupies your thoughts, controls your dreams, robs you of peace of mind, and rents the penthouse of your mind. You take this person or thing along on your vacations; he/she/it ruins your pleasurable moments, he/she/it affects your overall health causing you indigestion, asthma, headache and back ache as well as leave you completely tired and drained. This person then puts you on a lot of different medications.

As the old saying goes, you are taking the poison and hoping the other party gets sick. Ultimately this hurts you in every aspect of your life than the person or thing you are resenting. All you really had to do was: Let go!

The bad part is that when you stay resentful towards something or someone for a long time, your body gets addicted to the chemicals that it produces in the state of resentment and guess what? You become a resentment junkie. Now you are an official addict. Please read the section about addictions.

## Shame -

Have you ever felt ashamed of something? Why? Did you do what you did or said intentionally? Did you know what you were doing, you would consider wrong later?

If your answer to these questions is "Yes", then you need to understand yourself a bit better. Why did you intentionally do what you did? Did you do it for revenge? Did you do it because you wanted to feel superior? Did you do it to show them how much better you are? Did you just want to be right?

You see, sitting there and feeling shame and not analyzing it, is non-productive. Whatever it was that you did and for whatever reason you did it for, it was done in the past. Yesterday, you did not know what you know today. Every moment we grow. We learn. We did not know a day ago what we learned today. Shame is a low frequency emotion, which will only take you in directions you won't want to go.

If you did it for revenge, is because you perhaps at the time did not know, that we are all made of the same energy and there is no separating line between us. The only difference between you and

64

someone else, is the differentiating factor called: ego. Without ego, we would never feel the individuality. Ego allows us to have the individual experiences that we are having in life. However, when we let ego take the drivers' seat, we forget the original connection. When we forget, we curse and revenge and back-bite. When we curse and revenge and back-bite, we feel the low frequency feelings. And you know the rest.

If you did it, to feel superior, should I repeat what I said in the previous paragraph? The fact that you did not know that you are only talking to another instance of yourself… blah, blah, blah? Do you get the picture in how much of a difference it makes for you to get to know what you are made of? For me it eliminates a lot of nonsense.

## Worry –

Worry is always about the future. Imaginary things. Things that have not happened but what if they do? You are constantly consumed with the worst case scenarios and creating disaster recovery plans. Worry to a normal degree, to kick you into action, in doing something about the future, is good. When worry becomes chronic, the underlying fears and doubts can be truly paralyzing. It drains your emotional energy completely and takes a heavy toll on your overall health.

Worry also helps you in the anxious behaviour and feelings. Some people think that worrying helps them avoid bad things in their lives; or prepares them for the worst. How little they know that worrying is the problem and not the solution. This also becomes another addiction. A worry addict hardly ever faces anything in an easy way.

Here is s suggestion: if you really have to worry, put aside a couple of hours a day and schedule it in your calendar as the "worry hour". During the hour or two make a list of the worries and ONLY concentrate on them and try and see if you can solution them. Once that hour completes, take minutes of the hour and put the matter to rest in your head and don't worry again until the next appointment.

Anytime the worry shows up, remind yourself that this is not the hour for it. You will eventually wean yourself off in this way.

Also as I have mentioned before, worry is only if you feel you cannot control something now or in the future. If you really believe that you cannot control it, why think about it?

# Health Bits: Why do we need nutrition?

Nutrition or nourishment is the supply of materials - food - required by organisms and cells to stay alive.

A nutrient is a source of nourishment, an ingredient in a food, e.g. protein, carbohydrate, fat, vitamin, mineral, fiber or water. Macronutrients are nutrients we need in relatively large quantities. Micronutrients are nutrients we need in relatively small quantities.

The Macronutrients that we need are Carbohydrates, Proteins, Fats, Fiber and Water.

Micronutrients that we need in small quantities throughout our lives are Vitamins and Minerals such as: Potassium, Chloride, Sodium, Calcium, Phosphorus, Magnesium, Zinc, Iron, vitamin A, B, C, D, E, K and so on.

Having a lack of any micronutrient as well as having too much of it can cause minor and major issues.

## Are chemicals and drugs part of nutrition?

I want you to think about this for a minute and tell me what you think.

How are drugs made? Drugs have a chemical composition right? So let's say one drug brings up the insulin levels in your body, which the body would produce under normal and healthy circumstances and the other one mimics a chemical that your body would normally produce to make you happy or help you sleep and so on.

Your body behaves like a huge laboratory day in and day out. We produce roughly about 50 different known hormones and we are getting to know more and more. Every one of these hormones are important in the health and operation of our body. So for example lack of serotonin can cause depression and too much of it will bring about tremors, agitation, sweating and whole lot more side effects. Or dopamine, epinephrine, acetylcholine and so on....

Each one of these naturally produced hormones also work constructively with the macro and micronutrients to see the functions of the body are running smoothly. Without them operating and being in proportion, we are in trouble in two ways: one is that the lack of that hormone is going to bring about some sort of an ailment and on top of that, whatever this hormone was helping us absorb, is not doing its job anymore, so we will be lacking in some other sort of nutrient and hence another part also is going to start aching.  So everything is related.

So yes, every chemical we ingest is considered a type of nutrition. The same goes for the chemicals produced in our body due to an emotion.  So think about it the next time you feel angry, jealous, upset, anxious or frustrated.  What are you feeding your body through these emotions?  Will they help you in being well? A simple emotion can be behind whether you stay lean or gain weight. Whether a block in the arteries happen or a tumour is formed.  Spare yourself and try to keep your emotions in check.


## How do we get nutrition?

In order for you to understand how the nutrition works, I need to give you a quick briefing on how your cells operate.


We have some 50 trillion cells in our bodies.  Each cell has their own little organs doing the same job as your organs are doing for you. They breathe, digest, excrete, and reproduce and so on. They also have something called a membrane which is basically their skin.

Just like our skin, it has contact with the outside world and the inside world. And again just like our skin, it reads both conditions and will do whatever it is needed to keep the cell alive. You know like when you feel cold through your skin, the blood rushes to the skin surface to warm it up and to adjust your body temperature.  Your skin also is the biggest mouth you have.  Whatever you put on it, directly goes to the blood stream.

The perception of the skin makes a lot of difference to us.  If the perception of the skin is skewed, it can actually destroy life.  So remember this so far because I want to side track for a few minutes and come back to this.

There seems to be a few different assumptions that are introduced to us, which I need to clear up before we go on. First one is that we are made of different parts and the parts that won't work we can take out and keep going. This is when the doctors are not looking at how the parts are actually related and how they help each other out. It is common that we cut out the parts we think we don't need.

So they pretty much believe that if you take a complex structure, you can take it apart, study the pieces and when you know how each piece works, you put it together, and now you understand how everything works. Now if you know how each piece works, you can change them and control the environment accordingly. In a case like this the doctor looks into our biology, finds what is not working right, changes the part by cutting it or by drugs and believes that by this they will "manage" whatever it is they are suffering from.

Second assumption is that genes control life and we are victims of what we inherit from our families. This assumption of course have been over-ruled many times by newer studies but for some reason we want to hold on to the old idea of Earth being flat.

Third is that we need to compete to survive. Survival of the fittest. But it is now time for us to give up this old assumption and understand that we continue living through co-operation not competition.

On top of the assumptions, we also know that our cells are not the smallest pieces of our bodies. The smallest piece is called an atom. Or is it?

When we looked closer, we saw that not even the atom was the smallest piece of our body but it was the electrons inside the atom. Later we found out that there are really no physical electrons inside of an atom. They are just microscopic tornadoes of energy swirling around.

So what does this mean and how is it related to what we were talking about?

This means that there is no real physical structure to an atom. Which would mean our molecules that are made of atoms also don't have a physical structure, and in turn in means that our cells which are made of molecules don't have a physical structure and so it is the same with our organs and the entire body. So everything in our body that we touch and feels quite physical, it is really just made of energy.

Here is a scientific fact that you can explore: every atom and molecule gives off light and absorbs light. Meaning the vibration of atoms are in the range of light.

So every atom in your body is generating light right now. The energy you emanate is the characteristic of how healthy you are and how constructively your cells are interfering with each other.

You are a generator of waves, but in the meantime you are a recipient of waves as well. You know when you come into contact with someone who gives off energy that is like yours and vibrates to the same frequency, you feel good and you both feel powerful after you have separated and gone away. Yet someone else can drain you completely when you have left them. We talked about this earlier in the book on the topic of constructive or destructive energy.

We are the only creatures that depend on language to communicate. All other creatures read the vibration. We are also able to read vibrations, but because we have become too accustomed to "physical" reality we have forgotten how to do this. We have also been programmed not to pay attention to our feelings and listen to people. But by denying our feelings we have really forgotten how to use one of the most important tools we had been given originally.

Science has given the doctors all kind of facilities, like CAT scans, MRIs, Mammogram and Radiation Therapy. Say for example mammogram. This is not a photograph, it is an energy profile. So when you are looking at a CAT scan or a mammogram and you see these different colours, this tells you about the different frequencies, and then you say, "Oh, there is cancer" for example.

Is your doctor physically seeing the cancer? No. He/she is only seeing the vibrational energy of a cancer cell.

Your cells react to nutrition, drugs, hormones, and medication as well as energy vibration. As a matter of fact efficacy of energy signals is 100 times more potent than that of the chemicals.

So now I am going back to the topic of nutrition and we also touched on the chemicals that your body produces, and how important they were in absorbing nutrients.

The list of side effects on medications are so extensive due to the fact that you can never know what the person is feeling when they are popping the pill. You can ask them to have an empty stomach, but you cannot ask them to stop feeling. The chemicals and hormones released when we feel something changes the chemical composition of the pill we just took to manage something.

The second assumption we talked about was about genetics. Physicists believe that we all are collectively creating the world we live in. According to that, if I tell you that your life is determined by your genes and you buy into it, that is exactly how it will be.

We know today there is something called: epigenetic control. This means "control above the genes". So now I am going to express how your cells run the show. When this subject is looked at closely, you will see that only 5% of the entire population of earth are born with genetic defects. This leaves the other 95% with normal genes.

So let's go shortly back to: our bodies are made of cells and cells are living organisms and they live and breathe and give birth to new cells just like the big picture of them that we are. Cells also signal each other and communicate. If the signal is off, then we feel ill.

Three things can cause the signal to be off: trauma that has messed up the nervous system; toxins that pollute the system; and the most important is the mind; this is when you send the wrong signals in inappropriate times which results in malfunction of the whole thing.

On the surface of the skin (membrane) of your cells there are these little antennas that are sticking up. They are called receptors. They are responsible to tune into the environment around them and pick up signals. A signal can be something like a hormone, a chemical or nutrient that the antennas are looking for. So say for example calcium. Not all the antennas are interested in the same thing, they each have their own signals they are looking for and there is like

100,000 of them. So in order for calcium to be absorbed, the antenna that is supposed to pick it up has to be feeling alright. So the antenna picks up the calcium and starts to examine it and send information about it to inside of the cell.

So now another set of antennas get involved and they are called "effecter". These guys send the signals to the cell and let the cell know what is supposed to be done with it. Is it supposed to be digested, do they need to move a certain way, etc. etc.

These 100,000 plus receptors and effectors work in harmony to make sure all is alright. Can you wrap your head around this: more than 50 trillion cells and each of them with more than 100,000 antennas?

This gets interesting so that, the cells don't keep these receptors all the time. They practically shut down the ones that are not being used. So what this means is that if the antenna that is responsible to detect calcium is not there, then the absorption of calcium is not there. Lucky for us though, the cells will start raising the antennas back up when they see that there is an abundant of something is available again. This is why when you take vitamins, it takes a bit of time for you to see the effects and some people give up quickly and say, "It did not work for me".

Now on the side of our mind; our perceptions are everything. We have physical perceptions and mental perceptions. Meaning you see something and you have a physical perception like that is a knife. And then the mental perception kicks in of whether I can peel something with this or this can be used as a weapon. So it is then that you decide whether this is good or bad. The perception is crucial for our survival. And also it is what sets the fight or flight response in us.

Survival has two sides: there is growth and there is protection. Part of the growth is that we lose billions of cells on daily basis and get new ones. If this process does not happen we are doomed. We have to have proper growth and change daily.

Growth and protection work opposite to each other. Growth allows you to open up and take things in; whereas protection closes you up and will not allow anything to enter. Both of these take energy. Our systems are designed mostly for growth and occasional protection.

72

Let's face it we are not being chased by lions on a daily basis. Or are we?

See, when we are running away from the lion, our growth system is shut down and protection takes over. Once the lion gives up on us and thinks we are not so tasty after all, the system reverses again and growth kicks in. If we continue the protection mode longer than required, we are compromising our survival.

The more fear, worry, anxiety, rush, and stress you live in, the more of protection mode you are in. You are basically scaring yourself to death because of false perception. Our cells cannot grow in protection mode. Your body is smart enough to even prioritize your protection. Meaning if you have a cold, the body is going to attend to it quickly. BUT if you have a cold and the lion is also chasing you, then of course the body will deal with the lion issue first, because if the lion catches up, the cold and flu will be lion's problem not yours.

So do you see where I am going with this? This is all about emotions now. So when we feel danger one of our glands who is in charge of policing (hypothalamus) sends a message to pituitary and pituitary sends a message to adrenals and then the message is also relayed to all the 50 trillion plus cells saying, "get into protection mode, there is danger." So the adrenals produce the stress hormone. This causes for our muscles to be stronger especially arms and legs and all the energy and nutrients are sent that way. In the meantime the stomach and gut constrict and get smaller so the digestion is stopped.

We have created these daily lions that are chasing us. We keep ourselves in constant state of worry, anxiety, anger, and all the other goodies, and then when the cold and flu hit us, it takes a long time for us to get over it, because the lion is more important. Also when the lion is chasing, there is no digestion, so we eat even though we are worried and anxious and then the food does not properly digest and to make matters worse we take tums with calcium. The results of all this over time can be devastating to the body.

When we eat under stress that also adds to the pounds as well as indigestion, because the food is not properly digested and utilized. I have a trick question now: for those of you who are watching the news while having dinner, are you in growth or protection mode?

The another side to this whole thing is that when you are in fight or flight, your body strengthens the reflexes and so you are not really using your consciousness or it becomes super slow. As an example, when you are driving, you are conscious (hopefully), and then someone cuts you off and you immediately switch to reflexes to avoid the collision. When you are of course making decisions based on reflexes all the time, you make rushed and less than perfect decisions.

Think of yourself when you got angry at your partner or friend and just acted out of reflexes. I am sure you will recall a few incidents that you would do it differently had you been given the opportunity again.

As you see, you have this wonderful, amazing, intelligent structure in your possession. Can you start appreciating it more and praising this wonderful gift? Can you tell it how much you love it every day instead of blindly criticizing it? Can you give it some time off from the hectic environment we have created? Can you kiss it every morning for how gorgeous it is?

So by now, you should know what your emotion does to your nutrition. We are literally feeding our body with the nutrition of emotions. And seeing that we have tons of chemicals and compounds and hormones produced by various glands and organs in the body, each emotion of course will be targeting the nutrition in that area.

# How Do The Mind Powers Work?

So when our body is healthy, it operates in silence. You don't feel anything alarming. Another thing to remember is that the right side of the body is considered to be masculine and the left side feminine. So if you resent someone of the male gender, you may have health problems on the right side and likewise the trouble maybe on the left side if you have issues with a female gender.

The male side also symbolizes wisdom. So if you have been misusing your wisdom, you may get destructive results on the right side over and over until you use your wisdom properly.

Also the right side is the giving side and the right side problems may show a need to give in some area or way. You may have been withholding on something; whether it is love, money, or emotions.

Problems on the left side indicate resentment towards a female. Since the female gender also symbolizes love, if you have been misusing your power of love, or letting your love be misused by others, it can cause health problems on the left side of the body.

The left side symbolizes the ability to receive and then use whatever you have received wisely. If you have refused to receive a certain gift that was extended to you, or if you feel something good has passed you by, you have been cheated out of receiving something, then you may experience problems of the left side.

Also if you have gathered a vast knowledge of truth and spirituality and have not used it in your life or to help others, this knowledge stagnation can also come out as ailments on the left side of the body.

These twelve mind powers are: Faith, imagination, will, understanding, zeal, power, love, judgement, order, strength, elimination and life.

# First - the areas belonging to your conscious mind:

This area reasons, analyzes and thinks. It is located in the forehead, and all of our five senses. think, and say affects all your mind located from the the way down to the ponders, consciously the front of extends into What you deliberately, powers, forehead all throat area.

So the mind powers conscious mind are: understanding, faith, zeal and power. affected by will, imagination,

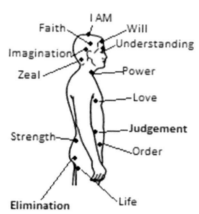

Misuse of any of these mind powers, almost immediately affects that part of the body. (E.g. sore throat for words of harshness). So now, knowing that these mind powers are located in the area of conscious mind, indicates that the problems related to eyes, ears, forehead, brain, nose, and throat are often caused by our most recent negative thought, or words from us, or directed at us, by someone else. So now, you can also learn, that you can get rid of illnesses consciously and easily.

# Second - the areas belonging to your subconscious mind:

The area of subconscious mind activity, is located in the heart and abdominal region. This is also the area of your deep emotional feelings and secrets. The area of subconscious mind, affects the mind powers of: strength, love, judgment, order, elimination and life.

When you have physical difficulties, in the heart and abdominal regions, it is normally because of unconscious emotions, and feelings that you may no longer even remember. Old hurts, prejudices, resentments, bitter emotions and memories of the past, that is stored in the subconscious area of the body. Diseases like: heart trouble, female disorders, kidney and stomach troubles, and various elimination problems are some that I can think of.

# Third - the areas belonging to your super-conscious mind.

This is located in the crown of the head. This is described as the "Christ mind", the "I AM" or the centre of divine intelligence and wisdom, because it has direct access to Universal life and wisdom. Your intuitive thoughts, inspirations, hunches, telepathic or other extra-sensory perception powers, are led by the area of your super-conscious.

There is a dynamic flow of energy from here to all 12 Mind Power areas. This is the most potent area of activity. Miracles can happen with the activation of this area. You activate this area, through prayer, affirmations (divine intelligence), and meditation.

# How The Three Mind Phases Connect For Healing?

You can release the dynamic energy of super-conscious, by daily meditations. Relax, breathe deeply and affirm: *"I am divine intelligence. I am, I am, I am. I am letting divine intelligence express perfectly through me now. I am, I am, I am."*

Sweep your attention from the crown of your head to the tip of your toes as you affirm this statement over and over.

Once you start using this mental drill daily, you will find that you are feeling better, more alive, energetic, peaceful and confident.

## FAITH:

This mind power is located in the centre of the pineal gland. You are using this mind power constantly. And it constantly affects your health, wealth and happiness. In infants, this area is very sensitive and soft above the crown of the head where the skull does not completely close until the child reaches the age of 7-9 years. During this period children show signs of extreme awareness and clairvoyance.

Whenever you are firm about your thinking about anything, you have faith. This area is related in one way or the other to all diseases and has equal power to overcome them. Pretty much whatever gets your attention is your faith.

When we talk and a word is spoken, a chemical change takes place in the body, and that is what this centre reacts to. Becoming master of your words, makes you the master of your faith and in turn the master of your health. One of the things that I always warn people about is owning the disease. Don't own your ailments. Don't say "my" headache, or "my" backache, etc. Say, "This headache" or "This backache" so to make it clear that you are temporarily experiencing them.

## IMAGINATION:

This is located in the vicinity of Faith and it is connected and related to faith. What you imagine, faith will manifest. So with this power and the centre you can imagine health or disease.

## UNDERSTANDING:

This mind power includes all forms of knowing described as knowledge, wisdom, awareness and perception and is located in the front brain just above the eyes. This mind power is coupled with the one above it called Will. These two are meant to work together, with the understanding leading the will.

78

The will wants to get things done in an outer or physical way, and often if we act based on will, we take hasty actions, and we can only wisely act when we follow and listen to understanding.

Understanding is natural to man. Your ears and the eyes are the organs that respond to understanding. You don't see "in" your eyes so much as you see through them, according to what you understand. The ears separate sounds according to your mental choice. They receive what the mind mentally accepts and refuse to hear anything else.

Usually then a trouble in the ear area means that the person is not tolerant of those who do not think the same way as he/she does. He/she most of the time wants his/her own way willfully. He/she is letting his/her mind power of will to rule the understanding. Someone who uses their understanding will have the least trouble in the areas of eyes and ears. The feet are also very much connected to understanding. And as you know we have nerves running at the bottom of our feet that is connected to various parts of our bodies, so not using understanding in turn can be the cause of many ailments we suffer from. This mind power responds to peace. A peaceful state of mind is a healing state of mind.


## WILL:

As I said before this is the twin brother of understanding. Your will most of the time wants things done in a forceful way and immediately. If you listen to your will, you will most likely make very costly mistakes in your life.

Having said that, you must also know that your will is wonderful. It is your lifeline. You have heard it in statements like: "he lost his will to live". Your body normally is the expression of your will. Your will is very important and it is very much needed for your health, wealth and happiness. But we must keep it on a short leash. We have to temper it with our understanding.

Willfulness brings tenseness and pressure and a tense mind ties knots in the nerves, muscles and tendons. For example using will all the time on its own, affects and hardens the arteries. Will also put extra pressure on the use of many organs beyond their normal capacity, which will leave them tired and impaired.

Will is often used as a destructive force. Almost all of the educational systems we have for our kids are based on breaking their will so that we have authority over them. Trying to change or break someone's will is committing a mental murder.

If you deal with disagreements in a willful way, this can bring about arthritis. The severity of this problem depends on the degree of person's stiff attitude towards others. Arthritis, just as easily as it physically responds to heat, it responds metaphysically to warm thoughts and emotions.


## POWER:

This mind power is in the throat area and has a lot to do with the use of words. Incidentally the thyroid gland is located in this area. They call this area also the "third ovary", simply because most ovarian problems in ladies are created through negative words. Even though negative words create trouble in the entire body, the throat area is more prone to them.

Every time we speak, we cause the atoms of our body to tremble and change their place. With this, not only we raise or lower our own body's vibration, but also we affect the people and living beings around us. This explains the fact that you feel tired or run down when you spend time with some individuals. You have heard the expression, "She nearly talked me to death." One can literally talk someone to life or death. Every word we say first affects our mind, then body and then our affairs.

Another thing to keep in mind is the tone of voice. It has far greater effect on our health and nervous system than we can imagine. Research has shown that when we speak words of love softly and from the heart, they tone up the vocal cords, sooth larynx and cleanse and restore swollen tonsils. Unkind words on the other hand, harden the arteries, harden the liver, and affect the eyesight and much more.

## ZEAL:

This is located at the back of the neck. The neck is a symbol of a kind, and flexible state of mind and attitude and it shows through how much a person is loving and compassionate.

This is the type of person who forgives without a thought of there being anything to forgive. They are yielding and non-resistant.

Have you ever tried to get someone else to think the way you thought he should and then later felt a stiff neck? Or have you tried to convince someone to do something you thought they should and end up with a tension headache later? This type of aches and pains usually are because the mind power of zeal was not properly used.

People, who develop this mind power, seem to have this special energy and power that makes them different from everyone else. They do seem to have some strange powers of accomplishment, and they express their ideas and talents that lead to greatness. And they are different from everyone who seem to be listless and tired all the time.

Zeal gives us the impulse to move forward. This mind power affects nose, ears, eyes, mouth and sensory nervous system. When we misuse our zeal by trying to force our will or way on someone else, or by burning up this energy through unwise activities, we will get a physical reaction often through one or more of our five senses.

The eyes may go weak or out of focus for example. Some become hard of hearing because they have been over zealous in making others hear their ideas to a degree that they have become incapable of hearing theirs. People who have sinus trouble or some kind of nose trouble are usually those with their nose in other people's business as they work hard for other people to conform to their ideas.

Misuse of zeal also often affects the throat. If you have ever gotten a sore throat for no apparent reason, check and see if you did not try to convince someone else to do what you wanted them to do. It could also be that you spoke negatively and with conviction, or you may experience difficulty with teeth because of the words you may have used in communication.

## LOVE:

This is located in the heart region. Anytime any of us violates love by showing hate, resentment, bitterness, fear and other unhealthy emotions, it will affect our heart and often the lungs, chest and breast area too.

We know today, beyond the shadow of doubt that minimum 70% of all diseases are caused by suppressed emotions. Regret, sorrow and remorse tear down the cells of the body. Thoughts of hate generate a deadly poison in the body.

Most people unfortunately misunderstand love. They think loving a person allows them the right to dominate and rule that person's life. These people also always end up with heart trouble. Domination and possessiveness affects the heart.

Love does not dominate or possess and it is not willful. Love is harmonizing, balancing and has a freeing quality of mind and body. True love frees rather than bind. Because of years of misunderstanding, this is why we cannot express love to anyone so easily anymore.

Misusing love not only affects our physical health, but it makes our homes, which is the place we should be looking forward to go to, often the most dangerous and destructive to our mind and body.

Heart is a pump. It circulates blood through several large valves. If anything constricts or limits the blood flow through these valves, then there is heart trouble. Feeling of being possessed, held down or forced causes a sense of restriction, limiting the activity of the valves and brining about various heart problems.

The thymus gland is also positioned in the chest behind the breastbone. This gland processes a type of white blood cell known as a T-lymphocyte. T-lymphocytes govern our immune system. So you can imagine if this gland is depressed what ramifications it can have.

## JUDGEMENT:

This is located in the pit of stomach in the solar plexus region. Misuse of this mind power can bring about a lot of different illnesses in the area of stomach and abdominal region. Those who are quiet complainers often have digestive problems. Judging affects the health of the person passing the judgement. Now if you accept or soak up other people's disapproval as well, you would experience upset stomach.

The ways that we misuse this power is by: fault-finding, judgement, and injustice. People who have the martyr complex and think that others have done them wrong, usually have stomach problems. Timid people, who feel life is unfair, are the same.

Pancreas is located in the area of solar plexus. It secretes insulin which as you know is vital to sugar digestion and metabolism. So misuse of this mind power of course can cause diabetes or hypoglycemia.

This mind power goes further because of where it is located and also affects Liver, kidneys, and spleen. Regrets for example can produce dangerous liver diseases. Your general attitude towards life also is recorded in your liver. Rheumatism, arthritis, neuralgia, inflammation, ulcers, haemorrhaging and organ displacements often are also the result of anger and agitation.

To remedy this of course we need to practice acceptance, forgiveness, unconditional love, compassion, and harmony with others, which will bring a warm glow and increased circulation to the liver.

I also mentioned that spleen would be affected in the area of this mind power. Spleen plays multiple roles in supporting the body one of which is that it recycles the old red blood cells, stores white blood cells and helps get rid of bacteria that cause pneumonia and meningitis.

## ORDER:

This is located at a large nerve centre just behind the navel in the solar plexus region.  So almost in the same area as the judgement. The word "disharmony" means "something is out of order".  If you are experiencing disharmony in mind, body and life and or business dealings, this means you need to develop your mind power of order. Order begins within.

There is always order in Universe.  When things seem out of order, we need to remind ourselves that the lack of order is not in Universe but in our own attitudes and emotions.  When things are not in order, don't rush frantically trying to make them right in an outer way. Instead of trying to make other people change, remind yourself that the lack of order is first within you.  If you can get your own thoughts and feelings orderly, then the people, situations and Universe will respond the same way.

When you understand that you have this mind power inside you, and you can use it any time, you will get rid of all tension, stress and friction.  As we realize this, we will have much fewer nervous breakdowns, heart attacks, and hypertension. There will also be a diminishing need for psychiatrists and mental hospitals.

A lot of physical abdominal problems can be due to disharmony or lack of order in emotions.  Women with female problems or pre-natal birth problems also need to pay attention to this mind power area.


## STRENGTH:

This mind power is between the hip-bone and ribs. We use this power instinctively in emergencies.  It is located close to our adrenal glands. These glands by the way are considered glands of emotion.

Strength is three folds: physical, mental and spiritual.

↳ The physical strength is the power, the energy, vitality of the physical body.

↳ The mental strength is the ability to achieve and be a leader, to be an expert in a field of work.

↳ Spiritual strength is the dedication to divine love, and acceptance.

On the physical side this mind power is related to material. Financial problems for example can cause issues in the lower back. Lower back pain can be caused by conscious or subconscious thoughts, either recent or past regarding your own or someone else's troubles.

The two adrenal glands on two sides of the kidneys, are considered the "glands of combat" and struggle, because they quickly react to anger, rage and fear. Cancer in the areas nearby is very common. Suppressed anger affects these areas in a great way. Now this is how important these tiny glands are to the body: if they are removed, the person dies.

Adrenals react very strongly to unhealthy emotional and mental conditions: jealousy, hate, anger, revenge, bitterness, worry, doubt, fear, and success struggle. When people overwork their adrenal glands, they feel and become weak.

Your mind power of power which was related to words you speak, plays a major role in the health of this mind power. This mind power also affects issues in the shoulder area. When we are grudgingly or unwillingly or with self-pity are taking responsibility for things, this area gets affected. Hip bone is opposite to shoulders. This is related to independence. When someone selfishly depends on others to support him/her, problems in the hip develop.

**ELIMINATION:**

This is located slightly above your base where you eliminate. When people hold on to negative feelings, emotions, past experiences and thoughts and don't let go, they may experience constipation. Things like possessiveness, or clinging. Now if they are possessed by someone else, this also can cause the same symptoms, as well as suffering from kidney, liver, intestine, colon problems, diabetic conditions, and haemorrhoids. To make matters worse, this mind power is very closely connected to the mind power of will on the forehead. The will, controls the circulation of life in the whole body. A tense will that is determined to have its own way, congests and constricts all the functions of the body, elimination being one of them. Type A personalities and people who are anal retentive and tense, usually have slow bowel movement.

There is no stagnation in healthy body. It is a perfect system of assimilation and elimination. We have many elimination organs, some of which are: liver, kidneys, lungs, skin, and intestinal tract. Strong negative emotions and strong will, hampers the action of these vital organs. The bowels also become constipated or loose because of mental poisons held in mind. Anxiety, irritability, resistance, worry cause constipation and if it is ongoing then the trouble becomes chronic.

Never relive or try to bring back your old unpleasant experiences. False judgements and criticism are always reflected in the organs of elimination. If the kidneys are over-working, try to get rid of fault-finding, sarcasm, criticism, unkindness, looking for the worst, picking out weaknesses in people and dwelling on their shortcomings can be some of the causes of the physical trouble.

When you think about your partners, husbands, wives, boyfriends or girlfriends, don't think of them as something that belongs to you. Think of them as creation of God. A part of you. A divine existence. A perfect being on their own. Give them the most unselfish love that you can.

There are two folds to this mind power: one is to eliminate errors and second to expand your good. Elimination of something from your life is always an indication of something far better coming. When there is elimination, you know that your life and your good are ready and trying to expand. Try and remember that every advancement means rejection of something old. Without rejection of our old cells, new ones cannot be created every second of our lives, and so where would we be?

**LIFE:**

This of course is located in the reproductive organs. Once again your mind power of power or your words prove to be very important. You can speak life to the parts of your body that seem to have given up and they come back miraculously working in perfect order. Most of us are only partially alive because we don't know that we can call out our energy of life.

One of the major contributors to illnesses in this area is limitation and oppression. PMS for example being so common is usually due to feeling restricted. The person is probably being dominated by someone. Reproductive organ disorders in ladies are usually related to a hidden resentment towards the husband, son, father or some member of opposite sex. When the mind of a woman is not gentle and soft, the fertility rate is low. Mind you, it is believed that one third of all cases of sterility in either party are caused by conflicts, hatred, fear, anxiety, jealousy and poor adjustment to marriage and so on.

Throughout the years I have come across a lot of couples trying to conceive and they are going through injections and everything else you can think of to try and have babies. The function of the fallopian tubes is that it unites the male and female cells. In high-strung women, the tubes are sometimes tightly shut because of nervous tension. Now, even when the tubes are open, and the male, female cells meet, they need the lining of the uterus to hang on to, which needs to be soft and relaxed. If it is tight and there are no ways for anchorage, then no pregnancy. With the same token, impotence in men can also be traced back to their resentment or hostility towards someone of female gender.

The mind powers of zeal and will are closely connected to the mind power of life. Our personality and temperament, as well as the state of our other glands, depends on the state of the mind power of life.

# Emotional Hunger Calls:

When we have physical needs, we normally attend to them and take care of them. It's cold; you turn the heat up or put on a sweater. You feel sleepy, you take a nap. You are thirsty, you drink. You are hungry, you eat. What do you do with your emotions when they come up? If your emotional hungers go unattended, they can lead to a wide variety of issues. When you do not respond to your emotional hunger, you end up feeling fearful, anxious, ashamed, insecure, aggressive or depressed.

Just as you need food for your physical nutrition, you also need emotional nutrition on a daily basis. There are a lot of us that are emotionally hungry and some downright starved. Not dealing with this eventually cumulatively causes a range of physical illnesses. The emotions that are not dealt with and buried alive, affect our perception of life and surroundings.

One way to go from the state of emotionally malnourished to well-nourished is through mind power of "power". Here we go back to the topic of words again. Use your power of words to nourish yourself emotionally and in this, changing the chemistry of your body. Since all our cells on a regular basis are checking their environment to see how they can behave and adapt to the environment, provide them with one that promotes health.

When you are around others please remember that they are not always in need of your upscale philosophies in how to improve their looks and lifestyles, but they are always in need of your unconditional love, regardless of how they look. Feed everyone love and they will feed you back and this way we all will feed each other's emotional hunger and have a healthier lifestyle. This is yet another reason why you would benefit from acceptance and drowning your judgements in love.

# Emotions and relationships;

The role of emotions in relationships is quite a bit misunderstood. When you listen to couples you hear things like: "Why do we have to talk about how I feel about things. My partner just needs to forget the past and be happy now. I've said I'm sorry and that I don't know why I do certain things, why can't she/he just get over it? Why can't we just move on?"

When we feel that our connection with someone we love is endangered, an internal alarm goes off. We respond to this alarm by what we have learned when we were kids. This is called the primary survival code, fight or flight. We are afraid that we are losing the very person we depend on. The loved one also hears this alarm in their head. Then we both get caught in this destructive cycle of action and reaction based on the same survival code.

Then we start playing the same scenario over and over again and we become confused on why these fights keep repeating. We basically get trapped in a negative loop-back. This of course takes us back to the mind-power of understanding that we talked about earlier. At this point we need to put the mind power of will on hold and stop the negative loop-back.

To use the mind power of understanding, first we need to slow down. We need to examine all parts of the disconnection. When we deal with "will" we are in panic mode. We feel overwhelmed, threatened, helpless, sad and rejected. We are then masking these feelings by fighting or fleeing from the situation. This of course will leave the partner confused, because they don't know why this is happening. The emotions that we are feeling of course are very basic, but we need to dig a bit deeper to understand the reason for the alarm.

So here are few tips on how to handle this:

- First and foremost we need to strengthen our trust.

- You need to be able to truly wear your heart on your sleeve and be willing to be vulnerable.
- Take some time to sit quietly and understand what are you exactly feeling?
- Calm yourself down
- Find out what was the trigger that brought this about?
- Pay attention to your body and see how you feel and where you feel the trigger the most?
- What do these triggers and sensations mean to you?
- What is your primary survival code for this? Do you want to run? Do you want to hide? Do you want to protest? Do you want to fight?
- Bring yourself together. But do it slowly so that you can formulate clear signals about what you feel and your emotional needs.
- Start the true communication with your partner. Express yourself with love and compassion. Bring each other back on the track if one is flying off the handle.
- Listen to hear and understand not to just respond. Clear your head from the answer you have already put together. Put yourself in their shoes. See the matter from their point of view instead of insisting on your own. You both need to practice this and be honest.

If none of this works, you may have to seek guidance from someone else to bring you the clarity that neither one is allowing to be seen. This is not a bad thing in a relationship. Someone else's view who is not emotionally invested can help you understand yourself better; and help you see dimensions and perspectives you were not considering before.

# Another Secret

Now there is another secret that I need to talk about, that might be causing health related issues. The ancient considered the right side of the body to be masculine and the left side, feminine. In ancient times and in old movies, you will see men fighting with their right arm, and defending with left. The healing secret is this: if you resent someone, of the masculine sex and gender, you may have health problems on the right side, and likewise the trouble maybe on the left side, if you have female problems.

The masculine side, also symbolizes wisdom. So if you have been misusing your wisdom, you may get destructive results on the right side over and over, until you use your wisdom properly.

Also the right side is the giving side, and the right side problems may show a need to give in some area or way. You may have been withholding on something; whether it is love, money, or emotions.

Repeated problems on the left side, indicate resentment towards someone from feminine sex. Since the feminine gender also symbolizes love, if you have been misusing your mind power of love, or letting your love be misused by others, it can cause health problems on the left side of the body.

Another thing is that the left side symbolizes the ability to receive, and then use wisely that which is received. If you have refused to receive a certain gift extended to you, or if you feel your good has passed you by, you have been cheated out of receiving something, you may experience ailments of the left side.

Now, if you have gathered a vast knowledge of truth and spirituality, and have not used it in your life, or to aid others, this knowledge stagnation, can also come out as ailments on the left side of the body. "Truth demands expression."

# Love Is All There Is

So many times the topic of happiness is brought up, when I am doing seminars or life-coaching lessons. It seems as if everyone is seeking something that they feel they need to chase and the cliché they always have heard is that: the happiness is inside you and it is not in external things.

There seems to be still a growing number of people that cannot find this "thing" called happy in them, and the only way to look for it is externally.

I have often started my talks on happiness with one note: When you ask me, how can I be happy, you are really asking me how can I give more love?

This of course is always followed by a blank look on the face of the person asking the question, looking at me with ears folded in and the head slightly tilted and then side to side. Sort of like the look I get from Bella my dog when I say something that she has not heard before.

Here are other things that I have been asked:
- Is there a way I can change the perception of this world that will change my experience?
- Is it actually possible not to ever be fearful again?
- Is there a possibility that we can actually forgive anyone that we think they have hurt us?
- Is there a possibility of us forgiving ourselves for the mistakes we have made so that we will never regret again?
- Can I actually be peaceful and happy while the whole world around me is falling apart?
- Can I actually put aside all my hang-ups about love and be able to truly love unconditionally?

My answer: "YES" to all of the above questions.

Our attitudes towards life follow our perceptions of our environment. Remember also that these perceptions have a value attached to them. These values will tell us if something is good or bad for us. These are learned values and not something we were born with.

Throughout the years, we have learned a lot of things that we have found out they were false at the root. We have two types of people: one type that will learn something and hold on to it with dear life as if that is the only knowledge that will ever be available, and it is the sacred truth; and the second, the one that learns things as he/she goes on and if by any chance there are some new findings on the topic, he/she drops the old belief like a hot potato and goes with the new one.

So going back to perception, it really is not the other people that are bugging us, but our perception of what they mean and our thoughts and feelings around that, is the hurting factor. This is one reason why I always say, when there is a conflict between you and someone else, always look for a conflict between you and you.

There are many ways in approaching what I will be discussing here, but the most important one is: *learn only love, as that is what you are.* What I have said here is describing both what you are looking for and how to achieve it.

Here are some of the things I can quote from *"Course in Miracles"* that are quite profound and worth thinking about:

- When you are occupied with helping and loving another person, you do not experience fear.
- You cannot successfully hide your fear from children and animals.
- The true contents of our minds are open to all; and in one level all minds are in communication.

- We are not confined to our bodies and we are not limited by physical reality.
- The mind, through its will to live, can affect a course of an illness.
- A preoccupation with the past, disturbs your present attitude.
- Our inner goals determine our experience. We are not a victim of this world.
- Love exists.

As we were growing up, we were taught to believe that past predicts our future and someone who is mature with a good head on their shoulder, carefully considers the lessons of the past when planning for the future. The truth is that past has only one lesson to teach us: *present is the only time there is.*

The trouble with our learning is that the past has created an "expectation", and we are constantly looking at the past and expecting the future to deliver the same. When we are looking at it this way, we are not being constructive and basing everything on fear. We do not trust anything or anyone and everyone is a potential enemy.

So this brings about feelings of guilt, victimization, and ambiguity about everything and then we start building talents of our own to depend on, such as manipulation.

When we do not feel loved, loving or lovable, we chase to control the outside reality in hope of bringing happiness into our lives. And because this then is something to achieve in the future, the present moment loses its value.

Happiness requires your attention to the moment of "Now". Try it; whenever you are fearful, you are not experiencing the moment of now, you are either ashamed of the past or anxious of future.

Fear stimulates the feeling of unhappiness in order for you to have a firm grip of the future. With this you cannot possibly feel worthy of being loved. Instead you are constantly in some sort of a guilt. You feel as if you have committed a sin that needs to be repaid and you will be punished for it soon.

We feel our guilt is private and some of us have a big inventory of it. Now sitting there brewing and steeping in this, all hell breaks loose around us and we take it as well-deserved. Holding on to this inventory is energetically costly and leads to emotional bankruptcy.

This type of an attitude results in existing, not living. At this point some even mistake happiness with pain, because they only feel alive when they are in the middle of a crisis. This of course brings them to experience more and more of the same in their lives.

The truth of the matter is that this kind of life seems normal to many. Most people do not make the connection that the choice between love and fear is really up to them. They choose instead to buy into other people's philosophy and accept the limitations of their environment.

If you think that you need to identify with the past, it is not so. There is an alternative. The world is not held together and running by us worrying about it. Your understanding and taking responsibility for your life, should feel like a freeing experience.

Far more than we realize, we only see the past in people we encounter. The funny part is, that this is usually our past and not theirs. To clear your vibrations, there needs be a change in attitude of genuinely wanting to see others as they are this instant. Allowing them to change. Most of the time it is us who do not allow any change in a relationship even though we claim so.

There would be very little that you dislike, if you allowed the past to be past. Your past experience can never tell you about your present love. Remembering and seeing are not the same. This is why memories are of so little use when you want to build a loving relationship.

All minds are joined, therefore any healing of any type is self-healing. Your inner peace will not only bring prosperity and health to you, but to others. Every healing happens from inside out. Love is our only function and destiny. To save yourself and others, the sooner you grasp the idea, the sooner everyone prospers.

All of us are connected, whether we are aware of this amazing fact or not is of no importance. Life goes on. But our unawareness causes misery for us individually.

There are no thoughts that you have or ever had that are considered private. Any thoughts that you might have regarding being a separate individual and cutting yourself off from life, will not affect life one bit. In other words, your belief in physical reality, does not change the reality. Your thoughts are frequencies that are sent out that are either part of the problem or the solution.

So now, if in mind you are joined with others, whether you like it or not, you are affecting them and they are affecting you. If you of course choose not to believe in this, and still feel separate, in reality would make no difference because you are able to separate yourself from others as much as the wave can separate itself from the ocean.

In other words, your low frequency thoughts and beliefs don't change the reality; they only do not contribute to your enjoyment of what is available. If the fridge is full of food and you are dying from hunger because you "think" it is empty, your thought will not over-rule the truth of fridge being full but it will rule your life in how much you can enjoy the food or die.

Quite simply, what you think can be the problem or the solution. Thoughts of love can get rid of loneliness, illness, pain and depression and on the other hand thoughts of guilt and fear can cause all that. Your body is a learning machine and its entry point is

96

the mind.  Whatever you have put into your mind will show through your physical body. If your mind is peaceful, so is your body.

Your ego will seek separateness at all times, because that is how it thrives and survives. Peace and inner quiet are the mortal enemies of ego. Love and peace come from the feeling of unity.

When you start understanding your true self as the spiritual being currently experiencing life in a physical form, your whole life starts to change.  This is when you fall in love with the source and its essence in all. This is when the sun looks brighter and flowers more fragrant and your friends and relatives more caring and loving, and nothing seems to matter but love anymore.  Everything becomes adorable, meaningful and amazing.  True mind and physical healing takes place and you feel at peace.

Our ego always prefers conflict in proving its individuality.  It would rather stew over a matter than just pass over it quickly.  To do this of course, it will use the "right and wrong" method.

# Principles of Healing

*One:* the first and foremost, is your understanding of the fact that the essence of your being is pure love. This principle talks to the fact that we are spiritual beings and connected in every way. Love cannot be hindered by physical things. Because of this we are unlimited. Love is all there is and the only real thing.

When you communicate with others, do it from love to love and not from past experience to past experience. This creates a communication that is seated in judgement, hence creating no positive results. When you communicate with love, your encounter is gratifying and healing.

I have been asked to define what love is and the only definition I can come up with: it is the absence of fear in understanding your unity with the ALL.

We have all had encounters with Divine/agape/unconditional love. If not in your dealings with an animal maybe in your dealings with a newborn baby. We all know what it feels like. We only forget to nourish it when we become accustomed to picking on others.

Divine love is not about giving, in exchange for something. It is not about seeing someone do exactly as you like them to do. It is not about right or wrong. It is about acceptance and purity.

What we currently have learned to do in our lives, is in the opposite direction to divine love. In order for us to love anyone, they need to be a certain way and try to fit-in.

As our newborns are welcomed to this world, we start saying, "Look at this face and learn what I expect from you. If you see me smiling, you have done something good. If you see me frown, stop what you were doing immediately. It is not good and not approved."

In this, from a very young age, we learn to cater to someone else's judgment of us instead of trying to just "be". In our later years, this brings tremendous pressure to our lives to a degree that I have seen some are happy in transitioning of some of the controlling parties in their lives and inwardly celebrate their death. How healthy is this?

Who do you ever see in their death-bed claiming, "I wish I would have had time to judge a bit more or argue a bit more or beat people up a bit more?" You would definitely see them say though, "I wish I had time to enjoy life a bit more." Parents frequently ask to be acknowledged by asking for respect in the most mistaken ways.

When you give true love, you are not concerned with the outer behaviours. You are not aware of any limitations. You are not preoccupied with time. You feel free and at peace. You feel "in love" – even though the society today translates being in love so differently.

Being in love now-a-days carries with it, certain written commitments and prenuptial agreements; none has to do with divine love.

We all say that we are looking for happiness, but when we are told the answer is found in love, we feel that is a tremendous price to pay. We rarely choose peace over conflict and love over fear and we believe in the satisfaction of revenge, being right and proving someone else wrong, gloating in the fact that we know more and humbling those who give us difficult times.

It makes sense to us to be harsh with our children to teach them gentleness; we believe in making some suffer for their actions in feeling that justice is served; we believe that pain can be pleasurable and that taking is getting. Then of course we are puzzled in why all these actions are not producing love and peace on Earth and mostly in our lives.

Having said all that, the only thing that is going to bring clarity to our minds is: Love. In order to be more immersed in love, we need to identify with what we really are; where we have come from; what is our source and how do we relate to the entire existence and the important role each and every one of us play.

To get into the space of love, first find out how attached you are to the physical. What decides your values? Is it the physical shape you are in? Is it the money? The house? The car you are driving? All of which are taking you away from real you. Have you ever seen a newborn being cocky about his pacifier while passing by another newborn? "Look mine is a Gucci. My mother is much richer than your father. I use designer diapers." Why is it that a newborn has no relations to this type of thinking? Because they are much more in tune with the source and where they came from and the divine love.

None of that matters when you experience true love. When two people meet and fall in love, even though they are experiencing Eros, which is the erotic love, there is a hint of divine love in there causing their eyes to be shut close to all other person's faults. Not being purely divine, when the erotic love expires, the love goggles are removed and they see fault.

As long as our bodies are here, our job is to use them as means to extend love in forms that could be understood and recognized by those sharing this planet with us. Health is inner peace; healing is letting go of fear and allowing love in. Nothing but peace, happiness, joy, health and prosperity can come out of love.

**Two:** Healing comes from inside out. Inner peace creates outer health.
**Three:** you can let go of the past and future. You can only change the future by your thoughts now, and if you are concentrating on what you did wrong in the past, the future is not looking too good either. Our fear of future usually stems out of the fact that we think what has happened in the past will repeat in the future in some painful way. With this attitude it would almost be impossible to be happy.

One of the greatest gifts you can give yourself is to decide not to be stuck in the past or be fearful of future and enjoy the NOW. Consciously release the past and forgive everyone and everything in it. Your past can only hurt you if you make it a part of your present.

*Four:* in understanding unity, give up all judgement. Become a love-finder instead of a fault-finder. We can learn to love ourselves and others instead of judging. Loving is the only true way to health and prosperity. Each moment of offering love brings us peace.

Let us try to remember that the very essence of our being is love. Our egos are constantly judging and condemning others and ourselves. Unfortunately many of us firmly believe that we have committed an unforgivable act, and the sense of guilt will be keeping us from repeating it again. This belief will only serve to bring us illness and destroy our peace of mind.

I have often been asked on the subject of forgiveness and what it entails and what needs to be done. My view of forgiveness is somewhat different than the rest I believe. I do not think there is ever anything to forgive.

Forgiveness does not mean that you swallow your anger and act as if everything is acceptable. Forgiveness is not showing patience; as in showing patience you are always showing resistance towards something and hence the patience. You can never say that you are patient against something you love. There is nothing in loving that you are resisting, hence no patience required.

Forgiveness of course does not mean that you act out your anger or once you have done it, you feel superior to the one you have forgiven. Forgiveness does not mean that you will go back to an abusive spouse, or let all the prisoners out.

Ego believes that if it forgives, it must translate this forgiveness into some behaviour. But true forgiveness does not require any bodily action. Forgiveness is an inner correction, enlightenment and understanding that lightens ones heart and frees us to live in the present moment.

The root meaning of the word "forgive" is "to let go". Forgiveness is the willingness is perceiving everyone including ourselves, as either experiencing love or feeling the need for love. Any form of attack from any source is a cry for help in wanting love. The cure: gentleness and love. Attacking one that attacks you, does not cure the attacker. Above all, forgiving does not mean that you will adhere to the attitude of "holier than thou" around people.

In understanding Unity with the Source and the ALL, and understanding the fact, that all anyone of us ever does, is simply choose from a menu that we have been offered in this plane; there is nothing to forgive. Everything is just an experience. Nothing personal. Let's face it, we are co-creators and not creators. The creator has already created all and in that all our choices in life whether we decide to be a philanthropist or a thief are also choices offered part of this creation and part of experience. Just because you chose to be the philanthropist and someone else chose to be the thief does not diminish the value of the experience nor leaves room for judgement.

All experiences are necessary and in that some souls have taken the responsibility into seeing that happen. They are to be respected for their choice and blessed for such a hard task they have undertaken. The choice they have made, violating the societal agreement often buys them many years in jail.

Trying to say I forgive someone, looks sort of like this scenario: you have gone to a restaurant and there are the options of lamb, shrimp or chicken on the menu. You choose chicken where your friend chooses the shrimp and yet another friend the lamb. In doing so, you turn to your friends and say, I forgive you for not choosing chicken.

And for those who constantly carry the feeling of guilt, thinking that God will be striking you one day for what you have done, in the above example is such that the chef will walk out of the kitchen and blame and punish every one of you for the choices you have made and condemning you, because he had a certain choice in mind. Does this make sense?

Neither does our beliefs on what God is and what he will do to us and his feelings of anger towards us. This amazing Source of Energy, has created ALL. Can you wrap your head around that? ALL means ALL not some. ALL means including the choices you make in this life. And ALL for the sake of experience. You have the choice to change your experience as often as you wish and that is the loveliest part of this life.

So now really, when you say, "I forgive you" what and who are you forgiving? In a conference on world peace where Mother Theresa was present, it was suggested that a form to be signed opposing nuclear-arms. When she was asked to sign, she refused in saying, "if I sign, I would be loving some people and not others as I will be taking sides in a controversy."

True forgiveness is based on reality. It overlooks the physical evidence gathered, from the point of view of a single body and turns instead, to the Universal truth of our reality. Each of us is innocent and loved completely by the Source. It understands that all mis-takes come from the ego and it is a part of the whole experience that everyone will go through to some degree. Forgiveness is a gentle vision that sees the goodness of the heart and the wholeness of the character and it recognizes the uselessness of condemnation in the process of growth.

It is not just the forgiveness against people that you need to consider. Some of us need to forgive animals, nature, seasons, the rain, the snow, the job, the nation, the foods, the dress styles, the government, the taxes and so on..... The more serious you take this physical reality the more there is to forgive.

If you forgive because you feel obligated to do so, you are missing the boat. Forgiveness is a gentle turning away from what we see with our physical eyes and searching for the truth that lies beyond the individual's ego.

*Five:* you are a student at all times and in the meantime a teacher to many. Create peace and love in other's lives with your words and actions. Search and find love in all, instead of their faults, regardless of what their behaviours maybe. Just as you choose to see the faults, you can choose to see the light of love in them.

Ego usually is a fault-finder. It does not care who or what is the object of its unhappy focus. In this ego is always seeking for individuality for the sake of experience. When we act out of ego, there is no sense of unity or wholeness in ourselves and our relationships. In that you cannot experience love, peace and happiness that follow. In a marriage that both parties are focused on fault finding, the relationship quickly dies; for the simple fact that neither one of them can do anything right.
If you ask a couple who are in such relationships to say a few positive things about each other, they will have great trouble in coming up with any positive points about their mate.

Most of us have a list of things that we do not like or accept about ourselves. Now instead of seeking this list out and forgiving ourselves, we then mirror these onto others in the form of fault-finding and mistakes. As if seeing someone else guilty is going to make us innocent.

It is very difficult for many to accept that what we criticise in others is often a reflection of what we have rejected in ourselves. We call others narrow-minded in covering up our own narrow-mindedness. This kind of fault-finding has become automatic and unless we consciously stop and contemplate the thoughts we can never be rid of it. We need to begin to question the validity of these faults and the effects they have on us and our relationships.

The amazing thing is that the love-finder is in all of us; we only need to start exercising it consciously at the beginning and later the autopilot shall take over.  By just doing this one simple step, your whole life will seem completely turned and different.  You will find more joy in your heart and a sense of constant happiness.  Your heart will sing at all times.  No more heart-breaks; no more disappointments, no more lack.  Only peace, joy, health and prosperity.

Each and every day share your unconditional love by many.  Let your inner child come out and play. Stop the seriousness of this physical reality that was meant to be a sand box to play in. Look at all the wonderful toys the nature has created and get busy playing.  Act silly without being fearful of being judged.

Guaranteed, those who judge you will be drawn to your natural joy and exuberance and their lives will be nourished in your presence. Choose to look on yourself and everyone and everything around you with love. Practicing this every day will bring you indescribable joy that cannot be touched by the events of physical reality. Will you choose to take this risk?

There is a prayer in the "Course in Miracles" that I really like; and it goes like this:

*"I am only here to be truly helpful*
*I am here to represent you, who sent me*
*I do not have to worry about what to say*
*Or what to do*
*Because you who sent me, will direct me*
*I am content to be wherever you wish*
*Knowing you go there with me*
*I will be healed as I let you teach me to heal"*

# Journey of Life

Life is a trip! You are going on this trip by the means of this physical vessel that you have been given. It is completely up to you in how you wish to travel, and how you maintain it. Do you want to travel first class, economy or standby?

No matter how you choose to travel, the flight pattern is exactly the same; you are born, you experience life, you transition. The quality of your experience between birth and transitioning is completely up to you.

In standby, you are gambling, in economy you are suffering and the first class is filled with goodies and joy. What will provide you this first class journey is: you making the intentional effort of buying the "Faith Airlines" ticket.

Faith, as we have talked before, in essence, is pure and unconditional love. Travelling on the "Faith Airlines" will eliminate your fears, anger, judgement, envy, jealousy, loneliness and depression just to name a few. Anyone can upgrade their ticket from "Fear Airlines" to "Faith Airlines" at any given moment. There is always more than enough seats available. For this upgrade to happen, all they need to do is change from victim consciousness to accountable and responsible.

Let me make something clear here; to love something does not mean you need to like it, approve it or even desire it. To love it, means you accept it as is and if it is not happening the way that will uplift you, you have a choice in moving on without wanting to change or rearrange it.

Understand that we ALL have choices and any choice we make is perfectly alright and we all have the right to experience life, as we are here to do. Not a grain of sand is left without an experience and all is done in love. If you can accept that, there is never a need to travel economy or standby because you need not suffer. When you are in the first class you can help others get there too, "*IF*" they are asking you how; but you cannot be in economy showing them how to live first class.

Travelling on the "Fear Airlines" goes against the nature, and the Divine Love. It will cost you your happiness, vitality, health, longevity and overall prosperity.

When you start travelling on "Faith Airlines", you will notice that the people around you are different. They are compassionate, loving, caring, and giving. That is the only type of people that can board that flight. The fearful people cannot ever afford to buy the ticket to this airline and hence if you have a current circle of fearful friends, you might need to be ready to leave them in a different airplane.

Everybody flying the "Fear Airlines" is infected with the "fear" virus. They got this epidemic through media, relatives, friends, co-workers and expectations. When we are kids, say we have a difficulty with someone and we get frustrated and angry. For whatever the reason our frustration seems to push the difficulty away. Since we have gotten the result we want, if it happens a second time, we react the same way. At this point we know that our frustration and anger pushes the problem away. Then we keep practicing until we master the art of anger and frustration.

In the same fashion we become really good at jealousy, envy, resentment, condemning, fault-finding, sadness, arguing and self-rejection. When we have mastered all that, we no longer need to pay conscious attention to it, and it becomes a subconscious act to behave that way. This is when we think we have lost control and when someone says, "Why do you get angry?" We reply, "I don't know. I have no control over it. It just happens."
Fortunately the cure is at hand. Faith! Faith even looks at fear in love. Your Faith power is so strong that it will cure and heal anything it touches.

I once heard an analogy somewhere where I cannot recall that was awesome and I would like to reiterate that to you:

Imagine if you lived on a planet that everyone suffered from a terrible and painful skin disease. Their entire bodies were covered with wounds and infected and very sensitive to touch of course. Everyone on this planet believed that this is the normal way the skin must be, and even the medical books confirmed it as normal.

When babies were first born, their skin was healthy, soft and glowing and then at five or six years of age, their skin also got to look like their parents and everyone else. What would be these people's behaviour towards each other? Of course they would try to stay away from each other and protect their wounds. They try not to touch each other because it is too painful. If someone by accident touches someone else, the person screams in agony and just to get even, will touch the person back. The funny part is that Love is still such a strong factor in their being that they still maintain relationships with others.

Now, here comes this day of miracle. You wake up one day and your skin is completely healed. No wounds, no pain, just a wonderful healthy skin. However, you cannot touch anyone because it hurts them and no one will still touch you under the assumption that it might hurt you. Isn't this how it is today?

Many are ill emotionally with fear so much so, that they will not touch love nor allow love to touch them. It is way too painful. The problem is that all the mental anguish we are suffering from, is labelled as normal and the few healthy ones are nuts. Our relationships are so emotionally painful, that the minute we hear someone mention the word love, we borrow two extra set of legs from the fellow near us and run away.

To protect ourselves we lie and we lie so good that we start building a whole belief system around it. The lying becomes second nature and we don't know we are doing it. When we actually understand that we are lying we try to justify it under the name of protection.

We build all kinds of barriers for ourselves and restrict our freedom. When someone says, "You are pushing my buttons." What they really mean is, "You are touching my emotional wounds, and I react because it hurts."

When you truly understand where people emotionally are, can you still get mad at them? Can you still judge them? Can you actually say anything insensitive to them? Those with wounds live in constant hell. What is the religious description of hell? Isn't it a place of suffering, fear, war, violence and punishment? What is the description of the lives of emotionally wounded? Isn't it the same? A life full of guilt, blame, sadness and suffering?

Let's put the lies we have heard behind and open our eyes to our real self – pure love. At the point of this transformation, what seems to be drama in other's lives, becomes comedy in yours. You are not wounded anymore. You are not hurting. You are no longer afraid to be who you are. You are no longer lonely. You feel supported and helped at all times. Whatever others do and say does not hurt you anymore. You are in control of your emotions. You are in control of your manifestations. You are no longer afraid to love.

The best moments of our lives are when we are playing, dancing, exploring and creating. These are all expressions of love. We are happiest when we express love. Try not to pass the mental illness to your children. Our teachers, parents and family did it to us, let's not repeat the experience. Do not domesticate your kids like you do a dog with reward and punishment. What we call education, unfortunately is nothing but a form of domestication.

The trouble is that we are so trained in thinking that this systematic education is required for us to live a good life, that when our children drop out of school we are completely panicked and frightened. We are accused of being bad parents in not being able to make our kids attend school and we buy into this.

We are born, and we learn the system of reward and punishment. We want to avoid punishment and we sometimes suffer anxiety over not being rewarded. When we were born we did not care if we were accepted or not, but all of a sudden this system is teaching us completely different set of beliefs than we were born with. The need to be accepted. The need to conform. All of a sudden everyone's opinion becomes more important than our own.

We start projecting unreal images of us to others so that we are accepted and internally we suffer, as that is not who we are. This suffering shows in the way of illness, anger, anxiety and frustration. So do you believe this leads to the path of happiness???

As we go on, we create various images for ourselves according to other people's expectations and we play many roles and we wear many hats. As a parent we must behave a certain way, as a child to our parent a certain way as a colleague a certain way as a teacher a certain way as a student a certain way and the list goes on. We almost never come in touch with who we really are anymore, as we are in constant pretence.

Our intimate relationships suffer most, because we feel closest to the one we are intimate with and in finding that we cannot even be ourselves in their presence, we fight, bicker and argue. Is that the path to happiness?

Most relationships start based on fantasy. When a man meets a woman he has this image of her in his mind that he thinks she will match and the same is true with the woman. Then he tries to make her fit the image he has made for her and she tries to make him fit the image she has made for him. In this relationship of course there are six images involved. How is this relationship ever going to be successful through the created fog?

Between the images we pretend to be and the inner image, we will feel lonely. Happiness seems unachievable because the gap is too huge. When in this state of mind, someone's adverse opinion of us can make a tremendous difference in our lives. "He is too stupid"; "He is too fat"; "She is ugly."

We become dependent on other people's opinion because we are domesticated. There is a difference between a cat and a dog. The dog walks in front of you and every once in a while will look back for your approval; where the cat just won't give a damn and is in complete touch with what she wants to do.

So many people suffering because of wanting to get acceptance and approval from others. Is this the road to happiness and happy relationships???

If you look at human body you will notice that we have two very strong alarm systems. When there is pain present in the body, that is an alarm that something is not right, so we look to fix it. When there is fear present, we know that there is something wrong emotionally and we look to fix it.

Sometimes we use these alarms to domesticate each other. We inflict pain on someone or emotionally make them fearful so that they can abide by the rules. Based on the same fear, we are constantly judging ourselves and others. Judging what we do and don't do, what we think and don't think, judging everyone and everything at all times. When you become aware of this, you realize why our relationships don't work with our parents, mates, children, coworkers and so on.

Here is the strange part of relationships: when you judge yourself and become self-critical, you will find things that you need to be punished for. You start feeling guilty and look for punishments to come to you in any possible form. So in a way you start mentally abusing yourself.

When people with relationship trouble come to me and tell me that their partners are abusive; a deeper look at the matter usually reveals this very simple fact that no one stands for more abuse from their partners than the amount they are offering themselves.

If one is in an abusive relationship, it is because they accept the abuse. The limit of your self-abuse usually is the limit you put on the amount of abuse you can receive from your partner. If anyone abuses you more than you abuse yourself, you normally and quickly walk away. Happy relationships have become: you abuse me as much as I want to get abused and I will abuse you as much you want to be abused, we are good together, there is a real good equilibrium going, it works.

If someone is complaining to you about an abusive partner and they have no idea why they stick around that relationship, you can bet your bottom dollar that he/she needs that abuse as a way of punishing himself/herself.

Every human being has a personal dream of their very own. We dream according to our beliefs and values. Not two dreams are ever identical. We need to start respecting other people's dreams. We can have thousands of relationships, but each relationship is only between two people. In every relationship we have, we dream a small dream together. Every relationship comes alive with two dreams.
Your dreams are made of emotions and your emotions are sprouted from two basic branches of fear and love. As much as we experience both emotions, one of them is the dominant one in our hearts and minds.

Let's check some of the characteristics of each basic emotion. Love is freeing, unbinding, and has no obligations. Fear is binding, clenching and is filled with obligations. Whatever you do out of fear is because "you have to do it" and whatever you do out of love is because "you love to do it."

Love is without expectation; and fear is filled with expectation. Love does not feel sorry or pity for anyone, only compassion. Fear feels sympathy and feels sorry and sad for everyone. You will only feel sorry and sad for someone, in whom you have no respect in their strength and choices.

Love respects you and understands your strengths and in that there is no sympathy and feeling sorry. Love is responsible, where fear avoids responsibility and would rather see you victimised. Anger, sadness, loneliness, jealousy, envy and revenge are all some of the different masks that fear wears. Love is unconditional, fear is full of conditions.

How many relationships have you seen that fear is mimicking love? I love you only if you let me control you, if you are good to me, if you fit my image of you. I will judge you against the image I have and in that I can pronounce you guilty. I sometimes feel ashamed of you because you are not what I want you to be, you embarrass me, you annoy me, I have no patience with you at all. In this relationship if you make a mistake you will be paying for it for years.

Should this relationship come from true love, then the whole scenario would change to: There is no if, there are no conditions. I love you for no reason for no justification. I love you the way you are and you are free to be who you are. In this relationship all mistakes are a one-time thing; you learn and move on and forgive.

All that I have said is not just between couples, but in any relationship. In every relationship you are only responsible for your part and not the other person's. In a relationship where one controls the other, there is no respect and in that there is no love. If you try to suppress the other person and take over the control of the entire relationship, be sure that this is out of fear and not love.

Think of your relationship like a game of tennis; would you ever attempt to get the racket from your partner and play both parts yourself? Does it make sense?

The quality of your relationship communications is also dependent on the two emotions of love and fear. Come from the space of love when you communicate.

One major note that I always refer to is for you to realize that NO ONE MAKES YOU HAPPY. Only you make you happy. You being happy, is you showing love. You can be in love and happy at the same time; but you cannot be fearful and happy at the same time. Love is not a concept, love is an action. The only way to master it is to practice it. You don't need to justify it or explain it, just practice it.

# Mind and Body Needs

We create a whole bunch of angels and demons for us. The act of intimacy has been considered a sin for a long while by many. The problem does not lie in the intimacy though; it is within how we manipulate the knowledge.

We have a whole set of beliefs about sexual encounters and how we will be punished in hell for them. But the instinct is so strong that we are willing to suffer an eternity in hell for it.

Then we have the guilt and we have the shame and by pointing fingers at those who are caught in the act, we try to make ourselves feel a bit more innocent. We have a whole set of beliefs around what a sexual behaviour of a man and a woman should be, and a man is always either too wimpy or too macho and a woman is always either too skinny or too fat depending on the judge of the day.

There are so many myths and lies about intimacy, which the rate of women not enjoying it, is on the rise every year. Self-image and just the pressure of performance, seems to be at all-time high. On top of that put the whipped cream of guilt and shame and evil and you got yourself a "perversion pie".

These rules and regulation we have placed on intimacy go completely against nature; but we believe them. We need to have a written contract to make intimacy OK. We need to present our words in the presence of many that we will be loyal to each other, and a one on one session will not do.

Now you are walking innocently on the street and this gorgeous woman or this Adonis is walking right pass by you, and you feel this incredible sensation and attraction. You cannot avoid this feeling because it is normal. Does not mean you are going to make the next move. When the mental and visual stimulation is gone, the body lets go.

Here is the catch. When you repress yourself from feeling what is, as something that is "OK"; the scenario plays itself in your mind much later over and over again. When you repress something, you think of it more and the body's reaction becomes stronger. If the first time around, you had enjoyed a guilt-less scene and let it go, you probably would not even have the same reaction if you see this person again.

Between couples, this can become a huge issue. The trouble is that when one of the partners makes the other one feel guilty about something this normal, the problem becomes persistent in the other's mind. Most infidelities in relationships happen because of the games our minds play, and the release of the tension of fear that you have been having.

The fear of being punished for an evil act. If this game goes on, of course it will be quite self-destructive. We have two different set of needs according to our bodies and minds. The body needs: food, shelter, water, air, sleep and sex. It is quite easy to provide the body with what it needs. The mind thinks and says, "These are _my_ needs."

The mind in fact, does not have any physical needs. Here is an example we can all relate to: our bodies need to be clothed. When you are cold, you go to your closet and find the first thing that is going to warm you up and wear it. When the mind thinks it needs clothes, you open the closet door and even though it is filled with clothing, you have nothing to wear.

People who overeat have the same trouble. When the body is hungry, you give it food and it is satisfied. When the mind is hungry, we binge. We have allowed for this to take over our lives quite a bit and this has caused the "not enough" symptom in our lives. The same is true, in intimacy. Those who are constantly looking for someone new to be with, have left this to be thought of, as if it is their mind that needs this activity.

Try to split your needs into two distinct categories: the needs of the body and the needs of mind.

The mind's instinctive need is to try and answer one question: "What Am I?' In this, it tries to identify itself with the needs of the body; I am the body, I am what I think and see; I hurt and I feel and I bleed. In this, the mind is justified to take over the body.

When you start splitting your needs, the more you realize you are not your body. In this process you let go of your stories and emotional pain and feel safe again.

As you go deeper into this process you find out you are not your mind, and you are not your soul, but you are this incredible force; that makes everything you see and feel possible. You will find that you are the force of life and nothing without you exists.

You are the force just passing through this vessel you call body, mind and soul. You are the force in every beautiful flower, in every singing bird, in every butterfly, in every ocean and rock. The whole Universe is being run by that force. You are life!

# The Road to Happiness

Just like anything else we have talked about so far, the amount of love you express and your perception, both play a major role in your happiness. Some people see happiness "nowhere" and some see it, "now here".

Your happiness is not hiding in some cave that you need to spend a lifetime to find. All spiritual masters and all spiritual books talk about the *"holy now"* and how to milk it. The one simple secret in milking the *"holy now"* is placing your attention internally not externally. Look inside you. If you spend enough time looking in, you will be amazed at who you would see.

This *"holy now"* represents a permanent potential in you, to experience love, freedom, and joy regardless of external conditions. You are the key to your own happiness. The only reason we are continuously searching for this thing called happiness, is that we have forgotten how to take advantage of this *"holy now"*. We are constantly looking to some imagined future, and have lost faith in the *"holy now"*. As long as you are looking into the world around you to make you happy, you are in for a disappointment. It is like looking into a mirror to change your looks.

The world around you is really only a mirror. Milking the *"holy now"* is about rediscovering yourself and your potential. All your potential currently maybe hidden under a pile of fear, doubt, guilt and mental conditioning of beliefs.

As humans, we have a lot of potential. We have potential for misery, sadness, pain and weakness and we also hold the same potential for happiness, joy and prosperity. What you focus on most, becomes familiar and what becomes familiar, feels real to you.

In a society, in which the focus is on tears before laughter, pain before joy and fear before love; only tears, pain and fear look real to us. Happiness seems to only come as a short burst just to give us an intermission in between painful times.

We are like fish dying from thirst. Surrounded by happiness yet not even recognizing it. Like the ugly duckling, we are constantly concentrating on and being fearful of, whether we are good enough, smart enough, cute enough; and all the things that we can be blamed and punished for, with no time to look inside to find what we have been searching for; though eventually we will find the truth.

Our misperception of self and God, has created great unhappiness for us. At any given moment, either you are remembering your true self, or forgetting. When you are remembering, you feel happy, joyful, smiling, trusting, generous and loving; and when you forget about your true self you become afraid, isolated and desperate. In the state of forgetfulness you protect, defend and attack.

So find out what makes you remember the truth, when you forget, and you have found the way to milk the *"holy now"* and be happy. In remembering and understanding your true self, first you believe, then you see the light, then you go towards the light, and then you become one with the light.

Happiness is your natural state of being. You hardly would find someone who does not want genuine happiness. So why is it that we have so many miserable people around? Just ask people a simple question and you can gauge where they are in their level of happiness.

How are you? Not bad. Not too bad. Not so bad. Could be better. Could be worse. Hanging in there. Still breathing. Can't complain. Okay. Getting by. No news is good news. Not dead yet. Surviving and so on.... We are having "near life experiences." Not quite living. Some of us are fearful of experiencing happiness of course, as I mentioned in earlier topics. Part of it comes from the saying we believe in: "better the devil you know." In this saying there is no change required. It is the familiar ground.

Happiness is much more than just an absence of pain. You need to build a relationship with it. When you keep your thoughts full of doubts, suspicion, criticism and fear, you are certainly not looking for happiness to show up. Next time you experience genuine happiness, watch your thoughts closely; is any of the abovementioned present? Or do you feel utter love and joy?

If when you experience happiness, your dominating thoughts are, "It's good while it lasts"; or "What's the catch?" or "What did I do to deserve this?" you are definitely shooting yourself in the foot. I remember growing up and our next door neighbour had a child the same age as I. In my times off, I could spend time with this girl and I would make her laugh so that she would be in rolling on the floor. Anytime this happened, her mother came in to tell her to stop her laughter; as any such laughter will bring much tears afterwards. Can you spell: scarred for life?

I remember her telling my mother, "Your child is not normal. I believe you need to consult psychiatrists as she is constantly smiling. This is blasphemy and will only bring about envy, trouble and invite rejection." I have since lost touch with that child, but if she has followed in the footsteps of her mother, she would be much in need of love now. She always shows up in my nightly love-cast meditations.

Because of such myths that have been handed down to us from generation to generation, we have all become "happychondriacs".

How many times you have told yourself, "When .... happens, I will be happy." Then the ..... happens and few minutes of joy is all there is. Take a look at the language we use to define our joy and you will understand how confused we are.

Have you heard the following phrases? I had a <u>hell</u> of a time; it was <u>awfully</u> good; it is to <u>die</u> for; I nearly <u>died</u>; I am <u>dying</u> to see you; she is <u>drop-dead</u> gorgeous; I love him to <u>pieces</u>; I love her to <u>death;</u> that is so_sick; etc... What we are doing is that, we are using the language of pain to describe joy and happiness. This is of course a learned and conditioned confusion.

Your inner self is not conditioned. You once used to know this inner self intimately and then you got distracted, and your attention got hooked otherwise. This true self has no "on" and "off" switch. It is always on. There are many different names for this true self. Zen masters call it your *original face;* Taoists call it: *the un-carved block* and the alchemists call it: *your inner gold* and so on.

Any time you act in alliance with your ego, you betray your true self. Your ego will only offer you illusions of separation, fear, loneliness and struggle.

In shifting from what you feel to happiness, you need to reconnect with your wisdom and light. It is usually the fear that something is missing within us, that leads us to look for happiness elsewhere. You overlook what is already here, and chase after it, over there.

You miss your *holy now* as you keep thinking about the time and space that is not here yet. You forget to be grateful for what is, but pray for more to come.

Our two little eyes, are always seeing bits and pieces of things, and we never have the time to step back enough, to see the big picture. It is only when we look with our hearts, that we can see the wholeness and the unity.
Great masters that we look up to, have always shown us that all we need, is already here. Great thinkers, great artists, great leaders, they all tune into, what is already here to see the solutions.

Imagine that! Everything here. Whatever you wish right now. Peace, wisdom, inspiration, prosperity; it's all here right now; because you are here. That is the big picture. That is what your true self is aware of.

You are what you are looking for. We are not here to "find" happiness and love; we are here to extend them. Real healing takes place when we stop resisting our true self. Here is a wonderful affirmation: "I am everything I seek."

Happiness is a journey without a distance. If you are currently not experiencing happiness, there is nothing wrong with you. Your perception may not be feeling well, but you are alright. Because of your perception your thoughts may be off, or you may be making wrong choices; you might even be seeing flaws in yourself and others around you; but your true self remains whole, and filled with love, waiting to jump out.

You can change all this if you like, only by giving yourself a break. Be kind to yourself. Stop the self-condemnation. Forgive, laugh and love. Happiness is all about being willing to be innocent again.

Look for the good in anything you see, and everyone you meet. See the sparkling light of source in their eyes, faces and smiles or grins. Mentally bow to the light of source, in everyone you meet today. Try it. I promise you have nothing to lose and all to gain.

## Are We There Yet?

When it comes to words of pain and suffering everyone has a story to share. We all have snapped, crackled and popped at one time or the other. We all have made mistakes and experienced what we called failures and illnesses and such.

You know how some nights you have a really late dinner, and you go to bed with full stomach and you have nightmares? The experiences you remember is also like that. This time instead of filling your stomach, you have overloaded your emotional circuitry, causing yourself a nightmare in this dreamland.

But nightmares usually do not become who you are, and they do not become your identity. Are you still identifying with whatever has happened in the past?

Remain true to your true self, by distinguishing between the experience and the identity. You are not your illness. Your symptoms are not who you are. No one failure is your entire biography. Mistakes happen in the moments of your life, they do not occupy the entire lifetime nor are they your nameplates. Pain is an experience, and not an identity.

As humans we do not only hold attachments to things we like, we also hold attachments to our sufferings. You just need to remember that whatever you identify with more, you will get more.

You will see a major change in your life, when you let go of your attachment to suffering. Take time to honour your experiences; smile at them and let them go. Every moment of your life, you are deciding on who you are; what you can or cannot do, what you do or don't deserve; and what you do or don't want.

Your success, prosperity, happiness, health and all, are written on a daily basis depending on these thoughts and the decisions you make behind them, and what you choose to believe. Let go of all the "I AM's" that you have built in your head and rebuild the list again constructively. Also do the same with all the "I Cant's".
Put your self-image in the hands of your true self, and see the true beauty you possess and your perfection. You are beautiful, and you can be whoever you want to be. You are one and united with all. Separation is purely an illusion. Albert Einstein called it: optical delusion.

I have said this through many books and many seminars and classes and articles, and I find it so important to repeat again, that you are truly not EVER separate from anything. In this, take a look at the flower and see your beauty. There is no need for you to envy looking like a movie star, you already do. He or she is another you. There is no time and space between you and the Source, the All.

You are the sun, you are the moon and you are the stars. You are all you see. You are the petal, you are the raindrop, and you are the morning dew.

Separation will not allow you to see how beautiful you are, and instead will show you all that you feel is wrong. You strive to make them right, by fighting against them, and resisting what is already perfect. In this, building the power of ego, placing your body in protection mode and not seeing true prosperity.

Remember always the first law of spiritual alchemy is that: the world changes when you do. You do not live in the world, the world lives in you.

There are three different views in psychology and the viewing of the world around us:

1. The world = my life = me
2. The world + me = my life
3. Me + the world = my life

In belief number one (the world = my life = me) you are getting no choices and whatever happens to you is your life. You are a victim. Whatever happens you take it, and it becomes a "dog eat dog world." People in this mode, usually rely on Murphys' laws a lot. They also take all suggestions from authorities as their truth, such as: at a certain age something needs to go wrong, at a certain economy they won't prosper and if they had a hard week at work, they can be sure that it will rain on the weekend.

The same group also suffer from over-exaggeration of life's smallest happenings. A bird dodo on their recently washed car is a disaster, and the stain on their favourite dress leaves them inconsolable for days.

In the second view (the world + me = my life), there is slight bit more hope. In this view they are saying that the world happens but "me" plays a role in it, and you may have access to some choices. In this view at least you know that you can make a difference. In this case, small mishaps become a nuisance but nothing really scarring. Your favourite soccer team losing is painful but not lethal.

The third view (me + world = my life), is when you see the world as your mirror. The world is the computer hardware, and you are the software. You become the "Micro" everything. "Micro-love", "Micro-soft", "Micro-kind", and "Micro-wonderful". You make it go around. Without you, there is no world. And the world will respond accordingly.

> "In me there is all of heaven;
> In heaven there is all of me."

The meaning of life is not a search, it is a choice. You cannot find its meaning in things. It does not mean anything on its own, we are the ones giving it meaning. Every single day, by all the choices we make, we make the world a meaningful place.
We talk about ego all the time, and how it wants us to be separate, yet there is no tangible truth about the existence of ego. So many people have died and have been autopsied, and yet we did not find ego in a single one of them. Obviously ego is just an idea. Not really something that we can surgically remove. Your ego is the sum total of all the "small ideas" about yourself and your limitations. Your ego separates you, and isolates you and just like "Dr. Evil", creates your "mini-me".

Ego lets you believe that Everything Good is <u>outside</u>. This is why so many people are looking for happiness outside of themselves. In order for you to look for happiness outside, you first have to deny that you have it. Your ego usually has a very limited perspective of you. Your ego doesn't believe and won't let you enjoy a "free lunch" and "no pain all gain."

You will be working "like a dog" as per ego, and life becomes a "bitch". To be happy, first you have to find the right job, the right girlfriend, the right house, the right car, the right amount of money in the bank, the right figure, the right wardrobe and the list goes on, making you chase something you already have.

Ego is your number one explainer. It will quickly explain an event as "good" or "bad". In explaining something as "bad", it will cause fear to set in. Ego will let you believe that fear and pain are in "things". It will never let you know, that fear and pain are only contained within the "meaning" you give "things". It will never tell you, that if you change that meaning, the fear will go away.

Life becomes hard, and things are never easy, if you really want it to be that way. Check your life philosophies to have a fear-free and pain-free life. What are your philosophies around matters of life, money, happiness, marriage, friendship, business, love, expectations and such?

Most importantly, what is your belief and philosophy about yourself? Because whatever you believe is exactly how your life is going to unfold. Remember that what you believe, becomes what you perceive. Whatever you believe in, your perception will work hard to gather evidence around it, to prove you right. A belief has no other power than what you give it.

Without you, your belief cannot exist. You are in charge of what you believe. The trouble is, sometimes we give precedence to what we believe, and our beliefs start ruling us.

Here is one of the challenges I have seen in peoples' lives: they try living in the moment, but hang on to thirty years of beliefs that are out of date. Pick a subject like relationship or happiness, and list all the limiting beliefs you have around them. Everything you fear, everything old and every expectation.

Now, take each of these beliefs, and ask yourself a simple question: "Do I want to be right, or do I want to be happy?" If you want to be right, then hang on to the belief; and if you want to be happy, release the belief and start building a new one.

Our perceptions are highly subjective. Every one of us sees things quite differently. This makes it impossible to distinguish what is right and what is wrong.

One thing that is worth mentioning, is that, perception is not your vision. Your eyes operate with six delicate yet strong muscles, performing over 100,000 movements a day for you to be able to see. Your iris, retina and optic nerves gather and organize information and send it to the brain at a speed of 155 miles an hour. Your perception is only one percent visual, and 99% mental.

Here is a very important thing about perception: you see what you want to see. ☺ As much as your eyes do the seeing, your mind is the one deciding what it sees and what you are going to focus on. This is why two people's perception of the very same thing, is completely different.

So basically you see what your mind is looking for. Does this tell you something? You are really seeing not the world, but your own thoughts. This is why the pessimist and optimist never agree, on what they see. They both see the world as they will experience it.

We really do not have any events, but we only have perceptions. Fear is a perception, so is love. Fear sees danger, and love sees beauty and safety. Everything is a perception. Pain is a signal to change your perception. There are always few methods to view and perceive things.

It is estimated that we have 2500 thoughts an hour, every hour, of our lives. Wow! That's a lot of thoughts. What is your mind full of? What kind of thoughts? Are they joyful or angry? Are they fear or love based? Do they belong to yesterday, now, or tomorrow?

Mental health, stems from your capacity, to choose your thoughts. That is the difference between pain and freedom.

If your child crams the ice-cream in the DVD player, what do you choose to do? Does a flat tire frustrate you to a degree that you get a headache? Do you experience cardiac arrest if someone gives you a personal criticism? Is it the end of the world if your computer crashes? Are you ready to pull the trigger if a friend lets you down? Are you writing a suicide note because you are having a bad hair day?

OK, OK, I know I am exaggerating a bit here but, if the little things are throwing your thoughts severely off, then my guess would be, that the bigger challenges would render you useless for days or weeks, or even months.

Do you have the courage to stop thinking all the negative thoughts, and let yourself be inspired and blessed and guided? Can you put enough trust on your inner self not to steer you wrong? Can you believe in yourself?

Ego, sends you after a wild goose chase, with a blindfold on. Ego, also believes in inhibitions; seriousness and formalities. Ego, bottles up God, labels it and sells it as a religion. Religions have taught us, to be afraid of God's wrath, and as long as we are afraid of God, we are afraid of everything there is. Everything frightens the one who is afraid of God, seeing that this energy is within all.

If you want to detoxify your soul from ego, then try to practice compassion, kindness, love, and the sense of unity. Love detoxifies ego. In detoxification, you find that God is beyond ego; it is immeasurable love; it is infinite intelligence; it is peace and it is the creative impulse within all of us. If your God is angry and revengeful, I would suggest you get a different God.

Your ego, uses something called "logic" to separate you, and make you think you are left alone, to figure things out. Your inner and higher self is the one that uses inspiration, intuition, vision and love to make things happen for you.

Ego, won't tell you this, but really, happiness is only one thought away at all times. One new perception, one new belief, one new decision away. Nothing but your thoughts, can help, or hurt you. Every day, the Universe is showing you, what you are thinking, and every day, you choose to blame the Universe.

For most of us, we think the thought, and feel the feelings, and then the feelings get in the way of our schedule. The truth of the matter is, your feelings _are_ your schedule. You may not have noticed, but your emotional healing, takes priority, over your career and social life.
Unless you feel like crying, keep smiling. Don't try to run your feelings through logic. Feel your feelings fully and completely. The feelings have only one request from you; they want to be felt. If you had to make an urgent call to a service provider, and you were put on hold for seven years, would you not be peeved? Well that is how your feelings feel, when you put them on hold.

Your entire healing process depends on feeling. To openly accept the feeling, and really feel it, you need openness and love. No judgements of any kind. You will feel pain when you are resisting your feelings.

Here is the kicker: there is no such thing as negative emotion. ☺☺☺ Feelings create emotions and they are what they are. In truth, there is no specification of what is negative, and what is positive, and again, the results of each emotion, is what we perceive as positive, and or negative, depending on our liking or dislike, and hence the labelling.

When you wake up in the morning, and you greet the Universe, be still and at peace for a little while. Set your intention for the day. Be, what you want for that day. For instance, love is very important to me. So every day I make a point in the morning, to be loving to whoever crosses my path that day.

This morning practice, crystallizes what you want to achieve, during the day in your mind. Do you want to lighten a room when you walk into it, or when you walk out of it? Decide. Be what you want every day. If you want love, be loving; if you want peace, be peaceful; if you want fun, be funny; if you want new, be different; if you want adventure, be open; if you want joy, be kind; if you want to receive, be giving; just be what you want. Life is not about competition. There is plenty to go around and we can all have all that we want to experience. Life is about being what we want.

Ghandi said, "Be the change you want to see in the world." This is because by changing the mirror, you do not change your looks. The world is mirroring you. When you change, the world around you will change.

Every single one of us, comes to this world bearing a gift. A very unique one. You are that gift, and you need to share this gift with others. Your ego is quite fearful of giving though. Ego believes that what you give, you will have less of. So all giving is considered a loss in its perception.

Your inner self is much quieter than your ego. It knows that giving is a treasure. When you offer smiles, your body registers that, and creates T cells; when you offer love, your heart gets the message. What you offer to others, you are affirming for yourself.

Giving, is always receiving. You arrive here with nothing and you leave here with nothing, so how do you justify gathering and not sharing and giving? When our lives are only around getting, our hearts wither and we become fearful and disappointed. Everything within your physical being and nature dictates giving and receiving both. Simple example: your heart. Giving and not receiving, or receiving and not giving are both lethal. This example is repeated within the entire nature around you.

The only thing ever lacking in your life, is what you refuse to give. This is the truth on all aspects of life: career, children, partners, and friends and so on.

The flip side of giving of course is receiving: are you a good receiver? Do you breathe life in? Do you allow others to give you as well? How much happiness can you handle? I would suggest you examine, find out and measure your receive-ometer.

Receiving is about trust, surrender, stillness, gratitude and loving. When you let go of your ego, and its sense of lack and surrender, receiving becomes easy. Let life give to you, so that in turn you can give; let your partner love you, so that you can love back; and let your workmates support you, so that their talents may unfold.

# Self-Acceptance

Accept yourself exactly the way you are. We are often too busy improving ourselves, so we forget to accept ourselves.

We often don't have time to relax and laugh and just do nothing. You are holy, you are an angel, and you are blessed. When you accept yourself your self-criticism and doubt and fear and judgements leave. You live naturally and orgasmically abundant.

Self-acceptance needs to be one of your priorities. Without it, you will push away love and you will sabotage your attempts at success and subconsciously choose unhappiness. Self-acceptance changes your perception of yourself. It is the most powerful healing experience you can ever go through. You do not have to do anything; you are magnificent as you are; be kind to yourself.

Many of us feel, nothing can happen unless we make it happen; we also call relaxation, downtime; time is priceless; and effort is power. Has it ever occurred to anyone, that we may be trying too hard? Too hard to be happy; too hard to be successful; too hard to be a good parent; too hard to be a good mate; too hard to be a good friend; too hard to attract a relationship or a partner; too hard to reduce weight, too hard to get rid of stress – now that's a funny one - too hard, too hard, too hard.....

What you try hardest to achieve, gives you the most grief, and brings natural bitterness. This is when you hear people say, "I have worked too hard to have this, and I'll be damned if......" What they are not realizing, is that they are damned to begin with, when they start working too hard for anything.

Here is a wonderful saying from bible: "consider the lilies of the field, how they grow; they toil not, neither do they spin: And yet I say unto you, that even Solomon in all his glory was not arrayed like one of these." – Mathew 6:28-9

Try today to swap effort for inspiration. Ease up on the struggle. Give up trying to make it happen by force. Commit to ease, truth and love. Believe in effortless accomplishment by simply looking around you and to the nature. There is no struggle there. Everything happens with ease. Make room for easier ways.

Having said all this, I know many who take pride and joy out of being drama queens. They are always after things they can dramatize. They actually go out looking for it. They look for heartbreaks and wounds. Ego loves struggle and drama.

It is through that the individual "I" is defined. Our very own personal drama. This is how ego establishes its unique worth. Our media and society plays a tremendous role in teaching us how valuable struggle can be.

We try to champion struggle, and believe that struggle builds character and knocks us into shape. As long as we believe in this, and look for struggle, we can forget about claiming our power and having wonderful relationships and understanding happiness.

But of course we also have the martyrs. Where they tend to believe that sacrifice is the only way to go. They use sacrifice to save a relationship; or make someone happy or for the sake of someone's success, etc. Be rest assured that sacrifice will not bring happiness, love and success.

Any time you feel like playing the martyr, think about this: sacrifice is a work of ego. Ego is your separated self, coming from the point of view of lack; you are not thinking with your whole mind. Sacrifice is never justified because there is always a better way. Sacrifice is not love. It may look like it, but it is not. When you lose, everyone around you will also lose. Sacrifice is guilt and fear. What do you feel guilty or fearful of? Sacrifice is not giving, it is a trade. Some use sacrifice as a form of emotional control.

The other topic I like to bring up is the topic of challenges and problems. Have you been taught that problems are a necessary and natural part of life? Can you think of a life without a problem?

In med-school and in psychology schools they teach you ONLY about problems. Anyone without a problem is either in denial, repressed or dead. Everything is a potential problem. A psychotherapist with patients without problems is like a dog without a bone.

Well let me tell you: there is nothing natural about problems. They only show, your inner world externally. Here is how you can deal with these unnatural phenomenon:

The minute you think of something as a problem, you are filled with feelings of fear and what if. If you change this perception into one of opportunity, then you start receiving inspirations, lessons, gifts and new options in resolution. We do not have problems, we only have opportunities. Einstein once said, "No problem is ever resolved at the level at which it was created."

In reality we experience problems and pain because of fear. If you just heal your fear, you have healed everything in your life. Our perceptions are very easily fooled by fear. Fear will even make you put on your victim costume.

I want you to take a real good look at fear and tell me at what time and space reality fear exists? Is it in now? Most likely is either in yesterday or tomorrow. Now is completely peaceful.

You may not want to start a relationship or a business because of what happened in the past. You maybe well-off financially now, but still working because at one time you were poor and you are fearful that if you quit working so hard, you may be poor again. People who suffer from bulimia are yesterday fearers. They used to be large and if they keep the food in them, they may get large again.

Many years back when I used to teach computer skills, in one of my classes I had a lady sitting right up front with the most painful gesture on her face. I used to teach the class with a lot of humour mixed as it lightened the atmosphere and the students were able to ask questions with ease. Every one used to laugh and have fun, but this one individual did not even crack a smile. As curious as I was, I left her alone.

Towards the end of the term, she had opened up to me and she started talking about the pain she had suffered in various areas of her body. I asked if the pain was still present and she said, "No." But her fear of that pain was still present. She was afraid that smiling, may bring back some of facial pain that she had experienced in the past.

Unfortunately, fear is your only obstacle on the road to happiness and joy. It is an inside job. It comes from ego and the feeling of individuality without faith and understanding that we are all one. You are never alone. You are supported and protected at all times, only if you begin to believe in it.

Fear is not in things and incidents, it is in the meaning you attach to them and your perception. Being present and living in the now is powerful. Let go of yesterday. Get rid of all your disappointments. Stop repeating these painful moments. If you get stuck in the re-runs of the past, you will miss all the present opportunities. Remember, your past is never held against you by anyone other than you. Guilt is a choice. Try to make your life guilt-free. If you live in fear, everyone will miss the gift you came here to offer.

Here is another way of getting rid of fear. When fear strikes you about any subject, say to yourself out loud, "I am afraid of...... because in the past I ......?" keep repeating this sentence and see the fear disappear bit by bit.

When you let go of fear and come to appreciate your power, at this point you have mended your relationship with yourself and those around you. You have become a family again. You and your mind.

You and your body are family again. You and everyone are family again.

Every night bring together the members of your family, your children, mates or anyone else you live with and share a few minutes sitting in a circle and appreciating the good things that has happened that day and offering gratitude to the Universe. Likewise if there has been something that has been hurtful bring that up and forgive. Forgive and appreciate each other as well. Thank each other and allow each member of the family to know your true feelings about them. Treat each night as if it is the last night you are spending with the family and you want them to know how much you love them.

When you make peace with yourself and your family, you make peace with the world. We cannot carry around hurt and wounds and be at peace. We cannot wish for the world peace, when there is no peace inside of us. We cannot wish for hunger to go away in the world when we have hungry eyes. If you play the role of a victim you cannot be happy.

Let love mean more to you, than any hurt you have experienced in the past. Holding on to old pain and wound, costs too much. It is truly not worth giving up your freedom for. When we play the victim and we are grieving, we have been kidnapped by our ego and have been led to hell and there we are waiting for the one who caused the grief to join us. The idea of revenge then becomes, let's both live unhappily ever after.
When you carry grief and revenge in your heart, you are carrying a grenade that blows up often inside you, leaving you into shreds. You become your own worst enemy. For as long as you carry revenge and grief, you are the casualty of your own war.

If you are holding on to grief, you must think you are a victim. Normally victims are constantly victimized because their energy seeks that. They have to prove a point. When you are looking for revenge, you are not looking for freedom, innocence, wisdom and love. You are derailed from who you are and you lose focus and your unity. You lose your powers. Revenge and grief are to you as kryptonite is to superman.

Here is an exercise I was told to practice as a child when someone was able to get on my nerves. I approached the person, held on to his/her hands and looked them in the eye and said, "Together, let's choose peace instead of pain. I will not use you as the instrument to hold me back."

Doing this, believe it or not, switches you from your ego to your unconditioned and non-domesticated self. It works like a reset button that changes your entire perception. With this, you both win.

People ask me, "How do you forgive?" I really don't know how to break this to them, but forgiveness is not a technique with 1,2,3 steps to it. You don't make it happen and there is no plan of action. Forgiveness is in understanding the Unity and total acceptance. It is only an intention. In wanting to forgive, you eventually learn, there is nothing to forgive. Choose to live happily *even* after.

Forgiveness frees you from the past, and in this you can live happily even after things are said and done. After the loved one has passed away, after the financial loss, after the boyfriend has left you and so on.

Choose happiness over your history. In all the forgiving you do, if you look at it you are forgiving your own thoughts. Nothing ever gets you into more trouble than your own thoughts. It is when you clear these thoughts, that you open room for inspiration. Dare to let go.

Letting go will bring more joy, intimacy, romance, relaxation, laughter, balance, abundance and peace. Attach yourself, if you want suffering. Let go, if you want happiness. Have you ever noticed that what you try to control the most, will give you the most grief? The only thing we need control over, is bladder. Control otherwise is not the answer to anything.

Trying to control, comes only out of fear. Control does not make your relationships safe. On the contrary it makes them quite fragile. We need to give up control if we want love. As blunt as this may sound, I have always risked saying that in any relationships, there are only two resolutions: one, accepting the person 100% as they are and unconditionally and knowing that even though they might have things that brush you the wrong way, they offer so much into this relationship that they are worth holding on to; or two, good bye.

Media has worked hard to sell us the idea that "control is power" and "you need to control your life" that we have believed it, and in that they also sell the leash for a very expensive price, giving you the fake feeling of being in control. The unfortunate part is that where there is too much control, there are no flow, abundance and joy.

When you are trying to take control all the time, your creativity is constipated. This causes variety of physical ailments aside from spiritual side of living.

Here is another way of looking at this: control and trust do not go hand in hand. Meaning, when you have trust, you do not need to control. Trust is an intention, and where you place your focus and power. Trust is dynamic and creative and it is beyond ego and fear. It will bring synergy and creativity into your life.

When you have trust in yourself, you show trust in others and external world. Not trusting others, only shows one thing: you do not trust yourself. Now the funny part is that, trust just like happiness is in us. We always have it; it is just a matter of where we focus it.

As the saying goes, "I have 100% trust. I have 40% trust in fear, 30% trust in self-doubt, 20% in certain failures, 9 percent in things going wrong and 1% in lots of hope." The key here is, where is the trust focused.

In relationships that don't work, there is always 99% trust that the other party is going to cheat and 1% that they might not. Remember you place your power where you place your trust.

# Synchoincidence™

What do you think of when someone mentions the word "Miracle"? The dictionary definition of miracle is as follows: "An event or effect contrary to the established constitution and course of things, or a deviation from the known laws of nature; a supernatural event, or one transcending the ordinary laws by which the Universe is governed."

I believe miracles happen to us on regular basis. We choose to notice or ignore them. If we try to and notice them, our lives become miraculous and wonderful and if we ignore them we lose one opportunity after another. The question is: "Would you know a miracle if it happened to you?" And how would you deal with it? And if you thought you could *make* miracles, what would you choose? What would be the first miracle you would manifest? I have dedicated this book and my life to teaching people how powerful they are and how they can create miracles in their lives on daily basis.

Have you ever thought about coincidences? What are they? Have you noticed how sometimes they form our lives? Let's say someone coincidentally dials your phone number instead of someone else and you strike a conversation with this person and you find out that he/she can be of great value for your business. You meet someone in the market or subway and end up getting a job that you really wanted in a company. You talk to someone as you are sitting next to them in a coffee shop only to understand that this person is an herbalist that can cure something in your family. Do we not call each of the above-mentioned a coincidence? Absolutely, we do. But notice how they also fit within the definition of a miracle. You can choose to label them as random occurrences in a chaotic world, or look at them as life-changing events they may become.

To me, every coincidence requires undivided attention. It is a signal from Universe to shift my life in a direction of manifesting my expressed desires. By understanding coincidences, you can capture their power and learn to create them at will, to create the beautiful, prosperous life you have been waiting for. Please take note that anywhere within this book when I speak of prosperity, I'm not only referring to wealth. There is also health prosperity, love prosperity, and much more. The title of this section: "synchoincidence" is what I like to call all coincidences that have happened synchronized to the time that you have been in need for them to happen the most. You are in need for money and all of a sudden someone sends you a cheque that they had forgotten about from long time ago. You really are craving for a certain food and your spouse shows up and he/she has brought that favourite food along. Your car breaks down in the middle of nowhere and one person that stops to help you turns out to be a mechanic or someone who can take care of your issue with the least effort. These are synchronized coincidences.

When you start appreciating and recognizing the coincidences in your lives, this is where the magic begins. The fact that you have purchased or given this book and you are reading it is nothing short of a miracle. This might be the single most important text that you needed to read to change the path of your life into positive direction. How powerful is synchoincidence™? Imagine yourself in the middle of a dark room with a flashlight in your hand. You turn the light on and shine it on a single area of this room only to notice a magnificent statue there. You think about the beauty of this statue and wonder if that's all there is. Now you decide to turn the lights on and once you do that, you see a huge room with all kinds of amazing artifacts. This is when you realize that there is so much more for you to experience and you are no longer limited to the view of one statue under the dim light of a flashlight. This is what synchoincidence™ does for you. It turns the light "on" for you. It allows you to make real decisions, instead of going through life with blindfolds and a flashlight.

There is a level of life that we are very used to, it's called: physical. This is where everything solid belongs. What makes it "real" to us is the fact that we can touch things and feel their solidness; we can smell things, hear things, see things or taste things. Everything in this physical life has a beginning and an end. So nothing is permanent. The law of cause and effect rules this physical existence and things become predictable. This is how many of our calculations take place, including weather forecasts.

We of course have available to us the quantum level as well. Nothing in this level can be experienced by our five physical senses.

Your mind, your ego, your personality, these are all part of quantum level. Neither one of these things is solid, but you know they are there. This level is also known as the level of information and energy. Now, the funny thing is that our physical level is made up of this level of information and energy.

This is one of the first lessons in physics we go through at school. They teach us that every solid item is made up of molecules. And molecules are made up of atoms. The atoms cannot be viewed, of course, through naked eye. We also learn that atoms are made of sub-atomic particles, which are in no way solid. They are just envelopes of information and energy. Everything we have around us is made of these non-solid envelopes of information. The reason they look solid to us is because everything in this level of life happens at the speed of light and our physical senses cannot register anything at this speed. We see something as a table or a chair because these energy envelopes contain different information, which is determined by their vibration and frequency. We cannot see the world around us as a ball of energy, because it is vibrating too fast for our senses. We can only register lumps of the information, which become the table, chair, mirror, etc. that we see. In physical level we constantly exchange parts of ourselves with others.

Let's now take a quick look at what is an atom. I know we have talked about it before, but I really need to drive this home. An atom is made up of a nucleolus, with a large cloud of electrons around it. The outer shell is not rigid at all. We make out solidity where the clouds of electrons meet, depending on how sensitive or insensitive our senses are. Our nerve endings and eyes are programmed to see this as solid. In the quantum level there is no such thing as solidity.

When you touch something, your electron clouds meet. You leave a bit of yourself behind within that object – although you do not feel it – and get a bit of that object's energy field in return. So every time you touch something, this transaction takes place and you come out a bit changed. This shows how connected we are to everything else.

We all are a part of each other. The only time we feel disconnect is when we solely depend on our five senses. If we could see ourselves at the quantum level, we would see how we flash in and out of physical existence. One moment here and one moment not and the next moment back again. The solidity and continuation is only what our five senses feed back to us. Just like when you are viewing a movie, you do not see the gaps between the frames, this works exactly the same way. Anything falling within this gap of existence is not viewable to us. As you probably have heard, they take advantage of this gap in commercials to send us subliminal messages. For example in the movie theatre they might use this to make you feel like eating popcorn where you were not thinking about it a moment ago. I believe your higher self uses the same technique to communicate.

Now let's talk about the level of consciousness. This is the arranging power behind everything. This is your soul. This is the presence within you. The one that does all the experiencing. It's at this level that birds and fish and other animals communicate. When you are watching a school of fish and one fish changes direction, in an instant they all do. The same with birds. No one really turns around to others and says: "Hey, I'll be going left now", they just all do it at the same time. This is instant communication. This is how everything in this world and nature is organized.

Physical science has not been able to explain this type of communication between animals. The animals live in the level of consciousness and synchronicity. They are in tune with their environment, and with each other. We also have the same ability, but because of all the things that we allow to distract us, we have forgotten how to use this ability. The mortgage, the telephone bill, the kids, the neighbour's dog, the anxieties, the fears, the angers and on and on, have completely distracted us from what we can do and derailed us. This is where coincidences happen. When you learn to live at this level, everything becomes available to you. This is where you create miracles.

In the meantime, some people still experience synchronicity. It happens all the time between twins, mother and child, pet and the owner. The interesting thing is that our bodies communicate at this level ALL the time. Human body has approximately fifty trillion cells. This starts with one fertilized ovum, one cell. This cell divides fifty times and presto you have a full human with fifty to one hundred trillion cells (to be safe, I will stick to fifty as this is variable). So everything starts with one cell only. As these cells are being divided, around 250 different kinds of cells appear. One becomes your teeth the other, stomach, spleen, gallbladder, tongue, skin, brain, etc. Each one of these cells does few million functions per second to keep you alive. Each cell also knows whatever other cells in the body are doing; otherwise the body would fall apart. Your body can only stay intact and operate normally if it is operating synchronistically.

Can you explain how these fifty trillion cells, each doing a million functions a second coordinate this communication of knowing how each one is doing? In order for you to do *any* simple function, say a handshake, you first have to think about what you would like to do. This thought sends a nerve impulse to your arm and hand, and you complete a handshake. Before this thought, there was no energy present for this action. But as soon as you have the thought, certain chemicals through brain are released, allowing you to carry this function.

We do thousands of functions every single day. From writing to typing to reading to eating to walking… These thoughts that generate the action, cannot be seen but without them we would be completely paralyzed. Our body then communicates in this fashion all the time and in synchronicity. There are 400 billion bits of information processed by our brains every second. Studies show that when we experience emotions, an electromagnetic coherent field is generated within the body. This electromagnetic field is then broadcast throughout the body. In a healthy body this synchronous function is regulated. When disease manifest, one of the rhythms of the body has gone haywire. Stress, fear, anxiety and worry are all among the biggest culprits in introducing disease to a beautifully functioning body.

Imagine a car that you have and everything is properly working. You take this car for a ride and put it under stress by not changing from the first gear to second, third, fourth or fifth as you speed up to 120 kilometers an hour. What happens to this car? I bet you, it will be dis-eased. These negative emotions interfere with your body's normal function and some part of your body feels constricted. This part of the body will fall off the synchronous communication.

Our souls exist in the quantum level. This is the part responsible for who we are and how we behave. This part of us is the extension of Source Energy. If we could live from this level, we could realize how connected we are to the Universe and everything around us. We would become the true co-creators and miracle makers we were made to be. All negative emotions would be lost. If we could make the connection between our souls and the Universe, synchoincidences™ would happen to us all the time and on regular basis, changing our lives.

Atoms are the extremely small particles making us and everything around us. A single element, such as oxygen, is made up of similar atoms. Different elements contain different kinds of atoms. There are 92 naturally occurring elements and scientists have made another 17, bringing the total to 109. Atom is the smallest unit of an element that chemically behaves the same way the element does. When two chemicals react with each other, the reaction takes place between individual atoms at the atomic level.

The structure of an atom looks very much like our solar system. At the centre of every atom is a nucleus, which is similar to the sun in our solar system and it contains the protons and neutrons. Electrons move around the nucleus in "orbits" just like planets move around the sun. The opposite electrical charges of protons and electrons keep the atom together. Sometimes depending on absorbing or releasing the energy, electrons will jump from their original orbit to a higher or lower orbit. When this happens, the electron has NOT actually traveled through space to get to the new orbit. One moment it is here and the next it is there. This jump made the electron go from one circumstance to another without passing through the circumstances in between. This jump is unpredictable.

Consider all the atoms in the world and all the unpredictable jumps. This makes you look at the world a whole new way. Scientists have been making many efforts to make sense of this phenomenon in nature, since even the least significant occurrences in nature are governed by this unpredictability; with no results.

All human creativity is based on this unpredictability. There are times, which one comes up with the most original idea. This idea does not actually originate in the person who worded it, but rather in the collective consciousness. This is why most of the time the same idea will originate to more than one person at a time. This idea had already been circulating in the collective pool of consciousness. The reason it occurred to this person(s) is because they were ready to receive this signal. This is where we can be geniuses, grasping a beautiful idea, when no one else recognizes its beauty. This is also synchoincidence™.

Concentrating on synchoincidence™ will bring more of it to your life. Try to learn and use them for what they are. When we want or desire something, we are looking at it from only one perspective: US. When your higher self is sending you a synchoincidence™, this is not only good for you but for many more that will come in contact with it. Learn to recognize and attract this subtle little guidance from your higher self to your lives. Learn to become a sensitive instrument in your surroundings. People, who are sensitive to the environment around them and live in an observing conscious mode, seem to pick up on the synchoincidences™ quite easily.

# Polarities and Intentions

"Fighting for or against" anything has become the norm nowadays. We fight against cancer, drug, war, abortion, environment, or let's use as an example, "fighting for peace" – which is the most amusing because it only confirms, at least in that singular reality, for that particular person, that peace doesn't exist. Also, when people pray for anything they "need", they are coming from a point of lack, asserting to themselves that what they "need" doesn't exist and they must do something to produce it. Fear usually tells us that we do not have what we "need".

Our ancestors knew that, whatever you put your focus on, you simply just create more of "that", even if "that" is what you do not want. We also know that creation comes from a thought that will stir a feeling causing an emotion. When you think, your neurological pathways are searched for the most used, familiar memories. When these memories are located, they automatically trigger an emotion – either fear, hate or love. Therefore, the Law of Attraction draws (attracts) into your reality not only that what you love, but also that what you fear - again, all starting with thoughts. Unconditional "Love", is the opposite of fear in polarity. You are either co-creating knowingly or not-knowingly. If you are aware of your emotions and feelings, then you are a conscious co-creator. This explains why you think you really want, desire, or need, something, yet don't experience "that" something.

If you believe that you do not create everything in your life, this means you are allowing yourself to stay in victim consciousness. Our world is based on duality. Duality will let you see realities through opposites. It will also allow you to experience both ends of the poles - good/bad, happy/sad, right/wrong, peace/war, etc., until you understand it, and no longer need to experience it. Unfortunately, most of cartoons, movies and storybooks are centred on victim consciousness. There is a victim, there is a villain and there is a hero.

When you truly understand that YOU are the centre of your own Universe, and the only one in it, then the realization will set in that if you perceive yourself as a victim, you must also be the victimizer and the rescuer, as well. If you don't find something pleasing, then take responsibility for "that" and be proud of this unpleasant thing that you have co-created and move on consciously and re-create something else. What you resist, you attract to you. Therefore, when you protest ANYTHING, you actually attract it to you since "protest" is a form of resistance. Please understand that responsibility and "blame" are not the same.

When you desire something, pretend as if it is already here. I am saying pretend, because at this particular moment you may not actually believe it yet. Feel how wonderful it feels to you. Once you know what you want, you need to experience the feeling of having what you want FIRST and stay away from the feeling of NOT having it. Feel yourself in that new car or new house. This is all it takes - Feeling Good.


So what you must really do, is first define WHAT you want. Next, you are going to find out WHY. The WHYs are the part of this deal that will stir your feelings and emotions. WHYs are your batteries, your electricity. Once the WHY starts swirling your feelings and emotions, try to stay there for as long as you can. Although 20 seconds is all you need, remember that the longer you stay in that state, the faster the results. Before you know it, the Universe will start bringing coincidences and synchronicities your way to put this thing together for you, right in front of your eyes. It's absolutely magical. But is it?


In the world of energy, anything we had, have or will have is already here. The only trick is to align to that frequency of vibration to actually make it visible to the physical eyes.


Intending, is just like wanting, but much stronger. Try to intend many little things during the day. Intend to enjoy the day every day. Turn your wants to intents. Immediately, you will *feel* the shift of energy behind this desire. It is no longer coming from a point of lack, but it is coming from a point of "I make my reality", "I intend". But please do not turn these two beautiful expressions into a mindless habit. These are strong words that, when used consciously, can manifest immediate miracles in your lives. Dare to intend. Dare to dream.

Dare to bring out the old dreams that you have put on the shelf, thinking that you cannot possibly have them. Take charge. Start co-creating.

# The Power of Intention

Every action starts with an idea in our head that is followed by the "intention" to take action on that idea. Everything in the Universe including the most mundane tasks of the day takes place through intention. Intention is the start of creation.

We are a powerful, superb, amazing and zealous being. This is our true core. Yet, most of us see ourselves as less. Why do we spend our days focusing on what we can't do, who we can't be, the problems we won't overcome and the dreams we won't manifest? The answer lies in our intentions. Because of its great ability to accomplish amazing results, intention and action must be directed toward results. This is called the power of intention.

When I started my business, Health and Life Coaching, back in 1976, I felt powerful and powerless. The feelings of power occurred when I gained more clarity of my vision for my company, enjoyed the rewards of great friendships, attracted new clients from my target market, collaborated with other creative and bright coaches and organized my office space to be more efficient. I felt on top of the world. I was able to expand my dreams for the future. My power of intention was focused on this manifestation.

After this great beginning, my power of intention became redirected because of my frustration at the lack of freedom I was feeling. As my dream business took off, I had less time to devote to planning new programs and auxiliary materials for my business. Once I became focused on the negative feelings, time constraints decreased my freedom. I started paying attention to the negative voices inside me, "I can't do it. I need a vacation. I don't have the power to innovate." These voices of doubt and fear overcame the great burst of energy that I felt in the previous weeks and my productivity plunged. The difference between one week's doubt and another week's successes is where I focused my power of intention. I took my attention off my doubts and placed it on how to grow and improve my business. I generated power by taking constructive action steps. In short, I redirected my power of intention. Now, after this tough period of feeling powerful and then powerless, I believed in myself again, my dreams, and my ability to create and manifest all that I am and have in the world.

Changing the direction of our intention can change our emotions and hence the results. We all sometimes have the habit of allowing ourselves getting caught in negative emotions. Usually when this happens, our energy is distracted to those negative emotions and away from taking constructive steps, especially the challenging, scary ones, to attain our goals. This is when we need to reconsider our intention power and put it to work and focus on what is best for us and having a clear idea of how we're going to achieve it. Then, once we have an objective and a strategy, take action! Action is the only way to move our desired result from being out there to reality. Keep moving slightly beyond your comfort zone. Notice the gifts that come your way. One day, you'll have accomplished your dreams and realized it was the power of intention that moved you there.

I'm not sure if you have heard of the Japanese art of object placement – Feng Shui. Feng Shui works best when you focus on what you really want to change in your life. Feng Shui is about creating an appropriate, harmonious movement and intensity of chi energy—the universal life force—in your home.

On an energetic level, we are connected to everything in our home. This means that the strength of our intention to change our life is an essential part of the success of our Feng Shui treatment. If we make generic Feng Shui adjustments that are not targeted to our personal issues and goals, we will not have a strong emotional involvement in what we are doing. Without emotional investment, it is difficult to trigger significant changes in our lives. Your thoughts are remarkably powerful.

Think of the difference in your own energy when you are excited about something, compared to times when you feel lonely, unhappy, or depressed. As you Feng Shui your home, support your actions with an attitude of eagerness and anticipation. When you constantly dwell on how dissatisfied you are with a life situation, your energy becomes stuck there. Apply Feng Shui with confidence, optimism, and a sense of adventure. This will keep you motivated and help activate the energy of your home. When you focus your mind on your reasons for making a Feng Shui adjustment and what you hope to achieve as a result, your Feng Shui will be much more effective. Activating Feng Shui or any other method you choose to use in your lives, with the power of your mind and intention is a crucial element to your success in life.

Intentions create synchoincidences™. Intent is the reason why when you are thinking of something, and it happens. It is the reason why some people instantaneously heal themselves of a disease. We as human beings have this power available to us. When we start seeing ourselves, not as individuals, but a continuation or a part of everything else in the Universe, the alive and conscious Universe starts to respond to our intents when we build our intimate relations with it.

Here are a few ways to shift your power of intention to get to the state of mind you want. These steps can be used at work and in other parts of life to achieve your desired results quickly and easily.

1. Watch your thoughts - If you are questioning why you aren't creating the result you want in your life, look at your thoughts and words, because they express your true intention. Focus on the goal, not the obstacles.

2. Seek support - Stay close to people who believe in you and remind you of who you are in all your power. Find three people today who can remind you of focus.

3. Become your own master - Arrange an appointment with yourself to work on focusing on what you want most in your life. Consider hiring a professional coach to help you along your path to what you want. Remember, even the greatest sport professionals have a coach to guide them to new heights.

4.  Get connected - Gaining knowledge that reminds you of what you want in your life is a powerful tool for focusing your power of intention. Find out what seminars and workshops are being offered and sign up for those aligned with your dreams.

5.  Create daily reminders - Create personal notes that remind you where you most want to put your power of intention and inspire you to action. These notes can be in your home and even in your office.

6.  Breath, relax and meditate - By slowing down, quieting yourself and allowing your energies to settle, you can reinforce the sense of direction in your life that you want to live and receive new inspiration.

7.  Make space - Clean up your office and life so nothing out there limits you from knowing the right intention for your life. Some activities which you might find helpful at work are: organizing your filing system, focusing on only three major projects at a time and completing your to-do list first thing in the morning.

8.  Only do what you love - Think back on your life. What are the things you most enjoyed doing, felt most passionate about? Try to include something you love in your life every day.

# Managing your beliefs

There are several beliefs in everyone's life, which we need to start managing:

*The first belief is* that there is an invisible and yet predictable life force within you, that you need to be aware of. This Source Energy with its divine, exquisite, organizing, intelligent powers takes the limited number of minerals that are in the nature, and organizes them into different things; some come out as snails, some as fish, trees, rocks, planets, galaxies, and some as you and I. What is important here, is that you and I have showed up in human form, but inside this physical form we still have that organizing intelligence, which is the creator within us.

*Secondly, your thoughts are* what you control and they originate within you. So you are the origin of what you choose to think about. This is the beauty of being a human being. As a human being, you can think what you want to think, and shape your reality according to it. Isn't this just magnificent? Everything starts with a thought. The thought originates with you. This is the first thing you need to comprehend. When you truly and completely understand that your thoughts originate within you, you will start creating your own life. *You ARE what you think about*, all day long. You have heard this saying over and over again that "As you think, so shall you be". No wise men ever came to say: "As you be so shall you think". You have the capacity to create your life.

*The third belief to promote* and nurture, is that there are no limits. Limits belong to the physical world and according to our thoughts and perceptions, we can have hundreds or thousands of limits placed upon our lives. The invisible world, the world of Source Energy, which remarkably enough is within all of us, has no limits. How many thoughts can you put into your brain? If the thoughts are formless and brain has form, how many formless things can you put into something with a form? The first has no limits and the second has many limits. It is your unlimited mindset, that is going to create the magic for you. It starts in your mind, and later on moves to literal manifestations in the physical world. You have to be certain in your mind that there is nothing that can limit you. Anything that you can possibly think of and imagine in your mind, you can produce in the physical realm.

*The fourth belief to* grow in you, so to create magic, is that your life has a purpose. Everything in the Universe has a purpose. You'll find that your life purpose as a human being, isn't really about what you do in your life, it isn't about your daily activities; it isn't about being a surgeon, a cab driver, a dentist, a homemaker, an accountant, a manager or a director. You will only see your purpose, as you detach yourself from these concerns with outcome, and shift your focus to: how may I serve? So, the only thing you can do with this life - since you can't take anything, collect anything and own anything - is to give it away. You showed up in a body, and you leave that body behind when the time comes, without taking *anything* with you. The measure of your life, will not be in what you have accumulated, but in what you have given away. And when you understand your life's purpose, you will see that your life is really about giving. It is about giving, sharing and loving.

*The fifth thing you* want to expand, is to overcome weakness by leaving it behind. Leave all your old habits behind. Starting with your thoughts! You have to change around the belief that "Life is hard" and "I have to struggle" and "I have to work hard" and "I have to set goals" and "I have to figure out a way to do it". Instead, understand the process of creating real magic in your life. Leave behind every single piece of behaviour that doesn't work for you or restricts you from having the miracles that you like for yourself. Whatever those miracles may be.

*The sixth belief is* that if you want to create miracles in your life, you have to make a thorough search of all things that you currently believe and have been taught to be impossible and then turn that belief 180 degrees. You have to understand that miracle makers do not know anything as "impossible". This is not a part of their vocabulary. You must understand that your doubt or your belief that something can or cannot happen, is *the only* factor that will either make your miracle, or keep it from happening. Doubt and fear are not the avenues to take to manifest miracles; you have to travel the route of knowing and trust. The Universal Law that has allowed for anything miraculous to happen to anyone, ever, has not been cancelled. It is still there and it is still available to you; and whether you know it or not, you are affected by it every day, every hour, every minute, and every second of your life. So, why not use it consciously? But first, you must take a look at all the things that you think are impossible for you, and change those beliefs around.

In my opinion, human cannot perform even the slightest act without inevitably triggering certain forces, which will bring about certain effects. It is utterly impossible to evade the law of cause and effect. What is possible, however, is to know what kind of forces one is unleashing by one's acts. I must say that I have always had great respect for farmers. I think they are the first moral philosophers amongst mankind. They were the first ones who understood that the intelligence of nature has brought about this beautiful, powerful and ever-present law of cause and effect. They were the ones who knew exactly "as you sow, so shall you reap". If we behave with cruelty, self-centredness and violence, sooner or later, we will be a victim of our own acts. Those who try to deny or reject this basic law become more and more estranged from truth. Their thoughts are torn by doubt leading them further from the miracles that they can manifest in their lives.

Each of us naturally imagines that we see the events and circumstances of our lives as they actually are and that we are objective. But this is not the case. We see the world and ourselves in it, not as it is, but as we are, as we are conditioned to see it. We see it through the lens of who and what we are. To know this is to know something great, because no one gets to view the world without a lens (a perspective coloured by beliefs, expectations and past experiences). Our mind processes all our experiences through this filter, and often our experiences get misinterpreted in the process. Discovering and seeing what is really going on in our life is actually far trickier than you might guess. In fact it seems almost impossible, because we never get to view the world without a "lens". The best we can do is exchange lenses (viewpoints, beliefs), and decide which is more accurate, or at least which one feels right, much the same as going for an eye exam to find the right lens to offset an eye deficiency.

In fact this analogy is quite appropriate in helping us to understand our present situation. If you find your vision is hampered, objects and people being somewhat out of focus and fuzzy - you don't say life is out of focus - you don't blame "out there". You know what you can do to correct your vision. You try a number of different lenses - some make your vision better, some make it worse, and eventually you settle on one that feels right. This is exactly the same with your life. The challenges and obstacles we come across in life are caused by what is inside us. Your lens is both distorting and creating your reality. When you change your lens, your reality will change.

Your minds' lens is constantly interpreting the events in your life. Every available piece of information is first sifted and weighed before coming to us. If an event or data is opposite to our beliefs, then it will be ignored to a very large degree, or distorted so to fit in with what our mind sees as reality. Now let's take this even a step further and you will begin to see how powerful your beliefs are.

As I have said over and over again, all physical reality is made up of vibrations of energy. The chair you sit on, the walls that surround you, your physical body, everything is made up of vibrations of energy. This is not a theory or concept; this is a fact known and understood by physicists. Our thoughts and beliefs are also vibrations of energy consisting of the exact same substance. Thoughts that are repeated again and again, followed by the same feelings and emotions, will gradually take an imprint on our subconscious. These imprints, in turn attract whatever correlates internally with us from outside. These formed beliefs now will channel our energy and act as a magnet.

The more we become aware of this and realize how our inner programming influences our experiences, the more of a co-creator role we can have.

Beliefs are just like another one of our organs. Without them, we are lost. They are our measuring sticks. They also form a major lens through which you see your life. If you cannot see well through your current lens you should not throw them away and say, "The hell with it, I'll do without them", but rather get a better, more suitable lens. We need to get to know ourselves as our subconscious knows us.

We form our experiences through our own beliefs and expectations – that is if we have examined our beliefs and they are not inherited. Our beliefs define our reality as the truth. They seem self-explanatory. They are a matter of fact. We accept them without a question. It almost never occurs to us to examine their validity. They are our invisible assumptions.

Once we understand how much of our daily experiences are influenced by these inner programs, the more we realize how crucial it is to examine them. This will need courage and discipline. But you must know that no one can change your beliefs for you, nor can they be forced on you by outside powers. You and only you can decide what it is you will choose to believe. The system I'm suggesting to you will, take a certain leap of faith.

You definitely cannot go through this process half-heartedly; as this will demand a genuine and solid daily commitment from your side.

Many times I am asked questions that boil down to this: "How do I create a miracle (of one kind of another) in my business or my life?" Often, the one asking considers miracles to be outside his or her ability to create. And that of course is the very reason why they don't create them. As long as your strongest belief about your miracle is that, some outside force has a hand in it and this force may or may not smile favourably upon your request, you are out of tune with the miracle vibration, and it's unlikely to show up.

My suggestion to you, the reader of this book, would be to review your life, looking for evidence of miracles you have already created. Simpler yet, look at the miracle your own body creates every second of this life. There is no other miracle closer to you to examine than that. This examination of Microcosm will give you a better understanding of Macrocosm.

Then analyze your vibration and see what you are tuned into? To manifest a miracle, work with whatever it takes to remember who you really are. Read or listen to inspirational words, get some coaching, take a workshop – it's up to you, but whatever you decide on, get busy with it consistently enough for your vibration to reassemble itself around the belief that you, as spirit, have the holy authority to create what inspires you. Remember, all the miracles that you can ever think of happening in your lives, have already happened. You just need to see them manifested and feel them with your five senses.

# Forgiveness

Most of the time when we talk about forgiveness, we think that it is something that we will give to someone else, after they ask, for something wrong that they have done to us.  There are few points in here that I need to clear:

Forgiveness is a gift that you are giving to yourself.  You are really doing nothing for the other person.  It's quite simple really.  Every time someone angers you, first you need to look and see if that person is mirroring you.  Second, when you are mad at someone, *you are* the one spending all your energy on THEM.  They do not really know the difference.  You get up every day and either few times a day or once a week or however strong this anger and rage is, you spend your moments of NOW thinking about who did what wrong in the past, instead of using your NOW constructively.  I call this: someone renting space in *your* head.  Let it go.  Forgive, so that you do not spend another precious speck of energy on them.

Forgiveness, challenges you to give up your destructive thoughts, about the situation, and to believe in the possibility of a fantastic future.  It builds confidence that you can survive any pain, and grow and learn from it.

Forgiveness, has nothing to do with another person because it is an internal matter.  This of course is a choice, but remember that *not* forgiving, puts you in a "victim" position not a "co-creator" position.

There is absolutely nothing so bad, that you cannot forgive. Absolutely nothing. Some of you I bet, are ready to argue that in the case of child abuse, the Holocaust, etcetera, the abuser has no "right" to our forgiveness and that forgiveness only leads to further victimization.  You need to remember, and I repeat, that when you <u>do not</u> forgive, <u>you are the victim forever</u> or as long as you carry the anger.  You are forgiving yourself.  In the case of extra-marital affairs I was asked the question that if one forgives, the partner will repeat the action.  Just because you choose to <u>forgive</u>, does not mean you have to <u>stay</u> in the relationship. That is only, and always your choice. The choice to forgive, is only and always yours.   Never forgive for someone else's sake.  Do it for yourself, and yourself only. Furthermore, forgiving, is not "approving" of the other person's conduct.  Forgiving is saying: "I know, no matter what you have done, you are just another face to Source Energy, and you have picked to do something from the menu of options offered to you, which I/we – as a society and community – disagree with and dislike".

You cannot have a loving and rewarding relationship with anyone else, much less with yourself, if you continue to hold on to things, that happened in the past. Whatever the situation, you need to make peace.  Without this step, it becomes quite impossible to be living the ever-present moment of NOW.

When you are forgiving someone, you are agreeing within yourself to overlook the wrong you think they have committed against you, and to move on with your life. It's the only way.  Non-forgiveness keeps you in the fight-back mode. Being willing to forgive, can bring a sense of peace and well-being. It lifts anxiety and takes you out of depression. It can enhance your self-esteem and give you hope.

Forgiveness is a wonderful and creative act, that changes us from being victims and prisoners of the past and to others, to liberated human beings at peace with our memories and ourselves. It is completely different than forgetting.  Forgiveness, means accepting the promise that the future can be more than just dwelling on memories of your past injuries and hurt. There is no future in the past. You can never live in the present and create a new and exciting future for yourself and your family, if you always stay trapped in the past. If you are at war with others, you cannot be at peace with yourself. You are the only one that CAN let go, and forgive! It takes no strength to let go, only courage!

Life is like an elastic that can either expand or contract, in direct proportion to your bravery and courage to forgive. Your selection to forgive, or not to forgive, either moves you closer to what you desire, or further away from it. There is no middle ground. Change is constant.  The same energy you use to hold on to something, is exactly the same energy you need, to create a new and exciting event in your life.  Forgiveness helps you move forward. No one benefits from forgiveness more than the one who forgives! Forgiveness is not considered a surrender as you may think.  It is a conscious decision to stop harbouring bitterness. In effect, it takes the poison out of our bodies. It cleanses our system.  You cannot take the poison and expect someone else to die. They will go on with their lives and you will be the only one continuing to suffer.

Forgiveness is the key to *your own* happiness. When forgiveness is given because you think you should, it is no longer forgiveness but an act of self-indulgence. Forgiveness breaks the cycle of hate, bitterness, rage and pain that is often passed on to those around you. Since your energy affects everyone around you, not only you are harming yourself by holding on to these feelings, but you are also causing a feeling of discomfort for those around you.  In the end, it is worth remembering, that all religions and religious books have recommended forgiveness over and over again.

Do you have someone that you have a hard time with? Maybe someone who is always late every time you see them? They end up being at least an hour late no matter what the situation. You have a hard time forgiving them for being late and you start to build resentment. All these strong feelings are signaling the Universe to bring similar feelings back to you. In this case, a resentful feeling.

You see, it isn't just about your forgiveness of another. When someone hurts you, it isn't just you. It is your spouse, your children, your parents, and anyone who is close to you. When you have all those strong angry and hurt emotions, it affects everyone. Not to mention prompting emotions of fear.

Forgiving will give you wings.  With it you can go above and beyond what has happened and let go of all the strong destructive feelings. You can then focus on your very own amazing life without having something to feel bad about.

Science has shown – as we have talked about - that everything is vibrating energy and that includes us. The more low frequency our vibes, the more difficult it is to manifest our desires. Equally, the higher our vibrations, the easier it is to manifest.

I know that we want to make everything sound more complicated than it really is to give it a feeling of importance. The laws of universe are truly simple; no matter how we want to see them be hard.

So to summarize what Forgiveness is really all about:

- Realize it's for you, not the offender;

- It is about taking responsibility for how you feel;

- Realize it's about your healing and not about the person who you have allowed to hurt you;

- Helps you get control over your feelings;

- A tool to help you improve your mental, physical, emotional and spiritual well-being;

- Knowing it is a choice.

- When you make the decision to forgive, you will probably have to revisit this choice many times. When you decide to forgive that's just the first step.

You'll go along with your life and think all is well. Then one day something will trigger the realization that you are still carrying some anger about the issue you have forgiven. Guess what? You get to decide again that you will forgive. You do so and in a few weeks or months the same issue arises again. You then go through the same process all over again.

This will probably happen several times depending on the depth of emotional scar. Don't worry, it's normal. What you will find, however, is that each time you go through the process your emotions are less intense. Finally, the day will come when you can recognize that you're thinking of the issue and just move on.

Don't get discouraged if the process takes a while. This is normal. Simply continue to move through the process and you'll find your energy being restored and your vibes being lighter.

# What is Thought?

Everybody thinks. There is not a human alive who does not think. Everyone uses their faculty of thought 24x7; but most of us do not know how to use it correctly. Thought is a force, a power. This is an instrument presented to human, so that they too, can be a creator much like the Source Energy. It is absolutely necessary for us to understand what thoughts are, and how they work. Thought is a force and an energy, but it is also an extremely subtle matter, which operates in a remote area far from the physical plane.

Think of a radio or TV antenna. We all know that they are used to pick up waves and vibrations. From the very first day you put them up, they constantly work to receive something from the atmosphere. Do you think after a year of collecting waves and frequencies they are any heavier than the first day you put them up? Of course not. Their weight and volume remains the same throughout their existence. They have been receiving something that is not material. Antennas pick up vibrations of certain wavelengths, which then they transmit to various instruments, which in turn is transmitted to others, triggering a physical reaction. Or let's take a simpler example: When I kick a ball and the ball starts flying into the air, I'm not really adding anything material to the ball; I'm just communicating the energy. This energy is going to make the ball go high up in the air, travel a distance, roll on the ground until the energy is used up, or an obstacle appears in its way.

When we formulate a thought, we do not touch the visible, dense layer of the matter. Thought communicates itself the same way as the kinetic energy communicates itself to the ball. Thought as energy, force or vibration is picked up by the antennas connected to certain centers in our bodies. When these antennas start to vibrate, they start transmitting messages to other instruments, and setting them in motion.

The power of thought is the greatest power that we have at our disposal. The world today, is in its current state, simply because of mankind's collective thinking; each nation is in its current state of peace, prosperity, poverty, or chaos, simply because of its collective thinking as a nation; and each individual is what he/she is, and his or her life is what it is, for the same reason. Our circumstances are what they are, simply as a result of our thoughts. What we think, we become; what we think is the cause of all our actions; what we think, attracts the circumstances and environment to us according to our thoughts.

What we think, determines what type of friends and associates will be around us; what we think decides whether we will be happy or miserable, successful or unsuccessful, healthy or unhealthy, prosperous or deprived, hated or loved. What we think, either builds up our character or pulls it down. What we think can overcome fate or reinforce it, can bring us into alignment with our superb destiny, or make us an outcast and a wanderer in deserted places. There is no limit to the power of thought, because it is a spiritual power of strong influence. Everything you do starts with a thought. Everything you do, you think about it first, even if it is something as simple as grabbing a glass of drink.

We cannot really say that one thought is more creative than the next. We ought to look at all thoughts, as creative. Having said that I would add that the potential of a thought to be a powerful creator or weak, is dependent on the emotions that are stirred up, but in any case it is still a creative force. Also, according to nature, urge, passion or certainty behind the thought, can make it more, or less effective. Thought creates a mould in the individual, where the ideas are poured and formed. Ignorance of this, does not excuse anyone from its effects. Whether we are concerned about business, health, or relationship, the fact that all our thoughts are creative, gives us the advantage of changing our thoughts and hence changing our lives. If you feel you will never find the person that is right for you, you will certainly manifest that belief. With negative beliefs, as Emerson has said, we are "mis-creating our worlds". Your world-creating creative mind is creating forever.

We have the conscious mind and the subconscious mind. The conscious mind collects knowledge and experience through the senses. It reasons and structures conclusions and passes these conclusions down into the subconscious mind. The subconscious mind is the one of action. It is accountable for all that we do. It is where the memories and instincts flourish. It is a pool of incredible power, which make life possible. But we know enough about its behaviour and workings that allows us to control it, and by controlling it, we control our actions, and by controlling our actions we form our lives, and triumph over what is called fate.

The subconscious mind acts completely based on suggestion. That is to say, it follows the thoughts that are sent into it blindly and devotedly. Therefore our thoughts decide what sort of action is brought onward. If negative thoughts are sent into the subconscious mind, then negative destructive action will be the expected result. If thoughts of weakness and failure are entertained, then weak actions leading to failure will unavoidably follow. On the other hand, if good thoughts are entertained, then constructive good action will be the result; and if strong, successful, thoughts are entertained, they bring on healthy, beneficial action, which leads to success and victory. It is impossible to have malevolent thoughts and bring on good actions. With the same token, you can say there are no thoughts that will bring about failure, as a thought of failure fulfilling itself can only be considered a success. You have succeeded in achieving what you were giving your thoughts and focus to: failure! So you are always a winner, whether you physically feel you have won or lost.

Life is not a matter of luck; it is not something out of our command; it is basically the result, or effect, of our thoughts. Therefore, by controlling our thoughts, we can rule and direct our lives to an almost unbelievable extent. As conscious thinking beings, we possess one of the best powers in the     Universe. How our lives turn out, is dependent on how we use this wonderful power.   You have probably seen those who carry lucky charms and protection amulets, etc. What these people are actually doing is playing a victim.  They are denying that they are responsible for what they get in life and blame some outside force (human, fairy, devil, evil eye...), and carry the amulets to protect them.  They are giving away their own powers to a piece of something like a rabbit's foot or a stone or anything else they would require to carry around for good luck. Living in NOW is the BEST protection against any malicious human or non-human influence.

Let me clarify a bit of what I just said. I am a big believer in stones and the power they carry within them and their effects in our lives. Every single energy formation has a certain effect in your life for sure. Every single movement, thought, word, feeling and emotion has an effect. Having an effect is different than "Good luck". You carry a pen around with you, because when you need to write, you have the instrument that allows you to do that. It is only an instrument to allow you do something. Carrying a stone or any other object around can be a reminder of a power you may have forgotten you have and it may affect your vibrations to be more positive, but it is never a matter of luck.

Most people mean well and want to do good and be good. But, nevertheless, most of us more or less are wrong thinkers. It is not generally known that negative thoughts are highly destructive; we indulge in them, thinking that they are harmless or idle. Actually, thoughts of impurity, anger, revenge, hate, resentment, envy, losses and grief; fear, failure, weakness, poverty, disease, decay, mortality and death, are all highly destructive. They are destructive to health and happiness. What happens when your husband, wife, children or anybody or anything you care for is late for arrival? I remember every time this happened in my life, my mother was worried that I got into some sort of accident or some other horrible thing happened. I finally asked her one day: "does it ever occur to you that I might be having a blast of a time and not thinking that someone maybe worried?" Why is it that we are programmed to immediately think negative as opposed to positive?

Negative thoughts literally break down the nervous system; they paralyze undertakings; they undermine the will and they cause us to make wrong decisions. This is one of the reasons why, when in the field of Orthomolecular Medicine we are concentrating to eradicate any disease, the power of positive thinking is practiced. Why do you think scientists do blind studies and then double blind studies? Blind studies are so that the patient is unaware of what is being administered, so they react to it whether it is a real medication or a placebo. But later they found that the expectation of the scientist plays a big role in the outcome through their thoughts and focus and hence the double blind studies where neither the patient nor the scientist knows which group is which.

Did you know that our thoughts could be controlled and synchronized in exactly the same way that a policeman controls and regulates the traffic? He holds up a hand and almost immediately the traffic behind stops. Our thoughts can be controlled and regulated in the same way. Unwanted, destructive thoughts can be arrested, while desirable and constructive thoughts can be encouraged. When we become masters of our thoughts, we become masters of ourselves and when we become masters of ourselves, we become masters of our lives.

We are all victims of suggestion. Strong-minded and immoral people intentionally influence others by suggestion, in order to take advantage of them. The hypnotist suggests to his victim that a piece of cold metal applied to his bare back is a red hot iron and immediately the flesh is scorched and blistered. The same as it would be the case if the metal were actually red hot. In this and many other ways, the hypnotist shows how powerful suggestion and the power of mind is.

We are affected by suggestion in more ways than we can count. We receive suggestions through eyes, ears, taste, smell and touch, unless we learn how to become positive-minded and work against suggestion in all its forms. We are unconsciously affected and influenced by newspapers, magazines and advertisements. Then, there is what is called "mass suggestion". It is very easy for a positive person to sway the thoughts and emotions of others. It is difficult for one of the crowd not to be moved with the crowd. This is why people, who in the ordinary way are sensible, become insensible on occasions of national rejoicing. It is also the reason why people who are peaceful and harmless in private life, may, when in a crowd, join in acts of violence. It is simply that the mass emotion gets a hold of them, controlling them so strongly that they get carried away.

It all starts with a thought. It is always thought that pushes us forward or holds us back. It is thought that gives birth to war and devastation or the noblest of endeavours. Thoughts require your feelings and emotions to touch matter.

Now, let's look at the subject of temptation. All of us are tempted in one-way or the other. What would tempt you severely might not affect me at all; but each of us are tempted in a way particular to ourselves. Temptation is just another way of suggestion. Temptation is the subtlest form of suggestion there can be. It is so clever that it seems impossible to oppose it in any way. With all this talk, I need to mention that many situations in our lives arise from the acceptance of suggestions. Poverty for example, is the result of acceptance of suggestion of poverty; so is disease, or any other trouble. To offset these suggestions, positive autosuggestions are highly recommended.

# What is your Power?

In the beginning, The Source Energy had an idea, a Thought, a Wish. Source Energy's wish was for you to become and so you were. You are an extension or an annex of Source Energy's Thought, Source energy's Will. Because you are an extension, your Self, your Spirit is created exactly in Source Energy's Own Image and Likeness. Source Energy's Thought has countless creative ability and YOUR thought being an extension of Source Energy's Thought, has the same power. That is why you can attain whatever you think about or believe in, and even right now as we speak you are achieving exactly what you believe in most. This rule is under no circumstances broken. The only differences between you and Source Energy are that: (a) you have forgotten What You Really Are but you are now remembering and (b) Source Energy created you in Source Energy's own image and resemblance, but you did not create Source Energy.

While you were busy forgetting, you have allowed your thoughts to create a world of havoc, made from fear and worry, and out of that, you have generated a world that is composed of exactly the things you fear and worry about around you. And because you are naive to the fact that you are at CAUSE, you think that there are such things as "idle"-thought that has no consequence, and that things just happen to you without your control. Now try to watch your thoughts closely, and I mean VERY closely, and you will never fail to realize that you often daydream thousands of negative, troublesome, annoying, aggressive and insignificant thoughts that very closely mirror what you experience physically. Watch your thoughts and you will see this to be true. Your world is literally taking shape from your thoughts and beliefs. There is no such thing as an idle thought. Every single little petty thought is a cause, which will have an effect at some level.

Because you are an extension of the Source Energy's Thought, with infinite power just like His Thought; and because, as you have noticed, science has proven that the physical world is actually a collection of energy that arranges itself according to Thoughts, the following statements hold forever true:

- You ALWAYS have free will.
- You ALWAYS receive what you ask.
- You ALWAYS find what you seek.
- If you knock, it shall be ALWAYS opened unto you.
- You can ALWAYS attain everything you believe you can.

You may not identify with all of the above statements at this stage, or at least, not ALWAYS. But they ARE true, nevertheless. Seeking is the same as finding. If you think that you are finding what you think that you are not seeking, watch yourself deeper. You will find out that at the very deepest level, you are seeking exactly what you have found. For example, if you feel that you are finding disagreement and poverty while you think that you're looking for peace and wealth, dig a bit deeper in an honest way and you will find that your core belief is that you are under attack, and something is capable of attacking you.

You can actually be attacked, and you live in a world of scarcity where failure is to be feared. Dig deep, be honest, then change your core beliefs and everything will change accordingly. Your world is always a reflection of your deepest intentions. Achieving is the same as believing. You are the Way, you are the Path, and the Truth of your world and what surrounds you, and follows you.

Your ideas, thoughts, visions and dreams, whatever they may be, good or bad, are the self-fulfilling prophecies of your future in what you may one day become or achieve. You do not need the help of a psychic to know what future holds for you, you can predict your life of tomorrow by looking at your inner self today. You can change your tomorrow by changing your inner self today.

# What is Certainty?

In order for your wishes to come true, you need to be in that frame first, right here and NOW, just like that. Simply decide and be. It is that simple, and the world will follow your decision. Being a state, is closely related to believing. For example, let's say you have a financial condition that is troubling you. You wonder to yourself: "why is it so, that no matter what I do or visualize or think, this financial deficiency is still with me?" The answer is in your core belief.

Do you deeply believe that you have the finances you need NOW, this very moment, or do you think you do not have them? Think deep. The question is not whether you believe you will have the finances, it is whether you believe you have them NOW or not. And do you believe in scarcity or in abundance? Do you think there is enough for everyone? Or do you think if someone else gets it first then there is little chance that there is enough left for you? Remember, the Universe follows you exactly to the thought. If you believe you will have the money *some* day, it will suspend your money till "*some day*". And since there are no real calculable values to "some day", then, that can be any day or never in this lifetime. And when that "some day" suddenly arrives without notifying you, and you start doubting, thinking "what if I don't have it", then it will respond likewise. So now you have lost that chance that you had "some day".

You are the Way, the Path and the Truth, and the Universe follows you. So, start by calling all your desires forward to the NOW by being certain that you have it already. Don't look for proof in the world. It simply shows you as you are. You are the evidence and the proof.

Certainty, faith and belief, are necessary parts of creation, whether it is success, wealth, health, prosperity or anything else for that matter. It is these ingredients, which give the Universe a green light to do as you wish it to do. Benjamin Franklin declared, "There are only two certainties in life – death and taxes." What do you think this belief will bring about? You see, you need to be certain before you get into that frame. For example happiness is a frame. How can you be happy if you are not sure of it? Other example could be creation of goals. How can you create goals without certainty? Not only they will not be accurate, but also their results will be affected. When you see a movie, what makes one actor or actress a better act than the others? It is their understanding and certainty of the subject and being able to be in and fit themselves in that frame, that makes them a good or a bad act.

Many religious teachers have come to teach us faith and certainty. This is not a new subject. But remember, as you read on, you'll see that faith is a lot like a frame. There is abundance in certainty. You cannot really speak certain, nor do certain, you can only BE certain. And the way to do that, is to simply decide, just like that, and let no other negation come to you. Everything is achievable to the degree that you are certain of.

"Fear is False Evidence Appearing Real." In reality, there is entirely nothing to be afraid of. Your Self has everything and is everlasting. Your Self is designed to never lack anything, it is completely self-sufficient. Your Self has it all already. It is never-ending. But its existence here on Earth comes with many false impressions. One of your purposes here on Earth is to overcome these false impressions. One of which is the illusion that there is scarcity. Where we know scientifically now-a-days, thanks to quantum physics and spirituality, as we have been advised over and over again throughout the ages, the abundance is all there is. If you ever catch yourself fearful of something, know that it is a figment of your imagination, and try to find out what that illusion is, because in reality, there is nothing to fear at all but the fear itself.

Fear creates the chemicals that, in turn, create all kinds of disease, not only physically, but also in your relationships, prosperity, mental stability, family relationships and everything else you can think of. Think of yourself when you were born and you did not know the

175

language and first you made a sound and little by little started pronouncing words and asking for things. You never told yourself: "well I'm never going to get this language thing straight, there is just too many verbs, nouns and pronouns". You did it without fear. You learned to walk and do many things without fear. Imagine how much you would not have done, if you had hindering thoughts.

When you pick up a phone to make a call, you know without a shred of doubt that you will not fail to pick it up and dial. The thought does not even occur to you that you may not be able to dial the phone. You do it with complete certainty. That is the level of certainty, belief and faith you need to have in yourself for the ever-present laws of the Universe and the competence and the potential of The Source Energy to work perfectly all the time. It is the certainty you need to have about the fact that you have it even before you ask for it, and in the guarantee that you have it all right NOW in this moment as we speak. If you think you do not have something, decide, NOW, that you have it, and you will. Do not say "but I don't see it". Do not work against yourself. Over time, it will become your second nature. Until then, do your best and always think that you already have it. Mind your mind. You can gain faith and certainty with practice. But it is faster to just decide once and for all that you have it. Just decide. NOW.

# The Creation Process

There is an order to creation: Being (Frame), Thought (visualization, imagination), Words and Action. Although you may not realize it, you create your experiences first in your Self, then in your mind, then by your words and finally by your actions, throughout your lives. It starts at the Frame (being) then goes on to thinking then to speaking and from there to acting. Acting is the stage where receiving happens and this is when we get to experience what we create.

Most people work like crazy all day long and wonder why they are not "successful" without focusing, nurturing or tending to their first three steps of being, thinking and speaking.  This chain of creation is the law of the Universe that cannot be broken. When you are thinking, you are actually devising ideas that shift the Universe in an assembly beyond your imagination. Your thoughts move beyond your head and physical reality. They form something at some level, in many places. For example, your thoughts and imaginations can be a cause to trigger the motivation in many others to act in particular ways that support your thought and wish, at the same time fulfilling their own needs. You are never alone. The system is one.

Once you think, you verbalize and speak of your thoughts. This sharing of your thoughts physically with other people, brings a kind of certainty and assurance. Then you act on your thoughts and words, bringing all physical systems needed into place that help "form" your thoughts into experiences on this physical plane. Try to comprehend that the physical objects you see are all an effect of your thoughts and others'. Thoughts, Words, Action are tools of creation.  Each of this three has a function. Some cause, some receive and experience the effect. They are completely different stages or levels. Level-confusion is the cause of a lot of misunderstanding and distress.

You confuse your levels when you think you can use the wrong level to create. You cannot create by action only if your thoughts and words contradict your actions. However, by acting the same consistently you can steadily change your thoughts. Let's say that you wish to learn how to think like a giving person. You can just do it now, think like a giving person. But if you find that not to be so easy, then act like a giving person, speak like one and soon you will start thinking as one. That is just a good programming method; it is not a cycle of creation. The only place you can think, speak and act is NOW. So don't wait for some "ideal moment". Just do it NOW.

# The Cause and Effect

This is the chief law that runs the entire Universe. It is the law number one. Every teacher, whether spiritual or scientific, has wanted to teach it. I'm sure you have heard at one time or the other, "You reap what you sow", or "You get what you give", or "What goes around comes around", or "karma", or "consequences", or "Every action causes an equal and opposite reaction", or many other parallel statements. Quantum physics is now precisely educating us how this works on a sub-atomic level. Things get better when your thoughts get better. They get worse when your thoughts get worse. THE WORLD IS ALL IN YOU.

You are THE CAUSE of everything happening in your life, whether you are aware of it, or not. To be happy, make and be a cause of someone else to be happy. If you like to have peace, teach peace and provide it to those around you, to have it. Cause and Effect works this way. Just like everything grows out of an idea and thoughts get manifested, your world also mirrors your imaginations and beliefs. Whatever in this physical reality you think of as real, is planted as real in your mind, and what is in your mind will affect you someday in some way unless you change your belief in it. This is an especially interesting subject as I usually get this reaction: "Are you telling me that building is there because I imagined it so? So why is it that everyone else also agrees that it is there?" I see the need to mention the power of group consciousness here.

The law of Cause and Effect is as functioning in the world today, as it was centuries ago. The original meaning of the word law, according to the dictionary, is "something set, placed, fixed and laid down".

The first grand characteristic that I would like you to grasp about this law, is that it is automatic in its action, and hence there is no possibility of escaping from it. Put aside all theories of heaven and hell and what you have heard about man being rewarded for good and punished for the bad he has done. That inevitably suggests to us the thought of an earthly judge, who may be biased or partially informed, or may be more merciful in one case and harsher in another. I prefer to speak of the law of cause and effect, because we know this is the law, which brings us the result of our actions with an automatic precision. No judges required. It is on auto-response.

In mechanics we know that action and reaction are equal, and energies and forces can never be lost. If you put so much energy into a machine, you will receive back from it as much work as a result. If you put a certain amount of energy into a word, action, or thought, you will attain a certain result from that. If you put a certain amount of force into a steam engine, you expect to get a certain proportion of work back. If you do not receive - what you know you may reasonably expect - from your engine, immediately, you look for a defect in your machine; it would never occur to you to say that the law of the conversation of energy is false. But when exactly the same law is working in our daily lives, we question it constantly. Why did this happen? Why did that go the way it did? Why am I sick? Why am I depressed? Why is my life this way? Why? Why? Why? For some reason we cannot see that evil follows evil and good follows good.

We often affirm that no laws of justice exist, instead of blaming ourselves for our own shortsightedness. We are, today, even though we might have forgotten, to a large extent, the products of the thoughts, surroundings, and the teachings of our childhood. Just as today we are bearing the results of yesterday, and the day before, so precisely we will bear the results of today, in the future. We have made ourselves what we are, and we have made our circumstances what they are. As we have sown in the past, so we reap now; and as we are sowing now, so unfailingly we shall reap in the future.

Unfortunately a great deal of today's religious teachings specifically includes a theory that we may escape from the consequences of our actions. This not only sounds fundamentally inaccurate, but it allows for unsafe conclusions to be deduced from it. If a man wishes to be an athlete, he must first train himself for the race. He cannot expect the development of perfect muscles by someone else doing the actual training for him. It has somewhat become easier for us to blame anything and everything for what we have in our lives without a moment of thought. If you put your hand into the fire, and it is burnt, you do not say "God punished me for putting my hand into the fire". You consider it a natural consequence of your action, and you know that anyone who understands physics could explain to you along scientific lines exactly what had happened to you, and why you have suffered. He would tell you that luminous matter is vibrating at an exceedingly rapid rate, that such a rate of vibration imposing upon the tissues of your hand had torn them apart, and so had produced the wound that we call a burn.

Acts are all the same to the Universe.  As an apple seed is not dearer to Universe than of a tomato seed, the same is true when it comes to acts.  Acts are looked upon as what they are, acts.  There is no judgment passed.  It is us that label an act as good or bad.  This judgment in our part is passed through couple of different factors: what was the outcome of the act and how did this act make us feel. The outcome of the act is what causes happiness or regret.  When you are vibrating positively after an act is completed and you feel connected to your higher-self, you have done the right thing.  When you do not feel that connection, no matter what the outcome, the act is naturally labeled as bad and you will try to hide it.

The phrase, "what goes around comes around" is not some Universal threat. That is just the way it is.  I'm sure most of you have seen the "lazy Suzan" trays.  This is a little or large tray that is placed in the middle of the dining table or inside the cupboards and it swivels to give you access to the spices or condiments you need.  Now think of everything you do as tangible and imagine that you are putting them on a "lazy Suzan" tray.  As you turn the tray things that you have put on it will come around over and over again.  If you have put sugar, you get sugar and if sour grapes, then sour grapes. In the "lazy Suzan" of the Universe, whatever emotions you put on the tray, are the ones coming back to you.  Remember that no energy is ever wasted and all your thoughts and emotions are nothing but energy that you have placed on the "lazy Suzan" of your life. Let's start taking responsibility of our actions and thoughts.

# What are Suffering, Happiness and Joy?

Everything you need is "within". Joy also comes from within, from Being in the frame of joy. Pleasure and pain are from outside. Joy never stops being joy. It is what spirit and being is all about. External things do not affect joy. The joy cannot stop and is ongoing when you are present in NOW and conscious and in touch with your Self. It is impossible to stop joy, but you can be blind to it by not being present in NOW, fully present. Let me give you an example of being present.

You are walking on the street thinking about all the things you talked about with the bank teller an hour ago, and re-experiencing the past over and over again, thinking about the things you should have said and could have said, and so on and so forth. In the meantime missing everything that is going on around you. You are investing your NOW, in the past so you are not present. Then you get home and re-explain the situation few times to different members of your family, and there it is again more of your time spent on the past. I suggest, if you need to vent about a situation, to put it behind you, do it only once. Don't waste all the NOW moments in the past.

Anytime you see yourself thinking about anything that happened in the past, whether it was a minute or an hour ago or yesterday or ten years ago, you are not present. It is at times like this, that most incidents and accidents happen. Joy is an eternal frame that belongs to NOW. It is not in the past or future. These times do not exist, except only in our minds. Take care of NOW and all the other time slots will take care of themselves.

Pleasure and pain are complementary and external. The same thing that gives you pleasure can potentially give you pain. Think about it. Whatever externally is pleasing to you, when it is absent, you feel pain. You feel the hurt of not having it. Also when something is giving you pain and it becomes absent, then from that absence of pain, you gain pleasure. The reason most of the time people are dissatisfied, is because of their dependence on these external factors.

The other anguish that can be caused by not living in NOW, is something that you may have had in the past or something you wish to have in the future. People get saddened thinking about what they had, and they have lost, whereas when they did have it, they did not really enjoy it that much. So they wasted their NOW, then, and they are wasting their NOW, now. Then come the words such as, "but if I had this or if I had that, my life would have been better." Dwelling on the lack and getting more of it, of course, is wasting all the positive creating one can do in NOW, over concentrating on a negative thought of lack. Why not enjoy what you have now and manifest all you like and desire now? Don't let your mind escape NOW. If you do, you totally miss the joy of NOW. Once you make living in NOW a habit, real Joy comes to the surface. From there on, everything will become enjoyable, even the most "painful" things will not bring you suffering and you will start praising life. Joy is a frame, Joy is Being, and Being is NOW.

Resisting NOW is ineffective. Resisting NOW is agonizing. What do you anticipate to get out of resisting what IS? Joy is always present in the moment of NOW. It is chronic, but you can choose to be blind to it. When you live in NOW, in accord with everything that IS, NOW; in that moment, you are in the best point to enjoy NOW and also create the next NOW in the most influential way, free of worry, fear, anxiety and negativity. Use your mind as a tool by activating it to create an intention of the next NOW. This very rapid and detached thinking should only take a few seconds. All our problems exist only in our minds – they cannot exist in NOW. NOW, always passes. All struggles exist outside of NOW, in the mind, and only when you use the mind in error.

# What are infinite loops and their starts?

These are the loops that rule your life and it is vital that you are familiar with them. They are:

*You experience what you create, and you create what you experience.* What this translates to, is that whatever you feel inside, the emotions and the thoughts that you go through, manifest and create the next moments of your world. Emotions are Energy in MOTION. Thoughts are also energy. If you are not cautious, your emotions can conquer your thoughts. For example, if you are always worried, you will attract, create and manifest worrisome situations to yourself. Consequently, you create what you experience in you.

To create, is to make something "observable". You also experience what you create. This means that the world around you, gives you, your experiences. Do you see how the loop works? What you have to know is how to break the loop so that you can change your experiences. This is like the chicken and the egg. Which one came first? What is the first source? Only it is not as difficult to answer this question. Your frame, your beliefs, your thoughts, your emotions, your words and actions come first. They are the ones starting the loop. They become created. Then once your world is made up, you look at it and respond, so you experience it.

You ought to learn to break the loop, whenever you see yourself in a condition that you don't like, which is repeating itself. You can very well change this by simply refusing to react to it, in the same way over and over again, and instead watch it without judgment, bring it into the light, learn which thoughts or emotions are causing it, and then change them. Don't try to change the effects. It will do you no good. It will not work! The effect cannot be changed directly; you absolutely need to change the cause. It does sound obvious, but many people still try to do it.

Here is another loop. *You see what you believe, and you believe what you see.* We have learned to trust our five senses, and so when you see something, you subconsciously tend to believe it is true, even though it may not be. Hence all the magicians earning money. What causes people to think it is real, is that they see what they believe. Read that once more. *We see what we believe.* Even though this Universe is completely abundant, we see it in short supply, because we have agreed and believe that it is. But for the reason that we believe this, we have made it scarce by false impression. Your belief has the power to create your world. So where does this loop start? Of course, again, in belief. There are two ways to resolve this loop. One is to change your belief, so that you can change the circumstances.

The other way to break out of this loop, is not to believe in anything limiting. Let's say you wish to be wealthy. You first need to believe that wealth is all that is there, and your world will prove you right. You know very well that you sometimes see things not quite the way they are. You even sometimes see someone and think they are a certain way, only to discover later that you were wrong about them. Seeing is very much a function of your eyes and mind. So you can break out of your painful cycles by just confessing that you have no idea what the meaning of what you see is. Children do this all the time. They are constantly asking what it means, expecting an answer. The answer will come to you, as long as you don't predict what the answer will be.

Our Universe is brimming with this creative power. It is endless, and it is ours for the taking. This energy flows freely and easily. When the time is right, a tree grows leaves, bursts into flower, and bears fruit. We get everything we need from this endless pool of creative juice. It does not matter if we are arguing a case in court, working hard at a job we dislike, or doing photography at a stream. The energy source is the same.

When we are open and receptive, we channel this energy. It courses through our beings, and manifests in an endless variety of ways.

When we move beyond our ego's boundaries, and reconnect with the Universe, the power and possibilities are great. Below the surface, beneath the layers of protective coating we hide behind, we are one. When we pour ourselves, back into the ocean of Universal creativity, we become one with it. We burst into our full vibrancy, expanding toward full capacity; we dip into the realm of pure potential.

When we are connected to the Universe, when we are open and accepting, anything is possible. This is the place where miracles happen, where our dreams manifest. The basic principle is really very simple: if we stay connected and are true to ourselves, we will prosper. Staying connected is not so easily done for many of us. But the more days pass since our departure from the womb, the more challenging it becomes to maintain an open channel with the infinite. The world seems to plot against our being true to who we are. We are told how to act. Parents, siblings, teachers, lovers and friends define us. We internalize these things, losing track of our own internal voice, our internal guide and make a whole belief system around it. We feel confused and lost. We wonder why we feel depressed and indifferent, even as we achieve more and more of our dreams. We wonder why we do not feel free.

We have to be fully present in the moment, to appreciate what is coming our way. It has to be what we really want, what our core beings want—not what we have learned we should want, or even necessarily what everybody else wants, and, we have to be genuine, fully ourselves. We have to be completely alive to really feel what is happening to us. We have to return to our senses.

We are constantly using phrases such as: "If I have _____ I will be _____." Fill in the blanks with beautiful, rich, sexy, etc., which is the illusion of the quick fix. The problem is that quick fixes take us further away from our true self.

This separation from our true selves, from the Infinite, creates a devastating void and an incredible amount of fear. From this place, nothing is as it should be. We look for safety in submission. We follow the rules. We become uncomfortable with differences that swerve not too far from our "norm," and so the legacy gets passed on from generation to generation.

Now, after all this said, does manifesting your dreams sound like science fiction? Just think of the possibilities. Manifesting what you want, is the ability to create what you want in your life, or really more accurately put, the ability to attract what you want to you. You are incredibly attractive. You're like a giant magnet, and you draw to yourself experiences that are in synch with your beliefs, thoughts, feelings, emotions, words and actions. If you're charged up with a lot of positive energy, then you're going to attract a lot of positive things. Of course, the opposite is just as valid - if you're charged with negativity then you're going to attract the negative stuff. It is important for you to understand how you're getting what you're getting. Once you grasp that, it's a cinch to become really intentional about what you're attracting, and to clear out anything that's blocking what you want.

Imagine that you have a huge pot, and you're cooking the dish of a lifetime. In fact you are, you're cooking up your life! And you throw all kinds of experiences, thoughts, and emotions and so on into this pot. The good stuff-positive energy-tastes great and the more of it you add to your pot the better it tastes. Negativity is bitter and horrible tasting and the more of it you add to this pot the lousier the taste! This pot of yours is huge. It's enough to feed you for a lifetime! So if you pop in a few dabs of negativity, it's not going to make a whole lot of difference. But if you stand on the side of this pot and start pouring it in, it's not going to be long before your dish tastes pretty dreadful.

Once you start getting really intentional about manifesting what you want, you're going to start pouring some serious doses of positive energy into that mix. You're going to become more and more intentional about what you throw in your pot.

You see, if life just happens to you, then there's really no point in paying much attention to what you're putting out mentally or emotionally. But if you have some impact on the end result, then that's a different matter.

As I have mentioned before and will again and again, everything in this Universe is energy including us. In working on manifesting what you want, what you need to know is that like attracts like. The more positive you are the more positive the energy you attract will be. I know this probably flies in the face of everything you've ever learned.

I'm sure you've heard "Go out and work hard and then you'll get what you want" or some variation on that theme a number of times in your life. But there's a problem with that... If you're out there pushing hard and not having a lot of fun at it (I'm not talking about the kind of working hard that feels just fantastic) then what you're throwing into your pot is bitterness and fatigue and resentment. Not very tasty!

When you start living your life in a way where you manifest more and more of what you want you're going to be changing your focus and making sure that you're very careful about what you put in your pot. The tastier that life stew of yours becomes, the more attractive you become. And those things that you want are just going to start popping into your life all over the place with no effort.

Things may not always happen in the order or at the pace you think they should. At times I have been impatient; I have thought everything should have happened yesterday. But time and time again as I stand at the end of a journey, in retrospection, it all makes so much sense. So often, I can't see the wisdom of it at the time. Trust your process. Remember to be loving to yourself. If you've been going 1000 miles an hour in the opposite direction, then it's going to take a bit of time to redirect yourself. But if you stay with it, and you intend to redirect yourself and live in a different kind of way, I promise you won't be disappointed.

# Why experiences repeat themselves in our lives?

Have you had times when situations kept repeating themselves in your life until you underwent a major breakthrough? There are various areas that you are probably aware of, like financial situations, marital problems, friendships, drug addictions, etc. Some people seem to always have money difficulties. As soon as they fix one problem, another one is awaiting in the horizon. Some people have relationship issues. They go from one bad relationship to the next, not knowing how it happened. This is why:

All problems occur from believing in a thought. Until you change your belief, the effects will keep coming back from different sides and in different ways, with the same results, because the Universe follows you. Nothing outside of you will save you. You can only be saved from your crisis permanently by changing yourself and your beliefs from inside.

So, how do you change from inside you ask? Well, the first rule of thumb to remember is that the problem lies in your mind. Therefore it cannot be resolved as long as you refuse to accept it in your mind and clear it. You cannot break away from it. Your problem originates from a lower level where all problems come from, and you cannot save yourself from it. Except, your Higher Mind can save you. Realize that you have a Body and you have a Mind. Your higher Mind, is still connected to the Spirit and The Source Energy. This Higher Mind is where your motivation, clearness, precision and lucidity come from. Your Higher Mind remains in its original mint condition, safe and sound. But because you have free will, it will never interfere. This higher wisdom kicks in, when you decide to let go and stop crowding your mind with regular noise and conflict that you are so used to. You will need to let go, welcome your higher mind, and allow it to interfere. If you talk to any great artist or scientist, they will declare that inspiration arrives only when one becomes still. Einstein, Michelangelo and Mozart and many others testified to this. Be free from noise, be still, ask your higher mind to show you the path, and you will for sure be shown. This is your own self and it will never deny your call. Only *you* can deny and block the answer. Once you admit that you do not know, stop resisting NOW and start being clear in your thoughts, you will see the amazing coincidences and synchronicities in your life.

To stop the suffering in your life, stop all attacking thoughts in your head on their track. If you don't, they will just get back to you. Angry people are constantly in situations that bring them more anger. Judgmental people meet their own spiteful conflicts, and so on. You cannot possibly judge a thing as being "bad" without reinforcing the idea in your own mind that such a thing is a reality. In other words, for you to judge something you would need to have belief in it. And because of this, you become available to be harmed by it.

If you give something or somebody meaning and power, you let that something or somebody borrow you and do what they wish with you. Why would you so voluntarily give your Self away? The same goes for believing in something or someone outside of you as a solution to your problem. Because you believe that thing or person is the solution, you reinforce the idea of lack in your mind, and that without delay, weakens you, because the Universe will follow suit. You are saying that you do not have what it takes to resolve this problem and the Universe answers that focus.

Another important point to mention is goals. Never set a goal out of fear – its results will be temporary and destructive. Set all goals out of love and complete certainty. When you start seeing things in a clear light, you start to create instead of react. When you set your goal, be certain that it will come true and that Universe follows your believed truth. Be completely certain, have faith in the system and its workings. Although you may not realize this at this time, but your power is expanded across the entire Universe and is in alliance with it.

There are no clashes of will and the Universe is welcoming of your goals. If you pay attention, you will see that nature always achieves complex outcomes using graceful ease! Let the nature amaze you! The Universe will bring in all the needed resources to you at the right time, so that your goals will work out on their own. You just need to trust, be certain and not interfere with its workings. Consider whatever and whoever you come in contact with and the ones that are in your presence at any given moment, as help to get where you like to get to. Hence, at every NOW, look around you and ask, "How is this related to my goals?" and you will discover an answer. Sometimes, the reason you are in a certain place or a person is with you, is to point out a mistake in thought that stops you from getting what you wish to get. Or they simply can be there to provide some information. Just listen, relax, accept, and do not hold back anything and you will see everything work out! Universe works effortlessly. Your resistance is the only thing that slows you down and gives you grief.

# Is there any level of difficulty?

Universe is abundant, peaceful and totally powerful, but we have the false impression of scarcity and anguish. When the illusions are dropped, the reality of the Universe is waiting to be exposed.

There is no level of anything being more difficult than the other in any manifestation! The only level of difficulty is in your mind and nowhere else. Anything is as difficult as you believe it to be. Anything is as easy as you believe it to be. Universe acts very accurately on your decisions and thoughts. When a decision is made effortlessly, its results are effortless. When you decide you are penniless and believe it, you do so effortlessly. You don't really need anything to make that decision. You just make it, sitting there in your chair. This same effortless decision, decides the world that is going to surround you. You could have just as easily and effortlessly decided and believed that you are very wealthy; and the Universe would make your world according to that. Your achievements are solely dependent on your decisions of how hard or simple it will be. Remember, there are no idle thoughts.

Every single little thought and emotion that flickers in your mind is a powerful yet effortless decision that causes a corresponding effect. If you believe that in order to succeed in something you have to take ten steps, then so shall it be. If you decide or think about all the risks involved, there is a very good chance that you will experience at least some of them, depending on the emotions they stirred up in you when you were thinking about them. Honestly speaking, we are the only ones who sabotage our own happiness and joy.

If you are indecisive and continuously changing your mind about your life, so it will be. If even for a split second you think "but what if I don't make it.." that thought will have some effect at some level. The Universe carries out even the most insignificant ideas and feelings precisely and flawlessly, for you. Remember, you are an extension of Source Energy. Source Energy's thought and your thought carry the same potency in power. There is no difference in difficulty to make a dollar or million dollars. It is just your thoughts and teachings that make you think one is easier or harder than the other. You believe there is a difference, so there is. This is your unlimited power.

In any case, an illusion is something that never existed. It only appeared to be because of a belief in it. There are no illusions that can be said to be more real than any other. Your only genuine goal should be to heal and change your mind, to reinstate it to its original magnificence. Everything else will tag along automatically.

# Victim Consciousness

The most common way of avoiding taking responsibility for our feelings, is to attribute them to another person or situation. The typical language we use is *"you make me feel,"* or *"it made me feel,"* etc. The amazing reality is this: you can always *"choose"* to feel, but no one can ever *"make"* you feel anything. As long as you persist in believing that outside events or people have control over your emotions, you will remain dis-empowered. Each time you use the terminology *"it makes me feel"*, you are saying, *"it has total control over my emotions"*. In other words, you are living in victim consciousness. What is worse, we often passionately insist that someone is making us feel a certain way, as if we are proud to be a victim! Someone does something we do not agree with and we proclaim, *"You make me feel"*, and our associated emotional behaviour is not unlike to that of a performing seal!

I had someone once in my life that would, if I were sitting or standing, accidentally kick me while passing by, and then say, "What is your foot doing here"??? I can tell you that it does not get any more amusing than that. It was my foot's fault for being there, but it was not his fault for not seeing or not paying attention.

We can only ever be victims of our own minds — and this too is a choice. More precisely, since the term "victim" denotes one who has no choice, clearly there is actually no such thing as a victim! We have been living lives that we constantly thought were at mercy of forces outside of ourselves. This in practice means that we gave power to *everyone* and *everything* over us.

From the moment we started walking and fell down or hit the wall, our well-meaning parents blamed the inanimate objects around us to make us feel better and why change the habit now? It works, and nothing ever becomes your responsibility. Being a victim is the easy way out.

There are many people around that will swear to you that their circumstances are <u>not</u> due to their negative thoughts. How unfortunate for them that I do not believe them one bit. Victim consciousness is nothing <u>but</u> negative energy being sent out. Hey, even if you leave your life in the hands of an object or another person, you are still responsible for what you are attracting to it.

The bottom line is, you CHOSE to give your control away. Try to give up this victim consciousness. We have been brought up to think that we are constantly at the mercy of others, luck, or chance. I can tell you that staggering number of people operate solely according to this guidance. Once you grasp and understand the Universal Laws, you will see that there are absolutely NO victims and there never will be. Everything is a result of choice. We, nevertheless, constantly point the finger of blame on others or situations. Should we fail at something, or if we can't do something, or if we don't have something, it's because…

So, here is the last word on this: if you continue to pretend to be a victim, you will never, ever draw to your life what you desire. A powerful shift happens when you switch from operating in a "victim consciousness", to a "co-creator" consciousness. The co-creator consciousness makes you fully self-responsible. Victim consciousness allows you to blame, and point fingers at people and things.

You will hear those who choose to have victim consciousness saying, "I wish this, that or the other were different, so I could feel better".

You will hear those who choose to have co-creator consciousness say; "I am the creator of my own reality. Everything that comes to me is what I draw to me. There is no force, person or condition outside of myself that has power over me. My complete control comes from within. If something happens in my life that I don't like, I will know it was a direct result of how I have been flowing my Energy."

Co-creators <u>know</u> that the Law of Attraction is always at work, behind the scenes of every event. Co-creators do not criticize their manifestations, but instead take full responsibility for them. They don't blame anyone, not even themselves, but simply do the necessary self-query to find out how they have been flowing their energy to attract and draw a certain situation into their lives. Then, they make the necessary changes within and continue to enjoy the journey of life. Co-creators are also very sensitive to their feelings at every moment, and are constantly guiding their powerful energy flow in the direction they desire to go. They know that no-one is a victim and that everyone they encounter is a powerful co-creator, even though they may not know it because of what they have chosen.

How do you move from victim consciousness to be a co-creator? First, you declare your intention that you want to do so. And second, by making a decision that from this moment onwards, you accept full responsibility for every single one of your creations.

Remember, the moment you blame someone or something, you immediately shift yourself back to the victim consciousness. But as soon as you realize and remember that you created this event or condition to be there, and become willing to stop blaming and looking to see how you drew it to you, you shift right back into your power position of the co-creator. You are reawakening to and remembering how truly powerful you are, in each and every moment, when you operate as a consciously aware co-creator.

# Words

Words are our primary way of communication. We have gotten so used to them that we use them without even paying attention, on regular basis. Our tongue and mouth have been put on autopilot. Words are, however, very powerful. Have you noticed how you can bite someone with a word and aggravate them, or praise and motivate them? Just by words. Amazing, eh?

In order for you to comprehend a word, you will need to internalize it first. For example when I say: "coffee cup", you hear the word and internalize it, before you actually understand it. In fact, you are consulting your notebook to see what that is. Only because it takes a fraction of a second to do this consulting, we do not really think of it that way.

Now, once you internalize a word, you attach an emotion to it. For example, I will say: cancer. Immediately you will remember someone in your life who has either lived through or died from cancer and with that thought, there is an immediate reaction of emotion - happy or sad. You basically "experience" every word you hear and say.

With the same concept in mind, if you speak the words that have sad emotions attached to them, you become sad and if you say the words with happy vibrant emotions behind them, you become happy. Have you ever felt energy-drain after talking to someone? There is one possible reason why this happens:

*What they were saying was completely opposite to "your" beliefs and you were constantly trying to defend your belief.*

It could be something positive they were saying, or negative. Nevertheless, the words had their effect. Now think of this: every day we are subjected to thousands of words through family, friends, newspapers, TV, radio, magazines, ads, colleagues, etc. Is it any wonder that some of us feel completely exhausted at the end of the day? Words surround us. Words are very important emotional switches that we have. They can switch us to a happy state or to a sad state. Depressed or uplifted state. Discouraged or encouraged state.

As I mentioned at the beginning of this passage, we have put ourselves on "autopilot". We use words habitually. This does NOT diminish their effect at all. Take a look at people who use the phrase "I don't have enough time" often and you will find they almost never meet their work deadlines. Take a look at someone else who uses the word "stress" often and you will see someone who *is* stressed. We need to be paying more attention to the words we use *if* we want to head in certain life directions "intentionally".

The most current commonly used expressive word of the day is "Sic" pronounced "Sick". We use it to describe how good things are. Unfortunately your subconscious does not spell. So it takes it, that anything is "sick" is good. Can you guess the rest?

Some people suffer from "circular reference", as I call it. They use negative words bringing negative emotions and they feel down after that; hence they use more negative words, causing more negative emotions and they keep doing this nose-dive until the body becomes ill or stressed and the "circular reference" does not stop. These same people can and have the option at any given time, to stop the nose-dive, change their words and feelings, and start flying again. Why not use a milder version of words if you really have to use a negative word in your life? Take a look at the following examples:

| Negative phrases: | Replacements: |
| --- | --- |
| I can't | (I need to learn how) |
| My problem | (My challenge) |
| I'm stressed | (I need a little peace) |
| I'm anxious | (I need to redirect my energy) |
| I'm exhausted | (I need to relax and refuel) |

And, of course, the list goes on… You can change your vocabulary and in turn change your emotions, which will bring about your future experiences. To take a key step forward in manifesting your desired future, pay attention to the words you use at all times. Live at conscious level. Turn the autopilot off, and start flying your own plane the way you *like* it to be done.

# Conditions and Reality

You hear, all the time, things like: *"if I get slimmer I'll be happier"*, *"if I make more money I'll be happy"*, *"if what is there was over here I would be happy"*... We are constantly looking for physical remedies outside of ourselves, to start enjoying life. Then, when it does not happen, we have unhappiness, dis-ease, and upset. In all the statements made above, we are also concentrating on lack, and on something we don't have. We are constantly concentrating on the mess we are in, and trying to fix it, and go back to "normal". Fixing, is resisting our natural energy. Fixing is a great low frequency energy. Stop fixing and start feeling good.

We have learned that the reality in our lives is something we cannot do much about, and if we don't like something, either we get rid of it, or accept it. "Get your head out of the cloud". "No one said life is fair". "Can't live with them, can't live without them". "If you can't beat them, join them". "Face the reality". I am sure at one point of your life, you have heard one, or all of the above statements. Yet, through all this, the real reality is just the result of how you flow your energy. You do not have to put up with ANYTHING. All you have to do, is to flow your energy differently, and act accordingly. Just because you are living in the "reality" of a jobless market, it does not mean that you cannot land a fantastic job. We create everything, from a little argument to a global war. "Intend" to have a ball and be joyful in *your* "reality". Do not make it the focal point of your life and it will cease to exist. Switch your focus. It is that easy.

We have many "motors" that we run during the day: there is blame motor, ticked off motor, worry motor, anxiousness motor and many more. When you see these motors running, find something, anything, to think about that will make you feel good and turn the low RPM motor off. Switch your focus. Now immediately start giving yourself a soothing talk and do it out loud. Feel as if a loving parent or a grandparent is talking to you: it is going to be OK love; everything is fine; it's going to be alright; you will be fine; and you'll be OK. You are loved; you are cared for. Comfort yourself like a little baby, until you feel calm and quiet inside and you feel that the noisy motor is not running anymore.  Stay in this calm frame as long as you can, and keep the focus off that disturbing motor.  Now, out loud and immediately after this, give yourself a talk.  A motivational talk like:  come on, you know you can do this, so get up and go get them boy.  You know you are smart and you know you are brilliant.  Get up and do it right now.

Right after this talk do something physical to make you feel good.  Go for a walk, polish your car, jump up and down, whatever physical activity you can think of that will put you in that normal frame of joy, do it now.  Focus on what it was that you desired, and think of it as if you already have it.  The phrase "fake it till you make it" is invaluable.  But in truth, you are really not faking anything.  In the world of energy, really, truly, all you can imagine and want is already here.  It just may not be in the frequency you are vibrating to; and all that is required, is for you to align.  So you see, you are looking at real reality, but because we are so used to "seeing is believing", that we call this "faking it".  Just because you have tuned your radio to a certain frequency, does not mean the other stations do not exist.  You just have to change the station.

Let me give you a quick example of this reality thing you are so hooked to.  Scientists did a research many years back in which they took two sets of newborn kittens and placed them in two different rooms.  In one room all the lines were vertical and in the other all the lines were horizontal.  Few weeks later, they switched rooms so to put the kittens in vertical room in horizontal and vice versa.  The kittens were walking and bumping into things as if they were blind.  The ones raised in the vertical room could not see or comprehend horizontal lines and the ones raised in horizontal line room could not understand vertical lines.  So you see, our physical vision lies to us on a regular basis and we believe it 100%.  So much is going on energetically and otherwise around you that you are not used to seeing and hence you do not believe.

Going back to what we were talking about, just give us a situation we don't like, and we will either throw our hands up in despair or blame it on fate, or we immediately seek revenge, which we often mask as justice.  Neither one of these actions will work and neither one of them will leave you with joyful feelings.  Stop wasting your energy on creating low frequency waves and start being deliberate co-creators. Stop being uptight over things. Instead, understand that the situations do not control you; you control the situations. Last but not least, stop depending on your physical senses as a one hundred percent accurate tool.

# Appreciation

How good are you in appreciating? Can you see a rock or a tree or a bird or a chipmunk or a car or anything else for that matter and get this really nice, warm feeling of appreciation?

Appreciation is the most powerful, when it becomes your basic approach to life. When you view living through the lens of appreciation, you can reap its immeasurable benefits. Appreciation, goes beyond the daily pleasantries of saying, "Thank you!"

You first have to be willing to overcome certain resistances to appreciation. For example, the reasons you give yourself, for why you shouldn't have to appreciate something, and/or why it won't work, or how appreciation is just too hard in this or that circumstance. The hardest thing for us to do, usually is appreciating someone, when they're not appreciating us. We normally think: "Why should I be the one to make the effort"? You have to be willing to change your thinking and feeling patterns that may stand in the way of being a full-time, hands-on, appreciator. You cannot use the power of appreciation only when it is convenient.

Most of the time, our first reaction is that of blame, denial, lashing out, avoiding - anything but appreciate. Then again, if you want to enjoy the full range of appreciation's benefits, you must release low frequency patterns of thinking and feeling, and replace them with appreciative ones.

Appreciation takes courage, and not everyone is courageous enough to take this path. Let's face it, when you choose thoughts of valuing and gratitude as your primary way of being, you are swerving off the road almost everyone else travels. You are saying no to blame, no to resentment, no to revenge, no to violence in any form, from bad-mouthing others to kicking a dog, and telling off a person. You are saying no to victim-hood, no to martyrdom, no to passing the buck, no to criticism, and no to humiliating yourself or others.

When you choose appreciation, you are saying "Yes" to being your own best friend, without becoming self-centred. You are saying "Yes" to seeing the best in everyone without being blind to their weaknesses. You are saying "Yes" to perceiving the greatest possible good in all situations, while being alert to what will or won't work for you. You are willing to stand up for yourself. You are willing to recognize and applaud what's good about yourself, what's good about others, and what's good about your life.

Appreciation takes guts. The good news is, it's doable, because everyone, without exception, is capable of appreciating, of finding value, and of being grateful. As a matter of fact, there is something you are grateful for right now. What is it?

No matter what is your current feeling of gratitude, you can increase and develop your ability to appreciate. Even when you commit to the practice of appreciation, you're going to find reasons not to appreciate this or that circumstance, and you're going to make up rationalizations for why you don't think you should appreciate, or why it's downright impossible, in certain situations. What you need to understand is that, when you start appreciating, you are sending out all these high frequency vibes, which will help you manifest more of whatever you desire, dream, love, and visualize. Appreciation will flood you with happiness.

When you first begin working with appreciation, it may seem as if the situation is getting worse, or not budging at all. The first thing to happen, when you begin to appreciate a loved one in the midst of a troubled relationship, may be that more arguments develop. What you may be missing is that the increase in arguments may provide opportunities for greater clarification of issues. When you commit to appreciating, no matter what, you have conquered one of the most challenging resistances.

When you look at people and events through the lens of appreciation, you increase the potential for good opportunities in your life. As Steven Covey notes in "The Seven Habits of Highly Effective People", you become "opportunity-minded" as opposed to "problem-minded". Once you begin to use the power of appreciation, more things, people and situations to appreciate make their way into your

204

life. Your today becomes very good, and your tomorrow full of even more joy. As Dr. Emmons writes in his article - The Joy of Thanks, "My colleagues and I are finding that gratitude, which we define as a felt sense of wonder, thankfulness, and appreciation for life, is more than simply a pleasant emotion to experience or a polite sentiment to express. It is, or at least can be, a basic disposition, one that seems to make lives happier, healthier, more fulfilling, and even longer."

You can easily figure out your level of current appreciation, by listening to what you say when someone asks: "How are you?" or "How's your day going?" Is your answer something like: "Oh, you know, OK for a Monday I guess." Or "Another day, another dollar." Or "barely hanging in there." Or "Boy, I could not believe the traffic today. It took me an hour to get to my last appointment." Or is it more like, "Excellent, thank you. I was lucky I got to my appointment in time, even though traffic was heavy."

The second response expresses an optimistic and appreciative view of life. Both responses acknowledge the traffic. Nevertheless, they send out a different type of vibration to the Universe. In an appreciative frame of mind, you don't deny what has happened, you just choose to perceive and interpret it in a positive or appreciative manner. You choose to see the benefits to you in the events and people that come your way, and you are thankful for them. The vibration of appreciation is the highest and the fastest vibration one can generate to manifest dreams.

# Relationships

*If you can feel it, you can have it.* Feel a great relationship and have it. Feel a lousy one and have it. Principle is the same.

I can hear you say: "Well, my case is different. How would you feel, if you had to live with this man or woman?" And then you will start counting all the bad things, or all the things that are bugging you about your relationship.

Tell me, what are you doing when you are telling me what is wrong with this person in your life? You are concentrating on everything that is bad or wrong about this person or relationship. Hello? Do you get it yet? Here is a trick to help you: when you are really mad at someone in your life, and you have been bitching and screaming about everything that is wrong, grab a hold of yourself for a moment. Sit down and write *anything*, absolutely *anything*, that you *like* about this person. See how your feelings and vibration all of a sudden change? You go from the low frequency feeling of anger and frustration, immediately to appreciation. Wow! This exercise would work even better if you could get the other person to do the same thing, at the same time. Before you know it, you are hugging each other, whispering tender words, apologizing and loving. Now that's it. Stay there. Stay in that feeling.


We are the sole creators of all experiences we have in our relationships. Not our partners, not our parents or relatives, not our mangers or supervisors at work. Take a look at your own energy flow to identify what is going right or wrong with all these relationships. If your partner has what you might consider a bad habit, and you are constantly getting mad over it, or concentrating on it; guess what you get? More of that same habit. You may think to yourself, "OK, I'm mad because my partner does not put the cap on the toothpaste after he uses it". You keep on concentrating on this, and the more you do, the worse you feel, and more low frequency energy you send out. You are going to ask, "So, how much worse can it get? He will still not put the toothpaste cap on"? And I say:

"Wrong. It can get far worse". Remember that the low frequency energies go out there and gather the other low frequency energies of the same wavelength and come back to you. This might mean a broken something, a car that won't start, a fender bender, a divorce, or you name it, depending on the frequency of the feelings you have sent out. The bigger the stir of emotions, the worse the outcome.

The culprit in all this is "blame". There is not a trace of high frequency energy that will flow through a thick cloud of blame. No way, not a chance! So, if you are with someone who does not want to change and you do, the universal law and physics *will* split you up, for sure. Start talking with your partner about what you want and why. Not about what you don't want and why. Then leave it to Universe. Either the partner will change and follow you in your dreams and desires, or you will end up following your own directions. Let it happen. Do not try to force your partner to change, because all you will get in return is more and more trouble. If it happens that he/she wants to do the same, then hurray, otherwise work on "*yourself*".

If you want it said differently, change your scenario, props and play. Let me give you an example: I know someone, very close to me, that constantly repeats to himself that marriage is a horrible thing. He keeps on saying that, if he ever breaks up with the woman that he is currently in relationship with, forget it, there will never be another. He also makes comments like: "If sex is all there is, then God should have placed female genitals on a tree trunk". Now, how do you think his relationship will be going, if he does not change this attitude? I have asked him this question many times. I have said, "If you are firmly holding onto all of this nonsense that you are holding in the back of your head, and you believe in it, how do you think your relationship is going to improve"? He always has this comeback: "Oh I'm not talking about the woman I'm with now. I'm talking *any* other woman". I don't think, after all the talks about focus and feeling, I need to repeat that this friend was walking himself right out of his favourite woman's life, do I? Yet when it did happen, he found himself blaming everything and anything, but his hidden beliefs and vibrations. He believed that everyone was conspiring to see that happen.

If he needed to get ahead and change this from happening, then he needed to change his play, he needed to change his manuscript. He needed to write a new manuscript and get rid of the limiting beliefs and NEVER allow anyone to recite another limiting belief into his subconscious. And believe me people do that, so often. We learn many limiting beliefs throughout our lives from well-intended friends, relatives, parents, teachers, associates, or even people you see only once in your lifetime - because you are buying something from them or selling something to them - the media, and the list goes on and on. It is your responsibility to see how these beliefs make you feel. If there is no joy generated in your heart when you repeat a phrase to yourself, then throw it away. It is just another hidden mental terrorist that you will take in and feed otherwise.

In the line of business that I am, whether it is health or life related, I have had a lot of people asking me how they can "help" this or that person. "My friend just lost his job, how can I help"? "My brother has cancer, how do I help"? My suggestion: Be careful. A helping hand is not always what it seems to be. Think about these questions for a second, and you will see that there is a lot of focus on the third party. The one that, according to you, "needs help".

You are building on other person's concern or pain and adding your own concern to it, which will send out a ton of low frequency energy, that cannot be good for either one of you. How *do* you help? First, you need to take care of your own feelings and put yourself in a "feel good" frame. Forget about other person for a minute. You need to flow high frequency energy out if you want to really help someone. Now, you can encourage, not ensure, that very same feeling in the person you are thinking about.

On the other hand, if you kept on thinking how awful it is for this person to be out of a job or to have cancer or any other thing, that lack-full vibration reinforces the lack-full vibration they are already in. Are you really helping them then? See them the way you want them to be.  Have a wonderful, positive, conversation with them, out loud, even if they are not around.  Direct the conversation towards this person's health and well-being; send them high frequency vibrations. *This* is how you help.  In other words, see the truth.  Granted, this other person may never find out what you have done for them, but *you do*.  Now, that's real help.  Aside from that, if they ask for help, then you can reach out and offer any help you physically can afford to give them.  Your physical and mental help must be congruent.


# Happy Relationships.....


How do you describe a perfectly happy relationship? I describe a happy relationship in a quality of communication you have as well as your level of acceptance.  Verbal, mental or otherwise.  Imagine living with a dog or a cat.  I am not going to change them; they are not trying to change me.  I am adorable the way I am and they are adorable the way they are.  I expect nothing of them, they expect nothing of me.  They give me unconditional love no matter what I wear or how silly I behave, and I do the same.  We have tremendous fun when we are out together. They don't embarrass me and I do not embarrass them, each on their own. My labels don't matter to them. I can be me and they can be them.  No masks to wear, no pretence, only pure love.

The dog does not try to show me how to play my side of the game and I do not try to show him his. We are always happy to see each other. If I have a lot of work to do and no time to play with the dog, the dog is happy to be by my side and let me be.  My dog will never insist on me engaging in an activity with him no matter what, and I will not insist on him engaging in play no matter what. My dog does not complain over mundane and simple things, and I do not complain about his muddy paws on the clean floors.  My dog does not blame me for how he feels and I do the same.

Here is the interesting part: most people have no problem having a relationship like this with their dog, but God forbid that happens between two humans. Why can't we allow man to be a man and a woman to be a woman and just accept them exactly the way they are. No expectations.

When you adopt a dog, do you ever think, "I expect you to make me happy?" Why do you expect that from another human being? You never think your dog is your "other half". You are complete without them and they are complete without you. There is absolutely nothing someone can do to make you happy or complete, if you are constantly miserable and lonely to begin with. Find your happiness first, before you hook up with someone. Your demand is an unreasonable one.

When it comes to choosing a mate, the question of the right man and the right woman comes up often. What is a right man or a right woman? I would summarize it so, that it is someone who is swimming in the direction you are going and not completely opposite to your direction. Someone whose views and values – emotionally, spiritually and physically - are compatible. The right man or the right woman for you is the one that you feel love towards exactly the way she or he is. Not the one that you will look at and say, "I don't like that, but it can change."

When you are adopting a dog, you never look and say, I wish he looked more like a cat. Oh well, it will change. There are millions of men and women out there. You can love them all, but most of the time there is one that will work with you like a key in a lock; that is called a match that works. When you find the match that works, treat them with trust, respect and love. Who will benefit out of this behaviour? Both. When you both become servants of love, unimaginable and unlimited possibilities open up to you.

Before getting into any relationship start loving yourself immensely. Here is why: imagine you are filled with love. You have love to offer to everyone and everything. Then one day you come across someone who tells you, "Look, I have all this love for you. I will give it all to you, only if you do what I say, and let me control you." What would be your reaction?

The other side of the coin is, when you have not built your self-love and this same person shows up and you are literally starving for love. You take the love they are offering and become their slave. Later even fearful in what if this person takes their love to someone else? What if he/she leaves me? I cannot live without him/her. And the devastating events follow.

People who are addicted to sex are those who are masking their love-starved beings through looking for glimpse of love that they might find in their moments with different people.

When you love yourself, your love will grow and attract more towards you. When you have love for yourself, you can be alone without a problem. When you have love for yourself you will never be bored or lonely. Please do not go out there shopping, while you are hungry because you end up with a lot of things that are neither needed nor good for you. This is a shopping tip that works for your diet as well as your relationships.

Your heart is magical. Open your heart. Refuse going around and begging for love, and ending up in abusive relationships. Be generous with your love towards all that are starving. What will make you happy is love coming out of you. Love without condition.

Every relationship has the potential to be wonderful or miserable; but it always is going to begin with you. Start being honest with yourself. If someone is holding love hostage, so that you first can cater to their needs and fetishes; run for your life.

Many enter relationships trying to find what they need in someone else; only to realize, it is not there either. Enter your relationships without need. You will find how different they are. Your perceptions will govern and rule your reactions to situations, hence causing a healthy or ill relationship.

If you can learn to control your assumptions, perceptions and reactions, you can change your life. You control your personal dream by making choices. Create a masterpiece of your life. If your beliefs are telling you that perfect relationships are myths and not possible, no amount of affirmations and visualizations are going to bring you closer to the person of your dreams.

When you start controlling your reactions, soon your eyes will see a different reality. Become a hunter. Hunt one routine reaction at a time inside you. Everyone in life has a price tag on them. This price tag is not monetary but measured in love. Actually it is measured in self-love. Your measure of love for yourself is your price. That is how you are going to trade yourself in the relationships, and how much you are going to stand for. Do not go out there looking for love bargains, because that is exactly what you will find in the garage sale of love. Life always respects your price. When your price is high, your self-abuse is low and vice versa.

Let's take our species out of the whole creation. Look at anything else but humans around. What sense of judgement do you have? Isn't everything perfect and beautiful? Isn't nature just perfection? Life does not need to be judged and justified.

Now try to put people back into this picture, but without the ability to judge. In this case nothing becomes, good, bad or ugly; everything just "is". You will never see a bunch of ants gathered in a corner busying themselves in idle talks, of which ant has done what and whether their actions are justifiable or not. Nor you will find any other creatures for that matter, with this attitude. If it allows peace in the nature, it will allow peace within us.

There is nothing in life more rewarding or challenging than a relationship. This could be at home, work, play or in love. Here is one thing that almost everyone misses, even though it is a very simple fact: The only common denominator in all of our relationships is "us".

What is your relationship with yourself? Are you at peace? The key to this of course is self-love. How do you start loving yourself? Only if you are authentic, genuine, and natural. These qualities will lead you to get to know yourself better, which of course will cause appreciation, acceptance and compassion.

Forget about all external things. No one else knows your soul as well as you do and the art that you have come here to create. To be yourself you need to listen to yourself and understand that you are the only ultimate authority on you. You are the CEO of your life! Behave accordingly.

Every little thing you think, do or say returns to you by the Universe exponentially. If you feel you are not heading in the right direction, you can always change direction, but you must realize the time factor in this time and space continuum. If you are flying a jumbo jet and want to turn around, it is going to require some time in doing so. You cannot be travelling at 600 miles an hour and decide to turn 180 degree on a dime. It will not work for you. And usually a pilot who is doing the turning will not get bored and say, "I give up. She ain't turning! It works for every other pilot but me."

Have faith in the delivery of the Universe. Just because you cannot see all that is happening behind the curtain, it does not mean that nothing is happening.

Accept all that you have done so far. You have only done your best given your understanding at the time. And everything you have done is the reason why you are where you are today and in the state of being that you are today. Accept and forgive yourself from anything you consider a mistake. There are never any mistakes, only what you chose to do at the time.

Never compare your experience to others because you don't know what they came here to accomplish. People that you have in your life and all of your relationships were your choices either directly or indirectly but never accidentally.

I know that the question of birth and the childhood dramas are now going to pop up, so let me make something simple for you. You did not start at the moment of your birth and you do not end at the moment of your transitioning. The energy that has manifested as the physical you, has always been and always will be. Yes you did choose your parents and yes you did choose your childhood experiences. Why? How would I know? If that was what you needed to experience, that is what you experienced.

If you believe that you begin and end here, then I can relate to the pattern of thought that you might be having in being a victim of circumstances. The point is, no matter how you chose to start this life, you always have the chance and the choice to change it to ANYTHING that you like right now!

So now, let me make one point about your Relationship with Universe clear. As we have talked about before, there are set rules under which the Universe operates in order for us to be able to function in this physical reality. For example you cannot ask your cat to change to a dog or vice versa. This violates our mass agreement as human beings. Now here is the twist: if you were to turn your cat into a dog or vice versa only for your own viewing and not for everyone to witness, agree and applaud your achievement, then knock yourself out because the option would be available.

When it comes to romantic relationships, by loving, honouring and understanding yourself, you extend this love to your partner and make the adventure sweeter for both. Now, our society's and cultural expectation is for people to be involved in some sort of romantic situation. They do not really consider whether the person is ready or not. This mass-assumption can prove to be hurtful to those considering themselves alone. Whether you are single or in between relationships, you need to realize that life affords you the times to just grow.

The other issue is that too often the relationships are measured by how long they last. Measure your relationship with love. How much love or fun did you have or are you having in your relationships? There is a great belief among us that says, "Great relationships withstand the test of time." Since when are the clock and the calendar measures of love, emotional growth or happiness?

It is a good idea to ask yourself a couple of questions before entering an intimate relationship:

1. Do you want a relationship because you want to hide from the opinion of others or blend with it?
2. Is the relationship meant to add to your happiness or create it?

Relationships do not make you happy, they only intensify what you are already feeling. Your partner like a mirror will reflect your attitudes towards life back at you. When in a relationship, if you feel in a rut, or as if you no longer need it, this is your soul yearning for a different interaction. You might have grown out of the boundaries of what is being reflected. And maybe, you are staring at a past picture, instead of the mirror and you are feeling frustrated. In other words, you are seeing what you were, and not what you are now.

The very first person that reflects you and becomes your mirror, you will feel good in their presence and see your true self once again as you are now. Do not fight this current and the flow. Allow the growth. Allow the relationship. Remember that no love is ever lost. We are eternal and timeless and so is our connection to one another. It is only our physical senses fooling us that something has gone out of our lives. The only thing that you feel hurting when a relationship ends, is your pride.

With the same token, it is futile and dishonest to enter or stay in a relationship under the perception that you will make the other happy in doing so. How often have you heard people say, "I just want to make you happy."

I am often puzzled by people trying to work on their "relationships" whereby they should be working on themselves, their perceptions and expectations. This applies to any relationship intimate or otherwise.

Here are some thoughts on your intimate relationships:

1. Shed all behavioural expectations you may have for your partner,
2. Dwell on what you think is right as opposed to what you think is wrong,
3. Do NOT assume and mind-read,

4. Let the other person love you in his or her own way – don't expect to be treated exactly as you treat them. People are unique and their expression-abilities are also unique,
5. Be compassionate in your communications – choose your words wisely or be silent. Complaints and criticism will never pay positive dividends,
6. Settle for not having the last word,
7. Communicate, communicate, and then some,
8. Accept full responsibility for your feelings.

At work the very first relationship you normally develop, is between you and the work itself. Everyone and everything else comes in at second place.

In your home relationships, be especially mindful of children. Do remember that they may be new to this plane of life, but that does not take away from their innate wisdom. Also remember that they are fellow adventurers and not just a smaller version of "you" who need to adhere to what you want them to. Whatever the child's unique personality, it is a part of the chemistry they have chosen to maximize the effects of this adventure and experience.

To understand and have better relationships in general, understand that all you come in contact with, is chosen by you. You before birth, and you now.

# Self-Fulfilling Prophecy

The concept of the self-fulfilling prophecy can be summarized in these key principles:

1. We form certain expectations of people or events.

2. We communicate those expectations via various vibrations.

3. People and/or circumstances tend to respond to these vibrations by adjusting own vibrations to match ours.

4. The result is that the original expectation becomes true and this creates a circle of self-fulfilling prophecies.

Here is a quote from a dictionary: "A self-fulfilling prophecy is a prediction that, in being made, actually causes itself to become true. For example, in the stock market, if it is widely believed that a crash is imminent, this may reduce confidence and actually cause such a crash. Self-fulfilling prophecy is sometimes seen as a manifestation of positive/negative feedback in human society. In short, because a given prophecy was known, and sounded sufficiently credible, it affected people's actions and caused itself."

Think about what I'm going to tell you for few seconds. What are doctors trained to do? Heal you. Sure, that is their aim. BUT as soon as they find out what is *wrong* with you. Yes, they do want to heal you. However, if they don't find something wrong, how can they make it right? The same as mechanics or many other business traits. Have you noticed that, when you go to a doctor even for a small checkup, you are either close to getting something or you have one foot in the grave? If your doctor told you that you have some pre-?!? condition and it is scaring the daylights out of you; just slow down, take a deep breath and see what is it that you are focusing on. The fear has completely taken over your feelings. The wrong emotions are stirred up and shaken, and you are heading towards what is normally called: self-fulfilling prophecy.

This illness will start soaring when you receive a diagnosis and, even more so, when you focus on it. Stop thinking about statistics of this disease that you have been given by your well-meaning friends, relatives, doctors and the media. No-one is doing this to us. If we are attracting negative things, we are vibrating negative feelings. We are co-creating at all times. And for God sake, never say: "I'm going to win this battle and I'm going to beat this thing". Please, pay attention. What are you focusing on when you say that? It certainly is not health. Defensiveness is nothing but negative energy.

I feel strongly, here is the place to repeat the mention of a textbook quote on the phenomenon of "placebo effect". "The placebo effect (also known as non-specific effect) is the name describing a phenomenon that patient's symptoms can be alleviated by an otherwise ineffective treatment, apparently because the individual expects or believes that it will work. Some of the best studies, are in the area of pain research. People can be conditioned to expect analgesia in certain situations. When those conditions are provided to the patient, the brain responds by generating a pattern of neural activity, that produces objectively quantifiable analgesia. Amazing! We of course cannot leave out the textbook description of "Nocebo effect". "The Nocebo effect", or the "adverse effect", is a result of negative expectations by the patient. Some patients who believe that they should be ill, can exhibit genuine symptoms. How does this work? Thoughts generate feelings, feelings generate emotions and Bam! You've got it…

Take a look at this example: it has often happened that, when you are talking about a certain type of food that you like, you mouth waters. Can you recall an instance? Why is this? This is because your brain does not know what is real and what is imaginary. So whatever it thinks is happening, is what will take place. If it thinks that you are having a sour lemon, it will immediately call for production of saliva, regardless of whether you were just *thinking* about the lemon, or actually had a piece.

For the Nocebo effect, someone goes to doctor, they are diagnosed with a terminal illness, with no cure in the horizon and given a certain expected life span, and they die exactly the day of. That is the Nocebo effect. You believe it, just as you believed the Placebo. In Placebo the person believed he/she will get well, in Nocebo they believed he/she will die. We are used to taking market statistics as our measure. So if 80% of people die yearly from a certain disease, when we get it, we immediately place ourselves in the 80% range and off we go. The bold individuals who dare to dream and be in the 20% heal and live for a very long time.

To me, statistics, is like asking: "what is the temperature outside?" and hearing the following answer: "statistics show that the average temperature at this particular time would be 67 degrees Fahrenheit." Does that actually tell you what the temperature is? So try not to depend on the stats and live your life as the beautiful unique creation that you are.

# What is Death?

I don't know for sure.  Maybe you have a clear idea?  This is how I see it. Let's imagine, you are an actor.  In order for you to play your role in an act, you put on a costume and give the performance of your life.  Once you come down from the theatre platform, what is the first thing you do?  Do you go home, bathe, eat, or sleep in that costume?  I bet not.  It would be quite an uncomfortable life.  OK, so you take the costume off.  What happens? Nothing.  You are still you.  Nothing changed.  You have just taken off your clothes and what was containing and covering you.  That's all.  Your higher self has simply "put on" your body, to act in this play we call life.  For the experience, and the fun of it.  When the thrill dies, it might take on another thing to do.  Just like an actor who will change roles and will not play in the same role the entire life of their career.   But it will not go away.  It can't.  It is pure energy.  You can't just kill off energy like that.  But even though you cannot kill it off, negative vibrations can kill off the physical body for sure.  And this is something we do and we are actually quite dedicated to.

So now, if you are focusing on the pre???? condition that you were diagnosed with, the negative emotions created from  respective feelings will disconnect you from your higher self so much so that your physical cells literally start to dry up from the lack of life energy.  Should this continue, healthy cells cannot be reproduced.  At this point, they end their physical existence and recycle themselves back into pure, clean, positive energy they were meant to be, and we go through an experience called: death.  This is only the end of what you know as your physical form, not *you.*

What I normally do, when I experience negative feelings, is that I take some time out.  I take my dog for a walk and I call these walks, "manifestation walks".  Throughout the walk, whether it is ten minutes or an hour, I focus on every single good thing in the world or in my life that I can think of.  I play out the talks for myself.  I lay out happy scenarios; I appreciate the way my dog wiggles her tail as she is walking while her ears flap up and down; I appreciate the beauty of nature and the silence around me, and focus only on  things that make me feel good.  Once I do this, I cannot help but feel positive vibes throughout the day.  It becomes pretty difficult to erase that silly grin off my face.


No matter how old you are, you can learn new tricks.  Old dog, young dog, whatever you feel you are, you have absolutely no reason not to change.  Don't make it a new year's resolution, make it right NOW resolution. New Year's Eve will only need to be another "NOW".

# The Evil Eye

As long as I remember, my parents, grandparents, neighbours, family, friends and associates were frightened by the "evil eye".

I would like to take a moment and examine what exactly is this phenomenon, which is being blamed for so many things going wrong in people's lives. Every race, religion and nation, in one way or the other, fears it, and has own remedies to ward off evil eye.

"Evil eye" is nothing more than a low frequency emotion, stirred by thoughts of envy, jealousy, or even extreme love. Yes, love. It is not just your neighbour or family giving you an evil eye, it can even be you, yourself. Some people will not accept admiring remarks, because they believe it may bring them bad luck or "evil eye". So, when you praise them, or anything of theirs, in any way, they will down-play it and say: "Oh, it's really nothing. I've had it for years". What they are really trying to achieve by this maneuvering, is to take "your" focus and attention away from themselves, or the praised item. How is this item affected? Well, let's say you are feeling exceptionally well and happy. Then you meet this person in a store, or someone pays you a visit, and they give you a compliment like: "You look so good and happy today". Once a person leaves, you suddenly don't feel that great anymore and depending on the energy that was spent on you, you might even fall sick. Then your children come home and say: "What happened? When we left you this morning, you were feeling all happy and good." Your answer: "Oh I met this person who gave me an evil eye and I became ill; I forgot to take my amulet with me today." What really happened was that this person saw you, absolutely adored how happy and lively you were and maybe, just maybe, behind that happiness and love a little feeling of envy was poking at them saying, "I wish I felt like this." That feeling of envy, sent the low frequency vibes out, and hit you like a ton of bricks, without either of you even realizing what was really happening.

The intensity of the energy sent, varies depending on the person sending it, and also the intensity of the feeling behind it. There are a variety of remedies, suggested by many, to "cure" or ward off evil eye. In my opinion, a little bit of common sense can save you from a lot of low frequency energy. The reason an energy of any kind might hit you, is if you are open and available to accept it. When your mind is preoccupied and you are not experiencing the moment of NOW, you are leaving yourself susceptible to any energy. Being aware is the key. It is like if you are crossing the road and not paying attention, you are susceptible to being hit by a car; whereas if you are conscious of your action, and in the moment you cross when the timing is right, hence no casualties.

Here is what I can suggest: typically, whenever you are affected by any energy, be it low or high, you are operating at subconscious level, as opposed to conscious. This is one state of operation that I consider taboo, IF you would like to be in control of your life. Please DO understand that, when you operate at the level of subconscious, many things happen to you that you do not realize. One example would be your daily habits. There are many things that you do during a day, that if someone asked you to explain how, you would have extreme difficulty remembering. I have even seen people driving from home to work, yet later having NO recollection of how they got there. Probably, you had that same experience once or twice. This is the most dangerous state you can be in. You are completely open to any energy, control, subliminal suggestions, etc…. just to name a few.

In a state like this, someone may give you a praise maliciously – trying to send off low frequency vibes, or quite innocently. In either case, if you are not ready to receive this energy, you are completely susceptible to be hit by it. As you know, low frequency energies are against the frequency rate of our higher self, and accepting such energy without awareness, can be quite detrimental to our lives and health. All this said, I would suggest that, if you want to ward off any negative results of any suggestions, projections, etc., you must live at the level of consciousness, at all times. BE AWARE of your surroundings, feelings and emotions. If you feel someone is trying to send you low frequency energy, just shower yourself with love in your thoughts and visualize a wall of love protecting you. In the meantime, offer a vibration of love to the person you are protecting yourself from. No amulets, no beads, nothing. Only your emotions and feelings will protect you. If, at the time you are receiving these energies, you feel scared, or are thinking to yourself, "what if (s)he is giving me an evil eye?"; you have then sabotaged yourself. So, SIMPLY BE AWARE.

Being aware is not only physical awareness of what you are doing, it is also the understanding WHY you are doing the things you are doing. For example, next time you talk to someone, or behave a certain way, or do something, ask yourself, "Why did I choose to do this the way I did?" This exercise will definitely keep you in awareness state.

Some of us, regardless of education, suffer from superstition. All different kinds of it. You won't do certain things at certain times, and if this or that happens it will be good (or bad) luck. There are certain shirts we wear to important events, you have this lucky underwear that you have never washed, and on and on. Let me give you another type of superstition. Imagine you are wearing a green shirt and I see you and say, "Wow! That shirt looks great on you. I think this is the best colour for you. I know people who wear this colour for its good luck effects, and as a matter of fact I think you should consider buying a lottery ticket while in this shirt. If I were you, I would wear this shirt more often." Well, I have obviously given you some very good feedback, and made you feel good in this shirt; but also cast a spell on you! From that day on, this shirt is going to carry completely different energy for you. You might even consider it sacred and wear it only on special occasions.

Do you see how your mind got corrupted with just a few simple remarks? Do you see how I made a plain shirt rule you? What if something should spill on this shirt or it burns under the iron? Do you realize the psychological effects of this bond that I created for you? This is just the same when we carry stones, amulets, rabbit's foot or

224

anything else for good luck.  It is time to realize that it is us, and our emotions, that manifest our good lucks and bad lucks.  Nothing else!

To cure, or rid yourself from various effects of low frequency energy, all you have to do, again, is to spend some time in your happy thoughts and send yourself some joyful energy and love.  No baths, no teas, no rituals, no incents.  JUST YOUR FEELINGS.  *Everything* is dependent on *your* feelings.  By feeling vulnerable, you *allow* other people's energy to harm you.

# Astrology

What do you think Astrology is all about?. Fate? Luck? Things you can't change? That little blurb of horoscope in the newspaper? No!! None of the above!

Today, astrology is predominantly defined as a view at how human personality and behaviour, can be conditional to the position of the sun, moon and other planets etc. Astrologers generally believe, that a person is born at a time when his/her soul is in harmony with the astrological energies, present synchronously, in the Solar system. Because of this divine correspondence, the science/art of astrology has been researched and practiced for thousands of years, in many different cultures. Astrology is based strongly on probabilities. Generations of astrologers have studied the planetary cycles, drawn conclusions from repetitive occurrences, and used this knowledge for their interpretations.

It is important to mention, the ever-popular horoscopes found in magazines, newspapers etc., are usually, strongly generalized predictions, and are based *only* upon the sign of the zodiac, that the Sun was in, when a person was born. Even though the Sun is important in the birth chart, it is only one of many indicators of a personality. The so-called sun-sign astrology, mostly serves entertainment purposes, because, of course, there are more than twelve different types of people in the world.

So what is Astrology? First off - Astrology is not so much a form of fortune telling, but rather a tool for self-discovery. Real Astrology, helps you understand yourself better. It invites you to examine your strengths and strengthen your weak spots.

As we all know, Earth is a planet. But there are also other planets. Our solar system is one of countless solar systems in the Universe, all of which, are parts of the gigantic whole and accordingly related.

There is a spiritual "something", a psychic "something", an intellectual "something", an astral "something", and a physical "something", in every planet. Planets are not just physical things, any more than we are just bodies. Look at the function of Sun, as far as we understand it. The Sun is the life-giver to our solar system. The Sun shines, on all the planets, but each planet, according to its conditions, will receive it differently. The Moon, the nearest significant planet to Earth, also influences us, both physically and psychologically.

So, all the planets, in one way or the other, have their direct effect on us. The influence of one planet, over another, is dependent on the angle of its position. The planets influence us, just as other people influence us, in our daily lives. We seem to hold a lot of mistaken ideas, about what we are, and what we believe to be "external" circumstances that create our present state. That is not true. It is neither the conditions, nor the circumstances, but the attitude we hold towards them, that matter. Our true attitude, held with regard to our own nature, gives us the power to survive any influence whatsoever. Neither good nor evil can come to us, unless there is good or evil within ourselves. If we are good, no evil can touch us. If we are evil, then, for the time, no good can touch us. Everything is within ourselves. It is ALL about you! If we deal the same hand to two people in gambling, one will lose and the other win. The same is true with life. Some see trouble, and some see opportunities. We *are not* the victims of circumstances, we *make* ourselves the victims.

The planets, just like other physical beings, are made of energy. They can, very much, affect our physical being, since they have larger energy (mass) as opposed to our bodies. However, we are also influenced by our higher-self, which of course has an energetic field far larger than any planet will carry. So yes, the moon does have an effect on our body, hence the word "lunatic". Our body is mostly made of water. In a same way that moon or any other planet may have an influence on the ocean to rise, they can have an effect on our body. The interesting part is that when you are in touch with your higher self, none of these really affect you. Yes, the location of planets can tell you what may be coming your way, but the decision to allow it or not is completely up to you.

Regardless of the larger patterns across generations and continents at work, we always have an ability to control our responses to circumstances. If "character is destiny" meaning that, as we make our character we make our destiny, then obviously we are in charge of our own fate, regardless of external fleeting circumstances. As one who is dedicated to understanding "the crossings between fate and free will", I have found only four things to be "destined" in this world: to be born when you were, where you were, to the people you were born to, and under what circumstances. Everything else in life is a product of free will. Even the time of our death is determined by what path in life we choose to take.

We are copies of this amazing Universe. Each one of us is connected with every other being. If we understand ourselves, we can be in harmony with all the rest. This would mean that any influence coming our way, could be used to do good for others and ourselves. In such case, there are no influences that can bring us either luck or misfortune, only our own emotions.

I do agree that the planetary influences enhance our tendencies; but there is no "Source Energy" above, to force us, and there is no possibility of us being pushed into following any particular tendencies, unless we want to be pushed. If we make up our minds, not to be influenced, then we cannot be; and we simply do not follow those tendencies. So, you make another kind of birth possible. We don't even need to try to "be good". All we have to seek is "do good". When you "do good", you are good. Each one of us is absolutely and unconditionally responsible for the condition in which we find ourselves. When we blame the planets for the conditions we are in, we are blaming the water for drowning a man.

There is nothing in astrology that compels you, to be defeated, or to be a victim of a circumstance. As an example, a dear friend of mine who is quite knowledgeable in the art of astrology, told me that couple of weeks back, we were experiencing "Mercury retrograde". Any retrograde is a slowing of the planetary motion, relative to its average speed. During this period, motion of the planet gradually decreases in speed, to a point of maximum slowness, then gradually increases in speed again over time of normally three weeks. In the case of Mercury retrograde, people speak of periods that interfere with communication. Informal communications, like writing, speaking and interviews are supposed to be affected, as well as electronics.

We will, most often, find misunderstandings between people at this time. So, normally, they would say: while Mercury is in retrograde, don't give a party; be extra aware of what you say and what you interpret, when chatting with or writing to friends; cut back on errands; and expect that the check will be in the mail longer than usual. While all of this is completely true to that science, I still have a firm belief that, once you know how this planet or any other planet may affect you, you CAN change the situation to your advantage, IF you are in touch with your higher self. Remember: if you know anything fully, then you can manipulate it.

In my opinion, there is no absolute time of ease or absolute time of difficulty. Each person has a unique situation. Just because everybody else is having a difficult time, doesn't mean you will. Your emotions – not anything else - rule your life, or better said: make your destiny.

# Mirror, Mirror on the Wall

I have noticed that, at times if I have been critical of anyone, it was because they were simply reflecting back to me a problem within me that I had not noticed! Which brings me to think to myself: have I been that way to someone? And the truth of the matter is, 99% of the time, the answer is: Yes! Become aware of this the next time you dislike someone's attitude towards you. Be honest inside yourself and you will see what I mean. So, next time you are a subject of someone's verbal attack, simply note his/her anger without feelings in any way attached to it. Let their anger flow through you like going through a sieve. Then, thank them for pointing out what bothered them! It is important to detach yourself from the situation, because that way you will not experience frustration, anger or despise, but rather the feeling of compassion. On the other hand, when we appreciate certain quality someone shows, we do that because we have those qualities in us.

Point to Remember: When we judge and label others, we actually label our own qualities, which we have learnt to suppress.

I am reminded of a Japanese folktale that I read some time ago about the house of 1000 mirrors. Long ago in a small, far away village, there was a place known as the House of 1000 Mirrors. A small, happy little dog learned of this place and decided to visit. When he arrived, he bounced happily up the stairs to the doorway of the house. He looked through the doorway, with his ears lifted high and his tail wagging as fast as it could. To his great surprise, he found himself staring at 1000 other happy little dogs with their tails wagging just as fast as his. He smiled a great smile, and was answered with 1000 great smiles just as warm and friendly. As he left the House, he thought to himself, "This is a wonderful place. I will come back and visit it often." In this same village, another little dog, who was not quite as happy as the first one, decided to visit the house. He slowly climbed the stairs and hung his head low as he looked into the door. When he saw the 1000 unfriendly looking dogs staring back at him, he growled at them and was horrified to see 1000 little dogs growling back at him. As he left, he thought to himself, "That is a horrible place, and I will never go back there again." All the faces in the world are mirrors. What kind of reflections do you see in the faces of the people you meet?

In childhood, some of us sang this song: "I'm rubber, you're glue, and whatever you say bounces off me, and sticks to you". We subconsciously knew the other kids were attacking us, while really talking about themselves. We just didn't know we knew. We merely knew this song would make them go away. What we were doing, was "mirroring". We were holding up a mirror to their face and they had to run away because they didn't like what they were seeing. Well, the concept hasn't changed, and neither have our reactions.

Let's fast forward now, to the state of adulthood that you are in. The one thing you should have changed, is the running away part. As adults, we can benefit from each other as mirrors. We need to learn to appreciate a "reflection" as a constructive encouragement. While our background, experience, and circumstances, shape who we are, we are responsible for who we have become. Realize that our strongest mirrors, are those closest to us - particularly in relationships. Because we're each other's mirrors, what we mirror for each other, are likely the very things that become relationship issues. Why? Because we forget that we already know this "I'm rubber, you're glue" concept. Rather than seeing our partner as someone reflecting what we truly need to see, and because we never learned how to stay and "communicate", we do the "human nature" thing - we either fight or flight, instead of looking *in* the mirror, or we verbally/emotionally attack our partner, while using lecturing as our defence mechanism. I think we need to change our songs to: "I'm glue, you're rubber", to realize and accept we're all each other's mirrors.

We need to learn and see our relationships as accurate mirrors that they really are. They are quite revealing in, where we need to go with our own inner process. We can learn so much about ourselves that would otherwise be next to impossible.

Nowadays, we tend to form relationships of different kinds, in order to satisfy our needs for love, companionship, security, stimulation, sexual fulfillment, financial stability, and so on. We are only concerned with an external form of a relationship we are building. And because relationships are formed for the above "specific" reasons, we try to control them the way we want. We try to change the other person to what we think we should have gotten to begin with.

Our relationships, with other people, are a good measure in reflecting exactly where we are in our own process of spirituality. Any, and every relationship in our lives, with our friends, co-workers, neighbours, our children and other family members, as well as our primary partners or even a stranger, can be a mirror reflection. This kind of relationship, where we are aware of the mirroring effect, can be quite a valuable source of both, healing and learning. We draw to us, and are drawn to people who match and reflect some aspect of ourselves.

Dr. Wayne Dyer had a really good analogy he put across in his book. He said, "When you squeeze an orange, you will get orange juice. When you squeeze a lemon you get lemon juice. What would I get, if I squeezed you now?? Anger, jealousy and hatred or kindness, love and compassion?" Isn't that beautifully put? I would add to this, that whatever you can squeeze out of you, is what you have attracted in your relationships with others.

I will continue this subject by telling you a recent story about myself. After being employed with a large corporation and working with many wonderful managers - for about six years, and being considered an exceptional performer year after year - I inherited a new manager. The reason I say "I inherited" is that there was a change in the layers of the organization and I became one of those managed by this lady. As the time passed, she became VERY critical of me. Nothing I did, seemed to satisfy her anymore. If I prepared a presentation and drew slightly longer cosmetic graph line, she called the document "inaccurate". We talked many times and it seemed as if we are not getting anywhere and finally she threatened to lay me off since, according to her, I was not producing "accurate" documents.

Seeing the documents I produced were 100% accurate, she started to engage idle workers to constantly distract me, burden me with unnecessary tasks and questions while I was working on documents, in hope that I would make an error she could later use as "evidence" of her claims. I simply could not understand what the problem was, so I started sharing my story with anyone and everyone, to see what it that I was doing wrong was. I spoke to family, friends, colleagues, past managers, her manager, her past manager, human recourses and even "Employee Assistance Program," to hear all of them unanimously say: "You are not doing anything wrong and she is just being jealous and nit-picking." This did not resolve my issue and I was later laid off from my job. The day she was giving me my papers to be escorted out of organization, I had a realization. "Oh my God. How blind could I be? She was me." At that particular time in my life, I had a partner, which I picked on everything he did. I didn't like this and I didn't like that. She was reflecting back to me at work what I was doing to him at home.

I could have avoided all the aggravations by simply realizing that, months ago. For this very reason, when I shook her hand and she said, "I'm sorry that it had to end this way," I replied, "I'm not. I truly think that you were an angel in my life and you pushed me in a direction that I would have never realized without you." I truly meant it. But she could not grasp it, and I believe she actually thought I was patronizing her. To this day, I hope one day, she realizes that I really meant what I said. She was my mirror. She opened up my eyes to what I was doing wrong. What better friend can you ask for in life? I can bet you that if you squeezed me then, you would get: "nothing you are doing is right" juice!!!

How many times have you heard of couples that break-up or divorce saying: "we grew apart"? I say: "nonsense"! Consider everything I have said about a mirror to be true and you will see: they didn't grow apart, they just didn't grow together. Their "internal" attitudes changed at different times, the "phase" difference in growth, causing different "reflection", so, a need to "attract" a different mirror. Should a couple have remembered the "I'm rubber, you're glue" song and "communicated", they might have learned to grow together.

I think the most powerful thing you can do when you are having difficulties in your relationships – whether at work or at home - is to accept the idea that you yourself attracted this person into your life, to learn a lesson about yourself and to create an opportunity to heal and grow. Often those we have difficulty with or dislike, and those who create difficult situations or feelings for us, are there because they are a reflection of some part of ourselves that we need to heal. We often do not recognize our own dark sides and need to use the situations we create for ourselves in the outer world, as ways to look into our own inner self. You can use such situations in a way that will allow you to heal.

Accept the possibility that you may have, some of the qualities or behaviours this person has, but perhaps you have disciplined yourself not to express them or show them - at least not openly. If you can do this and discover a part or parts of yourself that are similar to him/her, and if you can accept these parts of yourself, as simply being a part of what it means to be a human being, then you will be able to get close enough, to the parts within yourself, to help them heal. Once you begin this process of healing yourself and especially the acceptance part, you will be able to speak with, and even work with, this person with greater ease. Your entire attitude towards him/her will change, and it will be much easier for you to interact with this person in a friendly and healing manner. Remember, our main responsibility is to heal ourselves.

The moral to this whole section is: Don't be judgmental of anyone else! And if you must find a fault, beware that the same quality is in you. Ideally, we will see more positive qualities in others as we develop our own positive qualities. To learn everything about yourself, make a list of everything you dislike in others.

234

# Circular Thinking

"Did we not talk about this, at least ten times before and came up with an answer?" I asked him angrily. "This is the first time we ever talk about it." He answered back. It seemed to me as if nothing ever was getting through to him. Same subjects surfaced over and over again and, no matter how we were arriving to answers, I could almost be sure that it was going to come back again.

Some people are just like that. Although they ask you a question, they have already made up their mind, in what the answer is supposed to be, and when you give them a different response than they are willing to hear, they come back to the same subject over and over again, until they hear something close to what they originally intended to hear. When they encounter a problem, they are swept into a twister thinking. Their thoughts spin, twirl and whirl around in their brain, seldom under control and rarely productive.

If you are stuck with a nasty problem, or question, that goes in circles in your head like a spinner, you are caught in what is known as "circular thinking."

Circular thinking is a habit of repeating old problems, without a solution in sight. Soon the habit will make you physically fatigued and mentally worn-out. Circular thinking always occurs when someone lives on autopilot – meaning through his or her subconscious instead of being conscious. They sometimes genuinely do not remember that they have already talked about the issue, or they have already been suggested an answer.

Circular thinking is an ineffective way to problem resolution. It takes up all of your energy without invigorating you, and will, eventually, lead to depression. It certainly causes havoc in what you attract to your life.

People in a habit of circular thinking, may begin to worry about money, and are then sucked into their usual, routine, thinking about finances. Round and round they go, thinking in circles about poverty. Or, perhaps, they are concerned about health. Into that tornado of illness thinking, they are drawn right away. The same old thoughts, the same old fears, the same old channel… I have seen them think about one subject for hours and then, when they finally think they are over it, they think about it some more. An example of this was when a friend of mine went to a bank to open up an account. The lady at the bank was less than kind and he finally left without finishing the job and, all day long and many days after, he invested his thoughts and energy into that incident.

Those with circular thoughts, reel around in habitual hurricanes of their minds. What they do not realize, is that <u>old thoughts do not bring new solutions</u>. Even less they realize, that they are frustrating those who are not living in the same circular style. They hardly ever finish a project, either because they were too preoccupied with something else, or simply could not come to a resolution on *how* this project must end.

In the story that I started at the beginning of this section, what I found absolutely amazing was this: since I would be aggravated following this type of conversation, the person would turn around and blame it on something or someone else by saying, "Oh my God. Do you not see how this guy set the stage again, so that I get into another fight with you?" I have found that people who practice circular thinking are, most of the time, prone to victim consciousness as well.

If you are to be a co-creator, you *must* live consciously. Would it not be funny if the creator – call it God, Source Energy or anything else – kept on forgetting that they have already created, let's say a cat, and did it over and over again? Few suggestions that I can give you, are: Keep aware of what you think at all times and live in a conscious level. Be aware that you're in it. This is a very important step. Be kind to yourself. You need to realize that, in order for your mind and thought to be productive, it needs rest. Insert moments of silence throughout the day. Clear your mind, and shut out all thoughts, whenever you find yourself spinning on anything. You are spending too much of your precious energy, on "circular thinking". Try to find ways to stop this fruitless waste of time. Try to remember, when was the last time you had that same thought, and whether or not someone said something about it or offered a solution. If so, re-listen to the solution in your head. It might be different from what you wanted to hear, YET, a solution. There is, most of the time, more than one way of getting from here to there. When a room is dark and you want to see better, what do you do? Do you push the darkness away, or do you bring the light in? The second, of course. Therefore, instead of trying to stop your circular thinking, welcome distractions. Bring the light in.

Remember Tarzan? This is when I want you to find your inner Tarzan. Remember how he could fly from tree to tree high above the jungle, high above the quicksand and wild animals and other snaring dangers on the ground?

Try to be Tarzan in your thoughts for the next while. Imagine the most beautiful tree you have ever seen. Up at its top, is a new awareness, an awareness that holds the perfect solution. Stand up and say, "I am Tarzan in a jungle of my thoughts." Then imagine yourself, at the very top of your solution tree. Enjoy the view. Begin swinging on the trees through complete awareness. You will swing from a health tree to a wealth tree; and from a self-expression and creativity tree to a relationship tree. They ALL hold golden nuggets of solution. Up there, you are away from any danger of quicksand thinking, or man-eating worries. Swing, fly, and ascend into the soaring heights of awareness.

If your dilemma tries to pull you down to the ground of anxiety, worry and fear, smile and say, "I KNOW the answer is not down there. I am staying up here."

# Ego

Have you ever heard people say, "I do not have an ego, I have dealt with mine and got rid of it"? I say: "Hogwash". As long as you have any beliefs, and we always have beliefs, we have ego. You could train your ego, but could not get rid of it. Ego exists as one's illusion of being separate from everything else. Ego is the part of a person who's always comparing, the part who feels either superior, inferior, inadequate, or deprived. It is the one who grips and resists, who sees oneself as the subject and everything else as objects.

Have you ever thought that what makes you live, is also within your partner, cat, dog, tree, table and so on? You are just packaged differently. You share the same essence. There are many of us on the face of the Earth, and we don't look the same but we still are all one. How did we ever start believing that we were separate? Could it be that such belief is reinforced though years of conditioning? Could the conditioning be divide and conquer? Have we not gathered the same beliefs about our nationality, race or religion? Have we not been separated that way? All our religions dictate that if we follow this line of belief, we go to heaven and everyone else burns in hell. So what about people who were there before this particular religion came about? Obviously, they are going to be told: "Sorry. You're out of luck. You were born at a wrong time. Hell it is for you."

Usually, the amount of suffering we experience through our ego, when we are wrong, is directly related to the amount of joy we get out of being right.

Ego causes more fights, than almost anything else. It often comes from a desire to be more than we are, yet having an insecure feeling about ourselves at the same time. Thus, this often leaves us having a list of things to "prove" to others and ourselves, and with a need to be right. Ego is usually completely resistant to change. Once you learn how to deal with ego's resistance to change, your chances for success greatly improve.

Ego's main function normally is to help maintain the reality we have chosen, by getting rid of any ideas or suggestions that don't fit. We all have an ego, and ego takes its job very seriously. It is a matter of life or death for it, so it cannot allow you to simply be flexible and change your mind about things. In order for your ego to be successful in its job, you must retain the same old beliefs.

The next time you get into a disagreement with someone, recall what happened when you had a previous argument that ended poorly. You probably felt misunderstood and unappreciated, even if you got your way. Or, did you agree to the other person getting their way, because you wanted to end the argument? As you analyze the previous experience, notice what your attitude was, when you realized you had different points of view. Was it your intention to learn something about the other person's viewpoint, or just to prove a point of your own? Now, take an honest look at how the disagreement ended. How did you feel towards the other person? How did that person react to you? It may not be easy for you to be truthful. The ego makes it hard for a lot of us. But, until you are willing to risk the possibility, that your ego may have led you off track, you are less likely to have the kind of relationships you really want, especially if you desire closeness and intimacy.

To change this scenario to a friendlier one, and to be prepared, should you have a disagreement again, pretend that the other person is seated at a table across from you. Visualize the conclusion to the argument you had with them, dangling in the air. Now, pretend that you are leaving this situation, and going to another room where you will be alone. Did your ego follow you? I bet you, at this point your ego was dying to rehash the argument and give you additional ammunition to prove the other person wrong. Take a very deep breath and exhale slowly through your mouth, as though you're blowing gently on a candle flame without putting it off. This can be your way to release some of the tension, ego has created, and to acknowledge your willingness to look at the situation in a more objective way. Now, tell your ego to be quiet. You can ask this with complete authority and very firmly. Remember that your ego loves coming back and rehashing old arguments.

Take a moment to collect your thoughts. Notice the fears and insecurities stirred up in both of you, by this argument. What is it you want?  Most of the time, we want to have things like respect, understanding, love, give-and-take and easy companionship in our relationships and dealings. Which one of these qualities did you see in danger through this disagreement? Once you are clear about this answer, imagine going back to the room where the other person is sitting. As you take a seat, pretend you place on the table - right there between you – an image of the quality that you were looking for in this relationship. In fact, you can't see the other person without also noticing this image of respect, understanding, wholeness and love. With the image on the table between you, imagine you say something like this:

> "It doesn't feel good to have our disagreement end as it did. I want to return to the topic, to explore how my opinions and the way I presented them, affected you, and why you believe as you do, because you surely must have good reasons for your position, just as I have good reasons for mine."

Or, imagine saying something else in this line to convey your intention, which is to let the other person know, you want to learn from your disagreement.

It is possible, of course, that the other person may refuse to discuss the topic. However, even if the other person is not open to help you learn, and your relationship does not survive, you would have discovered a great deal. Learning about yourself is <u>never</u> a waste of time or energy. What you learn can be used in future relationships.

If you keep in mind what you want from a relationship and work on "controlling" your ego, you will have a good chance of having warm, loving friendships.

Also, take a look and see, how open you are to changes in your life. I recon, those of us who are open to change, and accept and embrace change easily, are those who have trained their egos to work with them and not against them.

# The Outer and Inner Worlds….

If you see something in your life that is not quite going the way you like, you will need to tweak the inner you. The way that I can explain this is: every morning before going out the door there are few rituals that you do. You will look into the mirror to see if your hair is okay, and if your complexion is looking right and if you are a man, you probably will shave to look clean and if you are a lady, you probably apply a bit of makeup to feel good.

Now, once you have done this, and you are taking a last look in the mirror before you leave, you do not actually reach out and put lipstick on the lips that are reflected in the mirror or comb the hair you see in the mirror or shave the mirror do you? The same is true in the world around you. You need to change yourself to change the reflection.

When we look at the material abundance in our lives and we feel the abundance or lack thereof, why would you run around trying to manipulate the things externally before fixing your own beliefs? You need to turn inwards and change your thoughts, emotions, beliefs and perceptions and words before anything externally is going to change.

When you see people running around and trying to achieve things on the external level first, this is because they think that the physical comes before their thought. When you start desiring something physically, remember that it is not your job to figure out the details. Your job is to "desire" for the sake of creating a different flavour of this experience. The Universe is your supply not the dollar bills. Let the Universe decide what vehicle to use to bring you what you desire. The physical steps that need to be followed, usually are not many, when you leave the hard work to Universe. In order to fix your internal world, you would need to gain internal harmony. Internal harmony starts by acceptance. If something is rattling your cage, fighting it, won't make it go away. "Accepting it", and I will even go as far as, say trying to have fun with it, will. The second step in coming to harmony is the understanding that events that happen in your life are only, and only for your benefit. If you have had a desire, then the Universe is rearranging things to see it happen. See the events for what they are. Things are almost never what they seem to be.

The most important step in my mind is to stop asking how. "How", is what delays your desire from manifesting, causes havoc and diminishes your faith. Try not to figure out how to get things.

When we feel as if we need to control everything in this life, we try to ask many "how's". This is generally what gets us into trouble. As strange as it sounds, not knowing how, will get you to your desire faster. By getting rid of the "how" factor, you are also freeing yourself from worry, anxiety and stress and opening your mind to many possibilities presenting themselves. In this, not only you have a healthier body but also your thoughts and emotions are that of focus and faith.

Ground yourself in truth as much as you can in understanding that your natural state is a state of abundance, health and overall prosperity and harmony. You are a miracle. You are prone to succeed. The cards are stacked in your favour in all areas of life. Embrace these simple truths.

# Achieving Goals

In achieving any goal in life, large or small the very first thing to keep in mind is the level of self-confidence you have. Without this one ingredient, you will not be going too far and if you do actually manage to go ahead, you will either give up, or once you get to the goal, it will prove to be non-lasting and end up in some type of disappointment or the other.

Many of us go around in our life searching outwardly to "find ourselves" and find our "purpose in life". Many of us even give up everything we have and travel to distant locations such as India and Tibet in search of these; where the answer has been with us all along.

We come here to this physical reality as an angel with a message. What is the message? You! A messenger in a physical form from the non-physical realm, with everything you need preprogrammed. You come from non-physical and at the end you will return to this non-physical.

As a new born, you are completely aware of what you like or don't like; and when you don't like something, you make it very evident. You are following your preprogrammed instincts of being happy, joyful and loving and you avoid all that is going to distance you from them.

As you start maturing, you start learning the labels for everything in order to be able to communicate with your species. Everything has a name, a symbol and a label. The more of these labels you learn, the less attention they will get from you. You used to look at a tree with fascination before you knew its name, but now, a tree is a tree is a tree; or it is a "beautiful" tree, "ugly" tree, or "scary" tree.

In a few years, you have learned the name for everything. The ones who came before you created those names and agreed on them.

Now you are buying into this agreement. We call this knowledge; and as the years go by we gather more and more of it. We learn what is "right" and what is "wrong" and what is "acceptable" and what is "not acceptable". What we "should" do and what we "should not" do. We learn all the agreements of the society we are born into.

The catch phrase in the above paragraph was, "the society we are born into."

When we are born in North America we learn only what applies here, the labels, names, behaviour, etc. The trouble is that these same things mean nothing elsewhere in the world. An "elevator" is only meaningful if you are speaking English in North America. If you say this label somewhere with a different language or dialect, it means nothing. The very behaviour that you might find offending in one country maybe quite acceptable in another.

With the same token your values and beliefs are based on the agreement of one society; and according to that same agreement, you judge the entire life on the planet.

Everything we learn is based on attention. If you do not pay attention to what I say, I cannot teach and you cannot learn. Everything about learning and teaching is based on attention. So you first start paying attention when you are very little to those who are playing a role in supporting you – your mom and dad.

They have you as the captive audience. Using this, they teach you how your physical reality should look like and they give you all the previously agreed-upon names, labels, laws, etc.

First we learn the labels and then we attach the meanings to them, so that we can make sense out of our communication. At this point of the period of babyhood – non-verbal but instinctive communication – is over. We are no longer innocent. This is when we start learning about perfection and everyone drills into our head, "oh well, we cannot be perfect, we are only human." From the point of view of any religion or spirituality this is pure blasphemy; out of pure victim consciousness! But not something I would like to get into details of right now.

Every single thing in this Universe is perfect. The consequences of hearing the lie that we are not perfect sets us up in searching for perfection and continuous judgement. We keep searching and we find in our search that everything is really perfect except us – because we call ourselves imperfect. The sun, the stars, the trees, the flowers, the animals, the insects and everything else is absolutely perfect. Even those of us with a disability are perfect in their disabilities.

Everything about us is perfect. But just saying this is not enough. The true belief in this agreement is necessary.

With our attention on the labels, we are gathering knowledge and we are allowing this knowledge to take over our mind and thoughts. As our knowledge expands we learn how to dress, how to look, what weight is acceptable, what lifestyle is enviable, what car carries a better image, what kind of profession will bring respect and so on......

We allow others through their agreements to tell us what we should or should not be, do or have and this seems completely acceptable. Never for a moment do we question our own uniqueness. We listen to all the opinions of others around us and we surrender and try to satisfy all.

This is when we lose ourselves and we start searching for something called "perfection". From the feedback we get from the society and from our own self-judgment, we lose our self-confidence and become solely dependent on labels and other people's wishes and desires; and this is when the drama begins.

We are at this point tamed. During the years to come, through the voices in our head we make innumerous agreements with ourselves and those around us. The most important of agreements are those we make with ourselves. These will tell us how we feel about ourselves and what we should or should not be doing in life and what is or is not acceptable. We even make agreements that we can read minds and we can predict what one is thinking when they say or do something. We make an agreement in what should insult us and what should be considered a compliment.

Everything that we agree on in our head, becomes the "truth". The fun part to this whole thing is that these agreements are different from even family to family within the same society. So now we start judging others according to the "truth" in "our" head. Even funnier is the fact that these so called truths are even varying in the same family. If you looked at yourself through the eyes of your parents or siblings, you will see a version of you that you will probably not even recognize; and likewise if they looked at themselves through your eyes, they would seem like a stranger to themselves. It is all a matter of perception you see. It is all about our own agreements.

Our interpretation of things in life is very much dependent on our original reaction to them. We create our very own reality in our head according to the knowledge we gather and our initial reaction and judgements on ourselves and others is based on that. We are originally born with awareness and then we trade that awareness with this knowledge. Later when we search for ourselves, we go back and find this awareness.

When we are a child we mistake the labels with magic. We learn them because using them seems to be rewarding. Later we use these same magical labels against our very own self; and by repeating certain labels, we start believing that we are non-deserving and imperfect. This is when we start sabotaging ourselves. The words we use against ourselves are the action of self-judgement and the result is the reaction of self-punishment in the shapes of guilt, shame, and depression.

This is why it is so vital for you to grasp the importance of the use of words about you and others. Your language and your words are what you will be delivering as an angel to all that surround you: to your loved ones, to nature, to so called strangers and most importantly to yourself. Practice extreme care in delivering your message. I cannot possibly overemphasize the importance of words you offer. Someone once said, "Words are your paintbrush and your life is your canvas."

Words have magical power in them as using them actually will produce feelings and emotions. Just hearing a word can bring about feelings of happiness or sadness, and some words can run a whole movie through your head in one instance.

Never use your word against yourself or someone else. Remember that everything is a part of you in this pool of energy and anything you say will affect you equally.

With your words and labels, you create your own life inside your head. The trick is to remember that everyone else has done the same for themselves. So what comes out of someone else's mouth regarding you or your life is only true in "their" head. Do you understand? That is not your reality, it is theirs and they are entitled to live their reality as you are to yours. So taking anything they say personally at this point sounds somewhat unrealistic.

The advantage you have here, is that you know about this, but others you deal with, may not have yet come to see it. This should make it easier for you not to take anything personally or stop making assumptions. We invent stories in our own head that we believe to be the truth, and according to that we judge and assume, and each judgement and assumption leads to more of the same.

Assumptions are nothing but mental indigestion. First you think a lot and all about "what if?" Our thinking brings fears. When the fears are born that we cannot explain, to feel safe, instead of asking questions, we make assumptions.

Now, let's take a little detour to another side of this to what we were talking about before: your beliefs being implanted in you as an agreement since childhood.

Looking into what you have agreed to, Santa, tooth fairy and Easter bunny, were few of these agreements when you were young before someone told you at a certain age that they were all lies. In the case of other agreements though no-one tells you so and you keep on believing it, never, ever questioning their validity.

We allow the false knowledge to take over us. In the process of taming us this whole knowledge becomes our book of commandments. We punish or reward ourselves and our loved ones and everyone else according to this book. We invest all our faith in this book and this is how we lose our power.

So let's see, someone told you when you were young that "you will never add up to anything", and you took this to heart and somehow you agreed to it, never questioning it. NOW, you are basing your experiences and life on that belief.

We cast spells on others specially our loved ones with such comments without even realizing. When you discover and get rid of these lies and false agreements, you will set yourself free; you will stop judging others and taking things personally or making assumptions.

Once we gain awareness in what we are doing, and question the agreements in our book of commandments, we are on the path of what is called "second attention." The first attention was when you were born and you gave all your attention to gather this knowledge.

On the path of second attention, you uncover all the lies in the book and have a fresh look at everything over again. You start paying attention to real you – the angel with the message. Do your best in questioning everything and listening to the answers with no judgments and no assumptions.

Challenge your beliefs by just simply asking if they are true. Are they your conscious agreement or an implanted, previously agreed-upon and outdated agreement?

This is when the self-acceptance kicks in and you start loving yourself unconditionally and break out of the chains and shackles that you have been carrying around with you and investing energy in all your life so far. When you start loving yourself unconditionally, the ones whose opinion were so important to you, see the difference in you and you no longer are an easy prey to them. Practice self-love and master it.

At this point the power and the energy that you had invested in the false agreements come back to you. You and your life both transform. Doubt is a beautiful tool that if it is used productively can prove to be irreplaceable.

Once we have gone through the whole questioning period and doubting and re-evaluating our book of commandments, we are ready to enter the phase of "third attention".

This is the phase of mastery. This is the phase where you no longer use words to gossip, and see all as perfect. At this point you have completely stopped judgement. This is when you see the God in you and everything else around you. This is when you feel the unity of the entire Universe. This is when you gain power to paint your life anyway you wish and no goal is too big to achieve.

This is when you become aware of your whole body and compare it to the Universe. Just like your body has many organs, so does the Universe. The organs of Universe are the plant life, human life, animal life, etc. etc. and the organs in your body are your heart, kidneys, liver, lungs, etc. Every organ in your body is composed of cells and every organ in the Universe is the same – the cells in the "human organ" being each individual.

Do the cells in your liver know that together they are one - your liver? Do they realize their unity? Do we as humans realize that together we form one organ in the Universe? Do we realize our unity? Is one cell in your kidney better than the rest? Smarter than the rest? Better dressed than the rest? With better social status? Do they care? The purpose is to do their best in what they are there to do, and maintain health and joy while experiencing their physical existence.

The minute you grasp this unity, you start living your life from the point of view of love. You can easily and freely express love to those you know and those you consider strangers – as in connectedness there are no strangers. Your labels no longer define you. Other people's opinion becomes ONLY an opinion.

This is actually when you start delivering the message you are here to deliver. Your presence becomes the message. You realize that you are here to experience the best of everything and enjoy life. You don't have to search for yourself anymore because you never left yourself. You don't have to search for God as God never left you – he could not. If the energy that created you leaves your physical existence, you will need to join back into the ocean of energy immediately and your physical existence ceases to exist.

There is no right or wrong way in your creation of your life. The three stages of attention I have mentioned here in the religious language are translated to hell, purgatory and paradise. Living in either one of them is the right thing to do for the person who is doing it.

At this point I like to suggest a label and come to an agreement on what it means to you. This label is "respect". I feel that respect begins with ourselves and then it branches out to everyone and everything around us. When you respect yourself, you accept yourself exactly the way you are and likewise in case of others, when you respect them you accept them the way they are.

Once you understand the concept of respect, you understand the concept of acceptance. You accept all as perfect. At this point you are not in conflict with yourself or anything and anyone else. When you respect others and accept them, you do not pass judgments against their lives and behaviours and allow none towards yourself from others. This is like a boundary. Others may choose to tell you their story, but that is all that is, a story. They are the painters of their own paintings. If they ask you for lessons in painting, then you may share what you know, otherwise allow them to paint what they wish and desire; it is their canvas not yours.

You CANNOT paint a bad painting. Everything is art and it is unique and perfect.

Now all this talk was just to bring to your attention your level of perfection and the fact that you deserve all of that you wish. Take a quick look around you. Who did you pay for your amazing body when you were born? Who do you pay for the air you breathe? Who did you pay for the earth? Who did you pay for all the birds and animals and insects? Why would a Universe give you so much if you do not deserve to begin with? This is the doubt I like to start in your head on your way to your mastery.

On your way to gain mastery you start developing your understanding about you, which will in turn make you more understanding of others. There are no victims in that scenario. You are the master painter. You are responsible for how the painting turns out.

As you are going through the journey of mastery, you might at times feel as if someone is pushing your buttons, it is probably because they have reactivated an old hurt in you that knowingly or not knowingly you have been carrying around with you. If I may suggest, next time you get upset at someone, take a deep look to see which one of your inner victim stories they are triggering in you.

Everyone in your life is truly doing the best they can with what they have. People can only love you to the capacity that they can love themselves. They can only forgive and embrace you as much as they can forgive and embrace themselves. They cannot give you something they do not have the capacity to give.

Remember that it is not your responsibility to make others grow and become masters, it is only your responsibility to make you grow and become aware. Your awareness and understanding frees you from any anger and pain and allows you to move forward with joy. I need also to mention that your joy and peace of mind is not determined by others and their actions, but by how you respond to them.

Another area of discovery would be to find out if you are still stuck in the past. Do you have a lot of could have, should have, would have and whys???? Here are some bullet points to help you through this:

- ❖ Understand that the events in the past cannot be changed by any means;
- ❖ Your painful experiences are your treasures, your diamonds, your prize motivating you to excellence;
- ❖ Understand that "some gifts come wrapped in sandpaper".

Remember that you are going through this self-mastery to build self-confidence. Check upon yourself every once in a while and take your pulse. Do you have faith in yourself? Does your self-talk in your head support you? Are you still dealing with your very own personal consultant in your head telling you how limited you are? Do you have the entire communication network in your head telling you what you cannot achieve? Is your smile hiding your personal pain?

Be reminded of all the truth we talked about in this section and further remember that our lives are just a living, breathing manifestation of our self-talk. Talk to yourself and others lovingly. One way that I practice with my clients in stopping the negative self-talks is that I ask them to imagine that the negative talk is recorded on a CD that is playing on the left side of their head and their positive talk is on a CD that plays on the right side of their head. Anytime they hear the negative talk, they take their index finger and physically press the stop button on the left side and the start button on the right side. This is called "Anchoring", in Neuro-Linguistic Programming and it has proven to be extremely successful.

# Emotional Integrity

Definition of Integrity: the quality or state of being complete, undivided: spiritual, or aesthetic wholeness: organic unity: completeness.

It is a simple thing, wholeness that is undivided. It is also a very elusive quality. Emotional Integrity is having our heart, mind and will unified. When we are in our emotional integrity we can act without hesitation or doubt. The phrase of, "my mind says one thing, but my heart says another", may be all too common in our lives. When this happens our will is divided and we hesitate with conflict of mind and emotions.

When we live our lives from a place of Integrity we do not doubt ourselves. We do not second-guess our words or actions. Ego of course has its own version of integrity.

The mind wants to believe that everything we do is within our integrity. We often work very hard to make ourselves believe that we have integrity. But, unfortunately it is a false sense of integrity. If we have to convince ourselves that we are acting in our integrity, we are likely to be wrong. When we are in our integrity, our mind does not have to tell us what we are doing is right. Our heart and will know and our mind follows without a doubt. Real emotional integrity doesn't come with a sense of being right. It comes with a feeling of love.

Acting out of our integrity means, we do not have to try. We just take action. "There is no try, there is do or don't". We don't concern ourselves with whether what we are doing is the right thing. We also don't have a need to justify or defend what we are doing to anybody. This includes ourselves.

The action comes from the heart and is with love, which is how we know it is right and true. It also comes with humility because we are acting on behalf of love and not for ourselves or a sense of righteousness. Words that come from Emotional Integrity don't corrupt our authenticity with chatter in our minds. Most people second guess themselves.

When a person with emotional integrity makes a mistake, or fails in their endeavour, they don't judge themselves. They know they did their best and the mind does not create an internal conflict with self-judgment.

The break in integrity is when our mind is divided. Our mind says one thing and our mind says another thing in contradiction with the first thing. We look at something we did in the past and we think, "I shouldn't have done that." Then we try to justify what we did because we don't want to accept our own judgment. We defend what we did to ourselves. We say to ourselves, "Well it really was okay because I got (blank) out of it."

We project a negative opinion to ourselves, and then we defend ourselves against our own opinion. When our mind is divided with conflicting thoughts then so is our emotions.

Usually a house in our dreams symbolizes our mind. It is the structure of beliefs in which we live. A mind just like a house that is not in Integrity is divided against itself. It cannot stand. It is frightening to face the truth because when we do, it feels like our house of beliefs will crumble. We misinterpret this to mean that we will crumble because we identify and attach so closely with what we believe.

This is the time for us to build up our spiritual courage. We have to have the courage to face and accept the death of our beliefs. When the false beliefs break, we find that the truth is still standing, because truth can always stand on its own. The truth does not need us to believe in it in order to survive.

This is the time then to start and create a new dream, based on Love and Truth. In a way you can see this as a resurrection. Death being metaphorical for the transformation of our mind and emotional state. In this process our physical body does not die. After we let go of out false beliefs, we regain our emotional integrity. Once we have the emotional integrity back we start creating new relationships based on pure love. We also get to realize that we are not our beliefs; but we are the force behind our beliefs and ideas. We are life.

The best way to test your emotional integrity is by paying attention to your mind and seeing how quiet it can be during chaos; and how much love do you have present.

## Integrity based Love

This kind of love, includes the following:

1. Completely trust yourself.
2. Stop seeking approval.
3. Stop creating unnecessary pain.
4. Appreciate that the space of the past is gone forever.
5. Mistakes mean growth.
6. Guilt is a waste of time.
7. Allow others to be on their own journey.
8. Forget competition - replace with passion.
9. Perfectionism is exhausting.
10. Positive language transforms into a positive life.
11. Replace manipulation with honesty & integrity.
12. Replace negative habits with positive.
13. Take small steps towards big dreams.
14. Meditate; take a walk, read the funnies, and then dissolve the problem.

15. Dive into self-development.

16. Always be kind, listen with love, be compassionate and lend a helping hand to others.

17. Learn the art of gratitude and compassion.

18. Jump head first into your bliss… risk it ALL!

19. Never, never, never, base your happiness and love on money, other people, your job or anything outside of you.

20. Love is simple. Love is always kind. Love always empowers. Love can't exist without integrity.

21. Last but not least, live in the moment of NOW!

    ✓ Truly enjoy where you are and what you are doing.

    ✓ Don't busy yourself with something else while doing something else.

    ✓ Learn from everything and anything around you all the time.


Learning to live deliberately means choosing to achieve all the things you desire. Every moment of everyday we choose our own reality. Your own awareness is your true self. All of your life can be managed effectively and deliberately when you begin to operate more and more as an aware human being.

# In the pursuit of happiness

So we come back to the topic of happiness yet another time. It seems to be a big deal to pursue happiness. Everyone's idea of what that means is quite different and it seems to be a moving target. You meet your friend today and he is awesomely happy and the next day depressed. Our external search for happiness has become so ridiculous that sometimes we hold on to our pains so that our happiness will stick around. We hold on to something slightly troublesome because we think if that goes away and something happy happens in our life, we might experience something worse later.

Each person's emotional happiness is behind a barrier of criteria. If they can meet that criterion in their own mind, they reward themselves with happiness. You can find these barriers by thinking about the things you say like, "I will be happy when/if…." Or "I will feel better when/if….."

To be authentically happy would mean for you to stop blindly chasing the false premises in your head. First spot them and let them know you no longer need them and replace them with a premise that will help you be happy consistently.

In my opinion and this is absolutely a suggestion, the fastest way to happiness that I have found have been the expression of love. Psychologists suggest things like: work in a meaningful career, spend time with friends, and take time to savour the day. Why do these things show up as activities to do if you want to be happy? How do they contribute to your happiness? They cultivate happiness because people express love when doing them.

They express love for their friends and family. They express love if they are at a career they like than the one they dislike. They express love when they are savouring their moments. We tend to believe that our emotions are a response to people and material things. One way that this happens is by the fact that we hypnotize ourselves with words like: "he makes me happy…", "I am so happy that you came to visit me". These phrases have the load implying a mental assumption that our emotions of happiness is actually because of the external happenings.

The part we missed was the "love" we expressed for the person in our life or the one who came to visit us. Where did that emotion come from? We created it. Emotions are invisible to our eyes so we overlook where they come from. We create our own emotions. No two people create the same emotion over the same subject matter.

The person that visited is just a trigger for us to create the emotion of love that we express, not the cause of it. When you are enjoying music, it is not the music that makes you happy, it is the expression of love towards the music that does that. So one underlying fact that determines how happy you can be is the expression of love.

The true and lasting happiness is yours if you decide to become self-aware and choose your happiness criteria in your mind at will. The reasons we generate different emotions than love can be sometimes because we tell ourselves that it is not safe to love.

Keep reminding yourself that love, if it is unconditional, is always safe. The key word here is "unconditional". The "love that hurts" is the type of love that is filled with conditions. Feeling happy, is an internally created emotion and is irrelevant to what is happening around you. Start loving unconditionally and find out how you cannot get away from happiness.

# Change

We are led to believe, from our media and fear-laden populous, that change is painful. I was speaking to a wonderful friend the other day and she kept saying, "People don't change." I just looked at her, without a word, I knew she truly believed the illusion that people don't change. On the contrary, I absolutely know that people change all the time. We grow, evolve, and as we get older we become more of who we truly are.

The science of deliberate creation has proven that we can change in an instant. How? The moment we speak the words of change, renewal, and affirmation, it is done. We have begun the journey to our new growth. Change never struggles. If we allow it, it will simply be. For example once you stop struggling with money issues you no longer will have them. The issue simply disappears.

This actually can happen overnight, in any area of your life. How? You need to know and understand that you have always had the ability to create as much prosperity as you desire…and that the energy of prosperity comes from you, not outside of you. Did you get that? It's important enough that it is worth repeating: The energy of prosperity comes from you, not outside of you.

Let's take a look at the area of health for example: spontaneous healing has been seen by many medical doctors who have seen or heard about at least one patient with a supposed terminal condition such as cancer, who miraculously recovered. Conventional medicine cannot explain Spontaneous healing due to the fact that they perceive illness to be separate from self. This means an illness can only be treated with manipulative procedures like surgery, pills, radiation, chemotherapy and a host of other medicines.

I speak everywhere and I love telling people the good points in changing their lifestyle… I love shocking people in facing themselves. I don't need to tell you why you need to change your lifestyle, when the time is right; you would figure that out on your own if it needs to be changed. My educated guess would be that you are reading this is because you feel one area of your life needs to be changed somehow.

Nothing can go on living without change. Change is constant. Change is mandatory. Change is living. Look at your body and everything else around you. Every single thing is going through change every second of their existence. The minute something does not change, they are bound to die. You could not be healthy, ever, if the cold you have, did not change. There would never be a change in season. You can never travel because that is also considered a change. You will always remain in the same position at work doing the exact same thing. BUT that is, if you made it that far, because in order for you to live and exist, every single cell in your body needs to constantly change and if they stop, uh oh.

To change, is to go on. If you are a Star Trak fan, you probably know part of the phrase I will be using next: resistance – to change – is futile. ☺☺☺ Learn to understand the value of change and become flexible. A flexible attitude towards life, will also guarantee many years of physical health ahead of you.

Change scares the daylights out of many. Why? It must be the fear of unknown. But, do you ever think about what happens in your body, every single minute? Change. Every seven years, you are a completely new you. Change happens without you even noticing. As a matter of fact, without this change we would die at a ripe old age of probably a month, if that. Without change we would not grow. Without change our wounds would not heal. Without change the fruits, vegetables and meat we are surviving on, would not be around. Without change, oxygen would not be there. Yet we all find this little corner we call "comfort zone" and sink into it, and don't ever want to crawl out of it.


Many people are stuck in a "comfort zone", a place with no surprises, no difficulties, just same old same old, day after day. These people have become content, and satisfied with what they have right now; if they are not, well, then there is someone or something to blame. It is as simple as that. The only group that I have ever met, who are not afraid of change, are babies in wet diapers. Even then, when they are crying, I don't know if it is for the fact that they want to be changed or are afraid of it :). Imagine, if one day, all the vegetables we try to grow, decided, "I don't think so. I like the stage of seed that I'm in very much and do not like to change." What then? Well guess what? If you are reading this book, you better be ready to change. Everything in this book is based on change. If you keep having the same thoughts you were having, and keep doing the same things you were doing, then you will for sure see the same results you were seeing. Change is the main step. Being afraid of change, genuinely limits what you can achieve! Living in a comfort zone, stops you from trying new things. Just try to run a business while staying in your comfort zone, and see what a total waste of time and effort that is to become.

Break away from the usual, to get what you want. As easy as this sounds, unfortunately for a lot of people, it is not. They want the future of their dreams, but can't bring themselves to do the things that will get them there. And all I'm asking for, is a change of pattern in thoughts and emotions.

Getting out of your comfort zone, means expecting and welcoming change. How DO you take that step out of your comfort zone? You have to believe in the fact that you are in control, and *know* that you can do anything. Next time that you think you have a difficult task ahead of you, don't let the fear of the unknown be a factor. Each time you confront your fears and insecurities, it will get that much easier to do. And your belief in yourself will grow accordingly. We can't go from ordinary to extraordinary and stay the same.

Seeing that we are on the topic of change I would like to touch upon one of the current most sensitive topics of health: cancer. I am talking about cancer as an example, but then this includes all other ailments of course. Earlier in this book I talked about the effects of nutrition and emotion on our health. Let me dig into this slightly and look at it from the perspective of change.

So we go on for years experiencing the low frequency emotions and on top of that the bad diet and stress and the self-created lions that chase us on a daily basis, and the result is a change in our physical biology. At the least a system that was PH balanced, turns a bit more acid.

So now what? The cells in the body that were enjoying the healthy alkaline environment all of a sudden are faced with a new environmental change and they of course freak out wanting to live and adapt. In order for the cells to continue living in an acid environment they have to change themselves to the type that can endure this. Hence the cancer cell. I know I am making this sound a bit simpler than it is, but I am trying my best to show you that the illnesses are not your enemy. You are. The illness is mainly an alarm going off in your body telling you that something major is happening. So what do we do? We take the battery out of the alarm or toss the alarm out. Will this help?

As a survival mechanism our cells need to change to cope to the environment. When the temperature outside is hot, you take your clothes off. When it is cold you put your jacket on. If you continued wearing the jacket through hot weather you would feel ill for sure. You change because it is needed to keep you alive and going. Your cells also change because of the change in environment and because they root for you and want you to keep on living. But how do we thank them? We don't try to change the environment back to a healthy state so that they can switch back to being themselves again. We instead put them through chemical warfare and we use words like "fight" which causes their environment to be even more so toxic, not to mention our ungratefulness towards a bunch of cells that are trying hard to keep us alive.

I encourage you the next time something creeps up in your medical resume, try to thank the cells for wanting you to live and go on instead of fighting them and try and change the environment that is causing the issue, instead of silencing the alarm or killing it. Let's Change!

# What Are Identities?

When we place enough belief, enough importance, enough emotional "charge" into an idea, we make it take on its own life. It then becomes an identity. Most people have identities that they wear like clothes in order to interact with others. In fact, most people use several identities throughout the day.

The challenge for most, is not to get stuck on automatic. Some identities may not serve us, as well as they did at other times in our life. The most valuable and empowering viewpoint to have about identities, is that you are not them – you are the creator of them! We can use our identities, freely at will, as tools for our convenience, to interact with others, in letting them know what we do, but not who we are.

Some of our identities are less than our true being. Some are victims and some are sick, some are mean, and some have addictions, etc. But, none of those are really us. Our true self is aware, compassionate, intuitive, free, joyful, creative, grateful, appreciative, connected with others and nature. It is all of our highest and our best! It is the real you - the silent, aware witness - behind all the ideas of you.

To become fully aware of all your actions and the others' view of you, sit and quietly observe yourself up to this point in your life. What would you say about yourself, if you were someone else? Honestly, make a list on how others see you…list everything.

When we practice self-observation and become very aware and present, our lives automatically starts transforming. We passively observe thoughts, pains, or fears as they come and go, the way clouds pass through the sky. Being the "aware observer" gives us

264

total authority over our choices in each moment and therefore our lives!

Self-awareness will allow us to become aware of and peel away layers of old pain, fears, stored anger, and a whole lot more. These things exist within us at our deepest subconscious levels. As we observe ourselves we become able to actively change our lives.

"Man cannot discover new oceans until he has the courage to lose sight of the shore." -Vernon Howard

The most valuable science in the world, is self-science. With a firm understanding of who we are and what we can do, we become magicians capable of creating the kind of lives we really want. Without self-knowledge we have no central attachment; we are like loose spokes in a wheel without a hub.

# Breaking Habits

What is the payoff? The first step in breaking a bad habit is to look at why you find what you are doing so convincing. In other words, what's the payoff for doing this seemingly negative thing? Since you've already classified this as a "bad" habit you may be tempted to say there isn't one. But look closer. There is always a payoff. Let's say your habit is yelling at your kids or spouse. What's in it for you? You let off some steam and feel a little better for the moment or it gives you a false feeling of being in charge and the authority. Or you have a habit of leaving the dishes unwashed? The payoff could be that you get to spend more time on the Internet! Or maybe in the past when you left it, someone else did it and it is easier if they do it, so why bother? There are always payoffs for any habit we adopt. It is the payoff that is leading us to do something over and over again, even if we feel bad about it later, or suffer any consequences.

What's the Trade-off? Next, take a look at the trade-off. What is it that you are losing by exercising your habit? This step should be easier. Just think: why is it that you consider it a bad habit in the first place? Yelling at your kids or spouse is a bad habit because: it leaves everybody feeling tense and tears down your children's and spouses' self-esteem. You are trading a temporary release of tension for the emotional health of your children or spouse. Leaving the dishes undone is a bad habit because your kitchen is a smelly mess. To have more Internet time, you are trading off having a pleasant living environment. When you look at it that way, it doesn't seem like you are making very wise choices, does it? There has to be a better way.

Time to Make a Choice! It's no longer an involuntary act because now you know that you are making a choice every time you perform this action. You are choosing what you value more: the payoff or the trade-off! Each time you start to do whatever the habit is, you actively choose. Which do you value more? The relief you get by yelling at your kids/spouse or their emotional well-being? Having more Internet time or having a pleasant place to live?

This pretty much puts you in the driver seat, allowing you to take responsibility for all your actions and outcome. Whatever the result you choose, that will become your life. You can now choose to have your spouse and children around for life, loving you, or you choose to yell and scream and eventually lose their respect or even the chance of them walking away.


The whole reason you formed your habits in the first place is that they filled a need. You had tension that needed relief, or you had a desire to surf the Net. As you break the old patterns you still need a way to fulfill these needs. You will not only be making an active choice to not do the old action but also you will be making a choice to perform a better, alternative action in its place. Instead of yelling, you might decide to go for a run every time you are feeling tense. Instead of letting dirty dishes pile up, you may decide to use paper plates when you are eating alone. Whatever the new habit, it isn't as important as whether you feel good about the choices you have made. After all, the reason you consider it a bad habit is because it leaves you feeling bad about yourself.

# What Do You Invest In?

During our lifetime, we make a conscious effort to learn about money, how it is invested, where to invest it, how to spend it, how to budget, etc. Hardly ever we take a course to understand how, when and where to invest our energy; even though that is the only true currency you have. What do you truly invest your energy into? This is crucial. This is far more important than how you invest your money. The energy of money depends on your energy. If it's not high vibration and proactive you are wasting your energy, period! What is most important to you? This is a good time to make a list of what is crucial to the quality of your life.

Energy is everything. How is your emotional, physical, mental, and spiritual energy? What matters to you most? Are you satisfied with your life? How do your habits of sleeping, eating, and exercising affect your energy?

How much low frequency energy do you invest into your life? (Are you angry, frustrated, resentful, and sad, etc...?) How much energy do you invest on others and their issues? How much time do you spend worrying, frustrated, or influencing other's to change? Be honest. How many hours do you invest in low frequency energy on a daily basis?

How much high frequency energy do you invest in your life? How productive is your time and energy? Facing the truth of who you are will IMMEDIATELY free up your energy. Defining your purpose will IMMEDIATELY free up your energy! Avoiding the truth, kills vital energy.

Eliminate denial, accept your situation(s), and deliberately create your desires. Why do we lie to ourselves? Lying often protects our self-esteem. Keep in mind; you are what you desire to be at any moment. Every minute is a new chance to do something different. Lying to ourselves is far worse than lying to others.

# Being Independent of Other People's Opinion

In our journey of life we encounter hundreds, possibly thousands, of people. Each one have their own ideas of who we might be. Many times they will voice their opinion of us. Sometimes we will like what we hear and at other times we will dislike or even despise what they say. It is the "good" that we hear that addicts us to this whole process and we start constantly seeking validation in others.

Because there will always be people saying things to us, we have to know for ourselves what it is that we are supposed to be in this physical reality. We have to know what we want and who we are. If we don't, others will create our reality for us. Then, because we believe what everyone else says, we will begin to attract those things into our lives and before we know it, we will be living a life that other people have created for us.

Always remember that: other people's opinion of you does not have to become your reality. You see, you have to know what you want in life and where you are going, so that you can create your own reality. By doing this, you will be able to attract the things that you want, not what other people are projecting on you.

We each have our own experiences to live through. Trying to please someone else in following their opinion of us of what we need to do, wear, eat, etc. can make life extremely stressful. We cannot possibly fathom satisfying everyone in our lives; and there is definitely no need for it either.

If you don't like the reality that you are currently living in, then you need to do two things. First, find out if you are allowing other people to dictate your reality for you. If you are, then stop listening to what people are saying and begin to create your own life.

Second, if people's opinions isn't the problem, then you need to begin to change what you are currently doing in your life. You will attract through your thoughts, emotions, words and actions. So, begin to change what you think, feel, say and do. Once you do this, you will begin to create the reality that you truly desire.

Remember the following pointers on this topic:

- When you seek approval from others, you allow them to convince you that it is more important to pay attention to how they feel about your life than you do;

- If what someone else thinks about you becomes more important than your own idea of yourself, you are not in a healthy position. Anytime you take action to try to manipulate or affect other's opinion or attitudes towards you, you are in a less than healthy position, because you are replacing your own guidance system with their opinion;

- You cannot criticize or condemn yourself to success, wellbeing and prosperity.

# What stage do you fit in?

Throughout our lives we tend to go through various stages. Well maybe. By that I mean, we can actually get stuck in one stage and never decide to leave because it feels better to us. But normally speaking for an aware individual who is after betterment of their mental, emotional and spiritual lives, there are four stages that they might experience.

## Stage 1 – Victim

In this stage we claim that life is doing something to me – This is the "They did it to me" story. Constantly asking: Why me? Trying to win favours from God and in the meantime sticking to gossip, superstition, blame, fear, worry, preparing for unknown negative future, living from the point of reaction, spending energy in defense and disaster recovery. In this we are also influenced by current circumstances and we react to immediate issues of the day; we are afraid of lack, loss, and not enough to go around

## Stage 2 – manipulator stage

In this stage, we are doing something about it by: exercising the right of dominion, learning about the law of attraction, monitoring our thoughts, participating in co-creation and taking responsibility, making it happen, understanding our own power, studying the one mind, field of unity, the creator, the source, and understanding that we are either in alignment, or out of alignment.

## Stage 3 – channel, vehicle, instrument, surrender

At this stage we feel as if something is operating through us – we seek the awareness of divine order, trust, truth, something takes us through a level beyond we ever dreamed of, we start surrendering to the next stage of our development. This is the one I call: stage of no return ☺☺☺

## Stage 4 – As Us

In this stage, we experience no sense of separation between us, life, God and unconditional love – we reexamine our identities, and the veil before our eyes seem to dissolve. This is when we see the Source closer to us than our breath.  We finally realize the connection with Source and all. Our life and the life of the divine becomes one. This is the stage of complete and utter unconditional love and acceptance.  This is where the mastery begins.

# Final Discussions

Last week I was watching the re-run of Super Soul Sunday by Oprah Winfrey – whom I greatly admire - and she was talking to another favourite person of mine - Dr. Christian Northrop.

As the interview went on, I realized how much of the things Dr. Northrop was talking about, was exactly what I had practiced for years and unfortunately very much criticized, shunned and ridiculed for saying so. I remember around 450 doctors walking out of a seminar right in the middle of my lecture on the effects of emotions on health. Can you spell scarring? LOL - just kidding I am tougher than that, and this was more than 35 years ago.

It is when Oprah started asking questions that I could not contain myself and like a child wanted to jump up and answer. So I decided seeing that I am writing this book, I would answer these questions as if that was "our" dialogue.

Oprah - Why do you think we are actually here? What is the purpose of human experience?

EL – We are here to "experience" what could not be experienced without the physical existence. You see, when you have an idea and you bring that idea into creation, without the actual experience, that creation has no joy. The joy is in the experience. If I create a pen and just leave it there, it is of no use. Nothing becomes of it. When I create the pen and place the laws around the use of that pen and then use it in many ways possible, love it, hate it, properly use if, abuse it, break it or preserve it for years, now these are all experiences that bring joy. Our purpose is to experience as many different versions of humanity as we can and in that we are safe and protected and loved and provided for, only if we just start enjoying.

Oprah - Are we to blame in our illness?

EL – Blame is not the game. Responsibility is. If you would ask me are we responsible in our illness, I would say; "without a shadow of doubt." All that is available to us is health. All we are made of is the pure, clean and perfect energy.  We are the ones introducing surges into this current and hence we are responsible and accountable.

Oprah - What is the calling you came to earth to fulfil?
EL – The experience of giving the message as I perceive it and sometimes feeling the feel and taking the chance of being misunderstood. Feeling as if I came from a different planet. LOL

Oprah - Can we heal from everything or somethings aren't gonna get healed?

EL – The matter of getting healed is completely ego based.  By that I mean our ego is the one that creates the individual within us. Dependent on how much we control it or it controls us our level of healing differs. I can surely say that someone like mother Theresa would have no problem being completely healed or better yet Jesus or Moses or Mohamed.

Oprah - What is the greatest truth that you can say that you embrace in your daily life?

EL – Unconditional love and acceptance.

Oprah - What is the most important thing about the wisdom you want to pass on to everyone?

EL – The oneness and unity.  Once this is thoroughly understood, faith becomes inevitable and once faith sets in, peace and joy become the side effects.

Oprah - How do you know enough is enough in helping people?
EL – It is enough to begin with.  Never try to help anyone.  In trying to help, you are seeing yourself above them or somehow superior to them.  BUT it is never enough to serve them.

Ahhhhhhhh! Got it out of my system and it felt great.  Thank you for reading it and sharing my imaginary experience.

God Bless you!

I AM EL

Be the Light

Made in United States
North Haven, CT
23 April 2023

35800512R00152